EQUAL PARENTHOOD
AND
SOCIAL POLICY

SUNY Series, Issues in Child Care
Marian S. Blum, EDITOR

EQUAL PARENTHOOD AND SOCIAL POLICY

A Study of Parental Leave in Sweden

LINDA HAAS

State University of New York Press

Figures 3.1–3.3 have been reproduced with permission from the National Social Insurance Office in Stockholm.

Published by
State University of New York Press, Albany

Printed in the United States of America

For information, address the State University of New York Press, State University Plaza, Albany, NY 12246

Production by Bernadine Dawes
Marketing by Bernadette LaManna

Library of Congress Cataloging-in-Publication Data

Haas, Linda.
Equal parenthood and social policy : a study of parental leave in Sweden / Linda Haas.
p. cm. — (SUNY series, issues in child care)
Includes bibliographical references and index.
ISBN 0-7914-0957-0 (acid-free paper) : $59.50. — ISBN 0-7914-0958-9 (pbk. : acid-free paper) : $19.95
1. Parental leave—Sweden. I. Title. II. Series: SUNY series in issues in child care.
HD6065.5.S8H33 1992
331.25'763—dc20 91-3433
CIP

10 9 8 7 6 5 4 3 2 1

Contents

Preface ... vii

Acknowledgments ... xi

1. Introduction ... 1
2. History and Development of Parental Leave in Sweden ... 19
3. Participation of Swedish Fathers in Parental Leave ... 59
4. Determinants of Fathers' Participation in Parental Leave ... 83
5. Daddies and Mommies at Home: Parents' Experiences with Parental Leave ... 129
6. Consequences of Fathers Taking Parental Leave for Gender Equality in the Family ... 153
7. Implications for the United States ... 187
8. Conclusion: Equal Parenthood and Social Policy ... 217

Appendix A: Methodology of the Study ... 231

Appendix B: Questionnaire and Interview Protocols ... 239

References ... 265

Index ... 289

Preface

This book was written because of three separate yet interrelated concerns.

Employment and parenthood are difficult roles to combine. There is no scientific evidence that human beings are biologically or psychologically unable to combine working and nurturing. Instead, social arrangements make it difficult. As more women enter the labor force, increasing numbers are faced with conflict between employment and family roles. More often than not, one has to give precedence to the other. ***Can new social arrangements be developed which integrate these two important activities?***

Historically, women and men have been socially assigned different tasks and responsibilities. Since industrialization, women have been in charge of home maintenance and nurturing while men have been associated with earning income. Women's entrance into the labor force has only slightly modified these distinctions. With the division of labor by sex, women and their activities (especially nurturing) are less socially valued, and women have less opportunities for economic independence and self-fulfillment outside the home. Men's chances for self-realization in the occupational world are limited by pressures to achieve, while their chances for a more reasonable balance between family and work is also curtailed. ***Can new social arrangements be instituted which call for a more equal sharing of employment and nurturing by men and women?***

Economic pressures on families have led to an increasing number of children having both parents in the labor market and to the growth of day care. There is evidence that having two employed parents is generally good for children, if the alternative care they receive is of sufficient quality. Most of the findings, however, are based on preschool-aged children and older. We know little about how babies less than one year old fare when both parents are employed and need to rely upon a child care provider. We do know that parent–child attachment takes time; some professionals suggest babies need at least four months home with at least one parent in order for emotional security and attachment to occur. We also know that parents often suffer anguish and guilt at leaving their children too soon. *Can new social arrangements be instituted which value children more and recognize the need for babies to be with parents, without parents' sacrificing economically and occupationally?*

These are the questions which motivated me to write this book. My search for answers led me to Sweden, the only society in the world which has officially struggled with these questions for a considerable period of time. Through social policy, Sweden has attempted to put into place new social arrangements which recognize children's needs for parental care but call for men and women to share equally employment and parenting responsibilities.

This book focuses on one particular social program designed to bring about this new social order, parental leave. Swedish parents are entitled to 15 months of leave with pay and job security at the time of child birth or adoption, to be used to care for their new babies. Both men and women are allowed and encouraged to use these benefits. I analyze the development of the parental leave program and its success in achieving the goal of equal parenthood.

I believe it is very useful to look at other societies for insight into the social arrangements that can promote social change. This is particularly necessary in the case of studying the issue of combining employment and parenthood, since the United States lags far behind other industrial societies in considering the problem and proposing solutions. On the other hand, I try to be cautious about generalizing the findings about Sweden to other social settings, since I realize how unique each society is.

I also believe it is useful to study a society at the closest quarters possible, and not make judgments from a distance. Numerous visits to Sweden over an extended period of time, supportive Swedish colleagues, and an understanding of the

Swedish language have all helped me gain an insider's insight into the society. On the other hand, I believe I have maintained the outsider's critical perspective, due to my background and training as a sociologist and because I am not Swedish in origin.

Lastly, this study was motivated by an interest in trying to combine the perspectives from a number of disciplines, instead of relying upon only one. Accordingly, I have attempted to interweave theoretical perspectives, research findings, and methodological techniques from a number of academic fields, including anthropology, history, psychology, political science and sociology, in order to gain a richer, in-depth view on the subject matter.

Acknowledgments

Several people provided important encouragement and assistance to me while I was researching this topic and writing this book. Ain Haas, Philip Hwang, Karin Sandqvist, and Joseph Pleck all spent a great deal of time helping me with this project, and I am most grateful for their support. Others who gave useful aid included Joan Aldous, Julia Brannen, Barbro Dunér, Jane Hood, Monica Widstedt Höeg, Michael Lamb, Ann-Sofie Ohlander, Eva Pramsten, Barbara Risman, Graeme Russell, and Lena Nilsson Schönnesson. I appreciate the cooperation of officials at the Gothenburg social insurance office (Försäkringskassan), including Sune Börjesson, Gunnar Carlsson, Elsie Ericsson, and Sven Gustafsson. Thanks are also extended to the couples who allowed me to interview them at length about parental leave. Finally, I greatly appreciate grants from the American–Scandinavian Foundation and Indiana University, which made this research possible.

1

INTRODUCTION

In every known society, women have had primary responsibility for the physical care and emotional well-being of small children. There are individual instances where men have become primary caretakers of children, usually in the absence of mothers, but in no society is it generally the case that men and women are equally responsible for child care. Anthropological studies of preindustrial societies have not uncovered any societies where equal parenthood is practiced (Katz and Konner, 1981). Studies of fathers in various industrial societies—including Australia, Canada, France, Germany, Great Britain, Hungary, Israel, Italy, Japan, Netherlands, Norway, Sweden, the Soviet Union, and the United States—have also documented that women continue to serve as the primary parent (Booth and Edwards, 1980; Bozhkov and Golofast, 1988; Day and Mackey, 1989; Haas, 1982; Horna and Lupri, 1987; Hwang, 1987; Mackey, 1986; Moss and Brannen, 1987; New and Benigni, 1987; Nickel and Kocher, 1987; Parseval and Hurstel, 1987; Russell, 1982, 1987; Russell and Radin, 1983; Sandqvist, 1987a, Ve, 1989).

Women's primary responsibility for child care takes several forms. Mothers have been found to spend more "solo time" with children, which means that they are home alone with the child more often (Katsh, 1981; LaRossa, 1988). Even when both parents are home, mothers have been found to make themselves more available to children and to spend more time in direct interaction (Bronstein, 1984). Gender differences are also evident in *how* time with children is spent. Mothers tend to be more involved in physical caretaking tasks while fathers are generally more actively involved in play and stimulating activities (Bronstein, 1984; Easterbrooks and Goldberg, 1984; Jones, 1985; Katsh, 1981; Sandqvist, 1987a). Not surprisingly, women are more likely than men to define child care as work, while men tend to regard it as leisure (Shaw, 1988).

There is also evidence that women typically are the ones most *responsible* for the care of small children. This takes several forms. Despite the cliché of "wait till your father gets home," women have been found to be more involved than fathers in the administration of discipline (Condran and Bode, 1982). When men participate in specific child care tasks, women are usually the ones who have delegated or assigned those tasks to them (Branson, Anderson, and Leslie, 1987; Kotelchuk, 1976; LaRossa, 1988). Women have been found to make more of the decisions in regard to children (Condran and Bode, 1982). Mothers have been described as the "psychic parents" who keep in their minds all the details having to do with children. One person described psychic parenting and the delegation pattern that often occurs in the following way:

> Yes, dad will take Mary to the dentist. But it was mom who (1) remembered that Mary needed to go to the dentist, (2) made the appointment, (3) wrote the note to get Mary excused from school and reminded her to take it to school, (4) saw that Mary brushed her teeth and wore one of her least disreputable pair of jeans . . . (5) reminded dad to take Mary the morning of the appointment, (6) paid the bill when it came in the mail, and (7) posted the next six month appointment on the family calendar afterwards. (cited in Benokraitis, 1985:253)

Not surprisingly, given their greater involvement in and responsibility for many aspects of child care, women exhibit greater absorption in the parenting role than men. Ehrensaft (1985) states, "Women *are* parents, while men *do* parenting." Women limit their outside activities more in order to be able to do child care; this particularly occurs for employment. Women often pick jobs combinable with child care responsibilities, are the ones who take an extended time off after childbirth to care for infants, work fewer hours, and stay home from work when children are sick (Hiller and Philliber, 1986). Recent research studies show that fathers in postindustrial societies are beginning to spend considerable time with their children and often rank the fatherhood role equal to, or greater in importance than, the employee role (Barnett and Baruch, 1987; Booth and Edwards, 1980; Cohen, 1987; Gilbert, 1985; Haas, 1988; Lamb et al., 1985; Mackey, 1986; Nock and Kingston, 1988; Pleck, 1983). Nevertheless, there is little dispute that couples practicing "equal parenthood" are few.

THE IMPACT OF BIOLOGY

Women's responsibility for young children is a cultural universal. Because women are everywhere more involved in the care of small children than men are, it has often been assumed that the reason must lie in biology. If parenting behavior had strong biological bases, it would presumably be virtually impossible to alter the *status quo.* What does research suggest about the impact of biology on parenting behavior?

A Maternal Instinct?

Scientists generally reject the notion that there is such a thing as a maternal instinct, whereby mothers are uniquely more capable of caring for children because of some hormonal changes occurring at childbirth or some genetic predisposition. Research on primates reveals that the ability to nurture is dependent on prior learning and the experience of having been nurtured oneself (Oakley, 1974). Studies of individuals with hormonal and genetic abnormalities allow an investigation into the particular effects of feminizing hormones or genes. Reviewing this research, Chodorow (1978:29) states:

> There is no evidence to show that female hormones or chromosomes make a difference in human maternalness, and there is substantial evidence that nonbiological mothers, children, and men can parent just as adequately as biological mothers and can feel just as nurturant.

Studies on humans as well as animals show that it is infants themselves, rather than any special set of hormones, which activate nurturing behavior in females and males alike (Chodorow, 1978).

In further support of the idea that there is no such thing as a maternal instinct, studies involving newborns and infants in hospital, laboratory, and home settings have uncovered no evidence that men are innately less qualified than women to care for infants. Research shows that fathers can respond as appropriately as mothers to infants' signals for assistance and, when given the opportunity, spend about the same amount of time as mothers talking, teaching, soothing, and showing affection (Belsky, 1979; Field, 1978; Hwang, 1985; Jones, 1985; Lamb, 1981; Lamb et al., 1985; Parke and Tinsley, 1981; Yogman, 1984). Observational studies of parent–child interaction in public places in fifteen different societies also showed that "men responded to children in a basic similar way [as] women" (Mackey, 1986:168).

If biology was an overwhelming determinant of parenting behavior, it would seem likely that we would find worldwide that only mothers performed child care. Evidence from preindustrial societies, however, shows that 40% of the primary care of infants is performed by people other than mothers (usually siblings) (Newland, 1980; Weisner and Gallimore, 1977). Analysis of data on a world sample of 186 societies (provided by Barry and Paxson, 1971) shows that only in 2% of societies are mothers the ones who exclusively or almost exclusively care for infants; in no society was it the case that mothers were the exclusive or almost exclusive caretakers in early childhood.

Children's Need for Mothers

More contemporary arguments concerning the necessity of a gender-based division of labor for parenting rest on the idea that children naturally thrive best when their mothers devote considerable time to care for them. This idea appears to be a fairly recent social invention.

In preindustrial times, little concern was shown for developing children's personalities, intelligence, and individuality. Mothers, like fathers, were too occupied with activities related to economic survival to pay much attention to small children. Writing about preindustrial colonial America, Margolis (1985:18) states:

> The mother–child relationship was enmeshed in the myriad of daily tasks women performed for their families' survival. They kept house, tended gardens, raised poultry and cattle, churned milk into butter and cream, butchered livestock, tanned skins, pickled and preserved food, made candles, buttons, soap, beer and cider, gathered and produced medicinal herbs, and spun and wove wool and cotton for family clothes. The wives of farmers, merchants, and artisans . . . often helped in their husbands' businesses as well.

Even if parents had had time to spare from productive activities to spend with small children, cultural ideology (at least in North America and Western Europe) would have discouraged them from being too attentive and nurturant. Mintz and Kellogg (1988:14) maintain that in colonial America "childhood was a much less secure and shorter stage of life than it is today." Infant mortality was high and children were expected to take their place in the world of work soon after they were weaned. Religious doctrines also depicted small children as being born with guilt and sin. In order to break down a child's will, parents were encouraged not to be indulgent (Margolis, 1985; Mintz and Kellogg, 1988).

Since industrialization, however, the status of children has dramatically changed. They are now regarded as being in great need of more than the physical necessities of life. The new market economy which emerged with industrialization, as well as dissemination of findings from research studies on child development, seem responsible for these significant changes in attitudes toward children.

The new economy required a well-educated, self-disciplined, and stable workforce. Childhood came to be viewed as a crucial time period in the formation of adult character; children were regarded as needing protection, education, and special nurturing in order to realize their full potential as individuals—and, consequently, as workers (Frykman and Löfgren, 1987; Glenn, 1986; Margolis, 1985). Women were seen as the ideal ones to do this special nurturing. They had been more involved than fathers in child care previously, and their characters were seen as uniquely qualifying them to do this special nurturing—they were regarded as inherently more moral, pure, and tender (Bosanquet,

1906; Rotundo, 1987). In place of women's former productive activities, women were now admonished to pay increasing attention to the quality of the home environment, the nurturance of the marital relationship, and most particularly children. The joys of motherhood were exalted; motherhood began to represent "the greatest achievement of a woman's life, the sole true means of self-realization" (Oakley, 1974:186).

As mothers took even more control of child care and domestic work, fathers were freed to pursue the new opportunities for paid employment outside the home (Bosanquet, 1906). Masculinity became defined in terms of men's levels of ambition and achievement outside the home, and the economic dependence of mothers and children on fathers became taken for granted. The "father as breadwinner" ideal had emerged (Demos, 1982; Pleck, 1987; Rotundo, 1985).

A new belief system, the "doctrine of separate spheres," had thus taken hold, whereby men were presumed to belong to the public sphere and women to the domestic sphere. This belief system reinforced the familial division of labor which made motherhood women's primary vocation and made child care more women's responsibility, while men's parenting role was defined mainly in economic terms.

In the first two-thirds of the twentieth century, the idea that full-time mothering was essential to children's proper development became more entrenched through the writings of childrearing experts (Margolis, 1985). These experts made false assumptions regarding children's innate needs, according to Oakley (1974). One assumption was that "children need mothers rather than any other kind of caretaker . . . a mystical connection binds child to mother and to mother alone." Another assumption was that "children need to be reared in the context of a one-to-one relationship" (Oakley, 1974: 203–204). Much of the evidence put forth for these assumptions descended from studies of the negative effects of institutionalization on infants (usually war orphans). From these studies, comparisons were made between institutionalized care and maternal care, with maternal care being considered not only better, but the one that all children innately needed (Oakley, 1974).

It was not until fairly recently that such findings were reconsidered. Institutionalized infants often lack adequately stimulating activity, as well as the opportunity to form emotionally secure relationships with caretakers; these do seem to be prerequisites for children's healthy development. On the other hand, these early studies did not test whether mothers were the only ones capable of satisfying these needs for children. Contemporary studies actually show that babies are capable of establishing intimate relationships with more than one primary caretaker, are interested in contact with both parents, and are likely to attach themselves strongly to both parents once attachment behaviors begin at about the age of six months (Clarke-Stewart, 1978; Hwang, 1985; Jalmert, 1983; Lamb, 1981; Nettelbladt, 1984).

Breastfeeding

Probably the only real, established biological difference between the sexes which is relevant to the division of labor for child care is women's unique ability to breastfeed. However, it is not at all clear that breastfeeding leads inevitably to a division of labor for child care between men and women, even in preindustrial societies where frequent childbearing and longterm nursing are often inevitable and necessary for group survival. At one time, anthropologists (e.g., Brown, 1970) presumed that constant childbearing and breastfeeding would lead to a strict division of labor in preindustrial societies. Pregnant and breastfeeding women were assumed to be unable to perform work which was far from home, was dangerous, or could not be interrupted. Consequently, men were obligated to take on such work (e.g., hunting large animals), which in turn made them unavailable for child care. More recently, feminist anthropologists (e.g., Friedl, 1975) have disputed this notion, using field data indicating that pregnancy and breastfeeding do not limit women's mobility or engagement in risky activities as much as commonly thought. These findings cast further doubt on the biological necessity for the division of labor for child care.

It seems even less likely that breastfeeding is a major barrier to men's participation in child care in societies where the work men do is not very dangerous or performed very far from home. In industrial societies, there are further reasons why breastfeeding would not be a major obstacle to child care sharing. Family sizes are small, and women prefer to breastfeed a relatively short time (if at all). With the invention of baby bottles and the development of sanitary washing facilities, mothers need not be present for infants to be fed: breast milk can be pumped and refrigerated for later use, or safe nutritional supplements can be used. It may still seem more convenient and simpler for the parent who can provide naturally for the child's nutritional requirements to be the one who stays home with that child. But this seems to be a matter of convenience rather than biological necessity.

A review of the literature suggests, then, that women are not biologically more suited for caring for small children. Nor are small children biologically programmed to respond only to their mothers' care. However, stereotypes and myths about men's and women's nurturing abilities might still operate to depress men's participation in early child care.

GROWING INTEREST IN EQUAL PARENTHOOD

A review of the research literature suggests that the types of activities associated with "mothering" (i.e., nurturing) and "fathering" (i.e., breadwinning) have been socially defined. These definitions may now be changing. In the past ten years, there has been a dramatic increase in expressions of interest in *equal parenthood*, whereby men and women would both be equally engaged in the full range of parenting behaviors which have up to now been the province of one parent or the other. Almost every American magazine and newspaper has featured articles about "the new father"—a man who is emotionally attached to his children and actively responsible for their care and well-being. These articles have not just appeared in feminist or women-oriented media. Even such traditionally male-oriented newspapers and magazines such as the *Wall Street Journal* and *New York Magazine* have featured the new father. Television commercials (such as ones for Kodak) provide visual images of fathers tenderly holding babies and toddlers, and magazine ads for pain relievers (Tylenol) and baby food (Gerber) stress the important role fathers play in choosing what babies need in order to thrive. Popular books about fathering have also appeared (e.g., Kyle Pruett's *The Nurturing Father—Journey Toward the Complete Man,* 1987). Opinion surveys document interest in a new mode of parenting. The majority of American men and women, as well as girls and boys, now believe mothers and fathers should be equally responsible for child care when both work for pay outside the home (Farmer, 1983; Hiller and Philliber, 1986; Huber and Spitze, 1983).

The expanding interest in men's participation in child care is generally attributed to changes in women's roles (Fein, 1974; Pleck, 1987). The rise in mothers' labor force participation has been particularly dramatic and influential. In 1950, only 12% of mothers of preschool-aged children were in the labor force; by 1987, 57% were (Blau and Winkler, 1988; Margolis, 1985). A commonly mentioned potential benefit of equal parenting for women concerns their employment opportunities. If women shared child care equally with men, they would presumably have more energy and interest in seeking self-fulfillment outside the home (Adams and Winston, 1980; Eisenstein, 1984; Hoffman, 1983; Huber, 1976; Levine, 1976; Smith and Reid, 1986; Yogman, Cooley, and Kindlon, 1988). Employers might give women workers more respect and become more willing to invest in their occupational potential if they knew that women were not the only ones who would take time away from work to care for small children (Hoffman, 1983; Newland, 1980).

A concern for the well-being of children also underlies contemporary interest in equal parenting arrangements. As more mothers are employed, some people look to fathers to provide more care for children. A more relaxed home environment for children has been predicted to be the result of an arrangement where either parent can do child care (Shreve, 1987). Some studies suggest that when men participate more in child care, they become more sensitive and able to understand children's needs (Grønseth, 1978; Lamb and Easterbrooks, 1981; Russell, 1982).

Increased interest in child development has also contributed to calls for greater participation of men in children's lives. Having two active parents is seen as providing children with dual role models, a "richer, more complex emotional milieu" (Ehrensaft, 1983), and an extra source of stimulation and unique experiences from which they can benefit (Ehrensaft, 1983; Ricks, 1985). Some studies suggest that high levels of father involvement are related to optimal toddler development in terms of developing secure attachments, social confidence, and problem-solving abilities (Easterbrooks and Goldberg, 1984; Hodgson, 1979; Pruett, 1987).

The feminist movement is often given partial credit for the rising interest in fatherhood. As women's identities have expanded to include occupational roles, some people have questioned whether or not men's personhood has been compromised by a one-sided focus on occupational achievement (Morgan, 1990; Pleck, 1987). Through increased participation in parenting, men might develop the more "nurturing" or "feminine" sides of their personalities (Ehrensaft, 1983; Russell and Radin, 1983; Yogman, Cooley, and Kindlon, 1988). Exclusive concentration on the breadwinner role often encourages men to develop only one side of their personalities: e.g., unemotionality, individuality, competitiveness, self-absorption, and toughness (Benokraitis, 1985; Giveans and Robinson, 1985). Bernard (1981) maintains that a one-sided focus on the "good provider role" has potentially high "psychic costs" for men. Men can depend too heavily on success in the breadwinner role to validate their sense of masculinity and bolster their self-esteem. When men let the role of father count as a "validating source," they are expanding the opportunities for succeeding at something and feeling good about themselves. Sharing more in child care might give men greater opportunities to enjoy the development of the child (Ehrensaft, 1983). When a sample of fathers in a large city was asked why they would like to spend more time with their children, the most common response was exemplified by this comment: "Time spent with my child is unique. There is nothing else that can make you that high or offer as much fulfillment" (Haas, 1988:26). Greater participation in child care seems to be a promising way for men to develop closer relations with children; there are some empirical studies that suggest a relationship exists between level of fathers' participation and closeness of the father–child bond (Grønseth, 1978; Hood and Golden, 1979; Radin, 1982; Russell, 1982; Smith and Reid, 1986).

While fathers are often regarded as obtaining important benefits through greater involvement in child care, it should be noted that not all observers agree that men have much to gain from equal parenthood. Polatnick (1983) maintains that men enjoy substantial advantages from avoiding childrearing responsibility; because they can concentrate on the breadwinner role, they can earn more money, prestige, and power than women can by being the primary parent. She also suggests that men will not want to share child care because of the disadvantages inherent in the role, including low status, drudgery, monotony, a long work week, being constantly on call, social isolation, and selflessness. An early proponent of equal parenthood admitted "the rewards of caring for a child are . . . hard to measure or hang on to. This is not the kind of experience men are taught to value. It does not lead to power, wealth, or high status" (Fasteau, 1976:63). While these factors may serve as important barriers to fathers actually sharing the parenting role, it is important to note that studies indicate that a large proportion of fathers—between one-third and one-half—are interested in a more nurturing role (Bradley, 1985; Haas, 1988; Jump and Haas, 1987).

THE ROLE OF SOCIAL POLICY

Advocates of equal parenthood would like to see this topic approached as a public issue and not merely as one resolvable within the context of individual families (Bernard, 1974; LaRossa, 1988; Zigler and Frank, 1988). Up to now, policymakers in most postindustrial societies have wanted families to conform to traditional gender stereotypes, with fathers viewed as breadwinners and mothers as the primary nurturers (Adams and Winston, 1980; Kamerman, 1983; Newland, 1980; Scanzoni, 1983). According to Lamb and Sagi (1983:247–8):

> [C]ontemporary legal and social policies in most Western societies do not facilitate paternal participation; indeed, existing practices more commonly restrict and limit the opportunities for male involvement in the family.

Consequently, fathers' rights to employment have been emphasized over mothers' rights, and programs which would support working mothers and fathers in combining parent and employment roles have been lacking.

A progressive approach to social policy "assumes the obligation of both men and women to support themselves, as well as to share jointly in the responsibilities of parenthood" (Lapidus, 1978:343). The changes most likely to promote equal parenthood involve employment practices (Lamb, 1983; Moss and Brannen, 1987). Progressives view working men and women as being in need of programs which would allow them to arrange child care without this negatively affecting family income. This calls for restructuring of work time and parental leaves with jobs guaranteed upon return. Policies that improve women's economic opportunities are also crucial; when women are economically independent, they can be more interested in an equitable sharing of child care responsibilities and better able to relieve men from the pressure of the breadwinner role (Levine, 1976; Roos, 1985). This progressive approach is increasingly being adopted by policymakers in Western Europe, because of a recognition of the importance of women's labor power and the effects of maternal employment on family life (Kamerman, 1983; Kamerman and Kahn, 1978; Nickel and Köcher, 1987).

SWEDEN'S INTEREST IN EQUAL PARENTHOOD

While some international bodies (e.g., the United Nations, the International Labor Organization, Council of Europe) have recently adopted resolutions that call for men and women to share economic and child care responsibilities in the family (Moss and Brannen, 1987), there is only one society whose policymakers have long advocated equal participation of fathers in child care—Sweden (Kamerman, 1983; Lamb and Levine, 1983; Qvarfort, McCrae, and Kolunda, 1988). Following Sweden's lead, other Nordic countries, particularly Norway and Finland, have become interested in changing men's roles, especially in promoting fathers' participation in child care through social policy; but this is a new development (Brandth and Kvande, 1990, Haavio-Mannila and Kaupinnen, 1990; Nordic Council of Ministers, 1988). While some communist societies (e.g., the U.S.S.R., China, Cuba) and some Israeli kibbutzim have long expressed a commitment to the goal of gender equality, none has consistently given even lip service to the ideal (enthood (Agassi, 1989; Ho, 1987; Jancar, 1978; L Newland, 1980).

Calls for equal parenthood in Sweden began 1960s, long before interest in "the new father" surfa [illegible] other countries such as the United States. This position quickly gained ascendance in the Social Democratic government, becoming represented in an official policy statement to the United Nations in 1968 and in amendments to family law in 1979 (Baude, 1979; Statens Offentliga Utredningar, 1982a). Equal parenthood is part of the Swedish ideology of equality *(jämställdhet).* According to the Swedish government,

> Equality means that women and men have the same rights, obligations and opportunities to have a job which gives them economic independence, to care for home and children, and to participate in political, union and other activities in society. (Statistiska Centralbyrån, 1990, my translation)

The goal of equal parenthood has led to various reforms in Swedish society. Maternal care practices have changed to encourage participation of fathers in prenatal care, parental education, and delivery. The national school curriculum mandates that *jämställdhet* be taught. Employment practices also illustrate the important regard in which men are held in the childrearing process. Fathers get two weeks off with pay at the time of childbirth, sixty days off per year per child with pay (shared with mothers) to care for sick children, two days off with pay per year per child (shared with mothers) to visit daycare centers and schools, and the right to reduce the workday to six hours for child care purposes.

However, the most significant of all Swedish reforms designed to bring about equal parenthood is parental leave. With return to his original job guaranteed, a Swedish father (married or unmarried) currently has fifteen months of paid leave to share with his partner so that one parent can stay at home for a newborn or adopted child. (An additional six months is available for twins.) As of 1990, the first twelve months of the leave are paid at the level of 90–100% of regular pay (higher if the employee works in the public sector). The last three months are paid at a minimum level, now equivalent to about $10 a day. Benefits are paid out directly from social insurance offices rather than from employers (which is the same procedure used to pay for sick days and short-term disability). The program, however, is paid for mainly by employers, through payroll taxes on all employees.

Sweden was the first country to institute paid parental leave for both mothers and fathers in 1974 (Sidel, 1986). The Swedish parental leave program remains the most financially generous and flexible in the world, and the one most directly tied to a commitment to the principle of equal parenthood (Kamerman, 1985, 1989; Moss and Brannen, 1987). At least five other societies allow fathers to take paid parental leave. These include all the other Nordic nations (Finland, Norway, Iceland, and Denmark) and Yugoslavia (Morgan, 1984; Nordic Council of Ministers, 1988). But none of these other countries' programs predate or are more remunerative or longer lasting than the Swedish program.

Policymakers have shown somewhat greater interest in *unpaid* parental leave for fathers, which is still regarded as a rather radical concept. At least twelve societies have government policies which allow fathers to take unpaid leave: the Netherlands, Belgium, Canada, Bulgaria, France, Germany, Greece, Hungary, Italy, New Zealand, Spain, and Portugal (Bureau of National Affairs, 1986; Mathews, 1989; Moss and Brannen, 1987). While popular interest in equal parenthood in the United States is high, a proposal to provide a modest amount of unpaid leave (12 weeks) to mothers and fathers had not yet been made into law as of 1990.

In contrast to what other countries offer, the generous Swedish parental leave program, based as it is on a commitment to equal parenthood, is a radical attempt to break the centuries-old tradition of women being responsible for children. Fathers' intense involvement with an infant in the first year of life during parental leave might set the stage for men's continued involvement in child care and the eventual realization of the goal of equal parenthood. If men were to be more intensely involved in infant care, through taking parental leave, perhaps children would come to be regarded as the equal responsibility of both parents, and children would come to know both parents as equally capable and nurturing.

A study of Sweden's unique parental leave program allows an exploration into many interesting questions related to fathers' and mothers' sharing responsibility for the care of babies. In this book, the following questions will be addressed:

1. Under what circumstances will a society elect to promote fathers' and mothers' being equally responsible for child care, through legislation and other means?
2. Given the opportunity, will fathers elect to stay home from work to care for their babies?
3. What are the barriers to men's electing to stay home to care for their babies?
4. What are the benefits and problems associated with men's taking parental leave? How do men's experiences with parental leave compare to those of women who have taken parental leave?
5. If fathers stay home and care for their babies, will this lead to greater gender equality in the family? In particular, will men continue to share responsibility for child care when they go back to work, and will men and women become more equal in terms of their interest and opportunities for self-fulfillment in occupational pursuits outside the home?
6. Can social policy be effectively used as an instrument for bringing about the end of such a cultural universal as women's primary responsibility for child care?
7. What are the prospects that men and women in industrial societies will eventually have an equal share in the caring and nurturing of small children?

ORGANIZATION OF THE BOOK

This book presents findings of an intensive study of the Swedish parental leave program, a study specifically designed to address the above questions.

Chapter 2 discusses the history and development of parental leave in Sweden. In particular, it covers the social, political, and economic circumstances which contributed to Sweden's having such a revolutionary stance on the issue of shared parenthood.

Chapter 3 describes the levels of participation of Swedish fathers in the parental leave program, and assesses these over time. Comparisons with mothers' rates of participation and patterns of leavetaking will be made. Men's participation in parental leave will be contrasted to their participation in other Swedish social insurance programs designed to encourage fathers' involvement in child care. Also described are Swedish parents' attitudes toward parental leave and potential reforms in the policy that would likely lead to more equal participation of fathers.

Chapter 4 reports on survey findings to test theories regarding the barriers to men's electing to stay home with their babies, even when there is an official policy allowing them to do so. Social psychological and social structural barriers are considered. Particular attention is paid to the role mothers play in the likelihood that fathers will take parental leave. These findings allow us to pinpoint the factors that are likely to prevent men and women from equally sharing the parental role in other societies as well.

Chapter 5 covers the extent to which fathers reported enjoying taking leave and the specific problems and benefits they encountered while on leave. Factors associated with fathers' having more satisfactory leaves will be explored. Fathers' experiences with parental leave will be compared to those of mothers who had taken leave.

Chapter 6 considers whether parental leave is an effective way of eliminating the traditional gender-based division of labor in the family. Survey findings are used to investigate if fathers' participation in infant care has the effect of increasing gender equality in the family. Specifically, the effects on equalizing mothers' and fathers' interest and involvement in child care activities inside the home and occupational pursuits outside the home are measured.

Chapter 7 discusses implications of the findings from Sweden for the United States. It analyzes the possibility that the U.S. will develop a policy like the Swedish parental leave program in the near future. It also uses knowledge gained about the actual operation of the policy in Sweden to predict what the consequences might be if the U.S. instituted a parental leave program.

The final chapter uses findings from previous chapters to discuss whether social policy can be effectively used as an instrument for bringing about the end of such a cultural universal as women's responsibility for baby care. The prospects for men and women in the future equally sharing in the caring and nurturing of small children are also examined.

This book is based on fifteen years of research, including two and one-half years of fieldwork and a major survey conducted in 1986. (Appendix A describes the study's methodology in detail.) Insight into the development, rationale, and administration of the Swedish program, as well as statistics concerning rates of participation of fathers in parental leave, were obtained through the reading of reports of investigations by Swedish government agencies and academic researchers, through discussions with agency personnel and researchers, and through three months of participant-observation conducted in two Swedish social insurance offices.

The findings on parental behavior and attitudes come from a 1986 mail survey of a representative sample of 319 sets of parents who had children in 1984 in Gothenburg. Gothenburg is a city of half a million inhabitants, contains many of the major industries of Sweden, and is the largest port in the Nordic countries. Mail questionnaires were sent to 721 couples who received parental leave benefits from two local social insurance offices for a child born in 1984. In all, 319 couples returned questionnaires—a response rate of 44%. Standard survey procedure of sending out several reminders could not be followed because official permission for follow-ups could not be obtained. Using census data, attempts were made to assess what biases might exist because of the low response rate. The responding group was found to be quite similar to the general population of Swedish parents in many important respects, including the percentage of fathers who took leave, social class, family structure, and family size.

Finally, intensive interviews were conducted with a small group of nine couples where the parents had shared parental leave fairly equally. These interviews were used to gain additional insight into fathers' motivations for taking parental leave and into their experiences while on leave.

Little research has been done up to now to examine government policies in terms of their effectiveness for bringing about gender equality (Ve, 1989). The purpose of this book is to critically analyze one such attempt, the Swedish parental leave program. This effort, then, is designed to fill a substantial gap in our knowledge about this topic. The questions this book seeks to address are of relevance to many other societies struggling with the issues of helping workers combine employment and family responsibilities and of enhancing gender equality. However, it must be emphasized that the results of this analysis cannot readily be generalized to other postindustrial societies. We must keep in mind that every society represents a peculiar configuration of historical, economic, political, and social forces. Programs that exist in one society cannot be readily adapted to another social setting, and a program which is successful or unsuccessful in one society might not yield the same results in another. Still, a study of Swedish society can help us gain new insight into the social forces likely to be associated with greater interest in fathers' participation in child care, as well as the likelihood of bringing about equality between the sexes through social policy.

2

HISTORY AND DEVELOPMENT OF PARENTAL LEAVE IN SWEDEN

Sweden is unique, in terms of both its long commitment to equal parenthood and its programs, like parental leave for fathers, that are designed to meet that goal. How did Sweden come to take such a revolutionary stance on the issue of shared parenthood, and why was parental leave adopted as one policy to further that goal? This chapter will argue that the Swedish government adopted an egalitarian approach to parenthood and developed parental leave in response to three concerns: worry about a low birth rate, a need to encourage women's employment, and a desire to liberate men from gender stereotypes. The unique features of Swedish society—involving the structure of political and economic institutions as well as cultural values—that led to the development of the parental leave program as a way to address these concerns will also be examined.

THE POPULATION CRISIS

Sweden's policy of advocating shared parenthood has its roots in a concern for the survival of the Swedish population, a concern that first arose in the 1930s. The worldwide Depression brought down an already low birth rate; if the birth rate dropped and remained below replacement levels, serious economic problems were predicted to be the result. A smaller workforce would have to support a growing number of older citizens, and declining levels of investments and consumption would depress the economy. Low fertility was a problem in most of Western Europe; however, Sweden had the lowest rates of all (Hatje, 1974; Kälvemark, 1980).

Some conservatives in Sweden expressed concern over the low birth rate in the late 1920s and early 1930s. But the importance of the declining birth rate in Sweden was brought to the attention of the public by social scientists Alva and Gunnar Myrdal in their book, *Kris i befolkningsfrågan, (Crisis in the Population Question),* published in 1934. The Myrdals recommended that the government, as part of a general plan of social security, subsidize the well-being of the family so that couples would find childbearing more economically feasible. Rejecting notions of coercive parenthood, the Myrdals recommended the abolition of a 1910 law that banned sale of and information on contraceptives, the liberalization of abortion legislation, and the addition of sex education to the school curriculum. The Myrdals also were strong supporters of women's right to employment, which historically has been seen by socialists as a prerequisite for gender equality (Hirdman, 1988). Accordingly, they proposed that the government take steps to help women combine employment outside the home with motherhood. In such drastic economic times, many people begrudged women jobs that could be held by unemployed men. But the Myrdals argued that women would have more children if government programs helped them combine motherhood with employment, that children would be better off with mothers who had a chance to fulfill their ambitions in outside employment, and that two incomes in a family would provide the economic security and comfort which are prerequisites for the willingness to bear and raise children. To critics who might reply that there were not enough jobs, the Myrdals answered that public works projects, sound economic planning, and a growing national economy would create enough jobs for all adults to work if they chose. Other countries experiencing drops in fertility rates at this time developed policies designed to encourage women to have children. What made the Myrdals' recommendations so radical was that they were suggesting that Sweden develop a pronatalist policy that made society, rather than individual women, increase the commitment to family life (Adams and Winston, 1980).

The Myrdals' recommendations were highly regarded by the

Social Democratic Party, which first took control of the Swedish Parliament in 1932. Their recommendations coincided well with the party's commitment to social equality, full employment, and enhanced material welfare. The Myrdals themselves were strong supporters of Social Democratic ideology; they may have used the population issue to gain support for social welfare policies that would otherwise have been opposed by more conservative politicians (Kälvemark, 1980).

The Myrdals' book touched off a heated debate about population policy and had a remarkable amount of influence in a very short period of time (Hirdman, 1988). In 1935 a Population Committee was formed to make recommendations for legislation. This Committee contained representatives from four political parties, and included Gunnar Myrdal as a full member and Alva Myrdal as a consultant (Hirdman, 1988). All parties basically agreed that some social policies were needed in order to arrest the declining birth rate. The Social Democrats were mostly interested in policies which would equalize the living conditions of families in different social classes. Liberals and Conservatives, on the other hand, were more concerned about equalizing the living conditions of small and large families (Hatje, 1974).

The Population Committee wrote eighteen reports during 1935–38 presenting the results of investigations and recommendations for legislation. The Population Committee generally agreed with the Myrdals' goal of voluntary parenthood. Accordingly, they recommended repeal of the law banning contraceptives and economic support for training high school instructors how to teach sex education; their recommendations, in turn, became law. However, the Population Committee did not recommend liberalizing the abortion law. A separate committee to consider changes in abortion legislation was established in 1934, and this committee had recommended extending the grounds for abortion to include exhaustion, poverty, interruption of education and career, social disgrace, and harm to an established relationship. These recommendations were not accepted by the Population Committee, not so much because of moral objections to abortion as much as a concern that making abortions widely available constituted a public admission that the conditions for having a child were not good in Sweden (Kälvemark, 1980).

The Myrdals' recommendations concerning mothers' employment rights were followed. The Committee recommended that working mothers' employment opportunities be protected by prohibiting employers from dismissing women for getting married or pregnant. This proposal became law in 1937 (Näsman, 1986). Recommendations from the Swedish Population Committee also resulted in the passage of a 1937 law granting mothers three months of unpaid maternity leave, six weeks before and six weeks after birth (Frank and Lipner, 1988). This form of voluntary unpaid maternity leave replaced former legislation which forbade employers from employing women during the two weeks before and the six weeks after birth; it was an improvement in that women gained job security. In 1939 unpaid maternity leave was extended to four and one half months, 12 weeks of which was to be taken after childbirth. In 1945, the time period was extended again to six months (Gustafsson, 1983). In 1955, three of the six months became paid (Statens Offentliga Utredningar, 1982b).

Sweden was not the first country to establish maternity leaves for working mothers. Indeed, Sweden's program was less generous than at least nine other countries which instituted *paid* maternity leave programs during or before the 1930s. These other leave programs seemed to have originated from a concern for low birth rates, as in Sweden. In addition, some countries were concerned about the health of mothers and babies in situations where mothers returned to work too soon. European mothers did not make up a very big proportion of the labor force at that time; nevertheless, there was some recognition that women were an important source of temporary and occasional labor power (Frank and Lipner, 1988).

Other Population Committee recommendations which became law included maternity relief (a lump sum of money given low-income mothers at childbirth), marriage loans (to encourage couples to marry at younger ages), subsidized housing for families with three or more children, and payment of costs associated with childbirth, prenatal, and postnatal care (Kälvemark,

1980). In addition to following many of the recommendations of the Population Committee, the Social Democratic–controlled government enacted measures to improve the economic situation of the family, including public works jobs and public housing. Other policies to improve the quality of Swedish family life included rehabilitation of housing to eliminate slums, a national health insurance program, and limited public ownership of industries providing the basic necessities of life (Forsberg, 1984). Another Population Commission was established in 1941 to recommend additional legislation which would promote childbearing. At that time child allowances (a yearly stipend to pay for children's clothes, food, and medicine), as well as free school meals, were instituted (Hatje, 1974).

Welfare policies led to dramatic improvements in Swedes' economic standard of living, job security, and health; poverty was virtually eliminated (Adams and Winston, 1980; Hadenius, 1985). In the 1980s, Sweden tied with Norway for having the highest per capita income in the industrialized world (Qvarfort, McCrae, and Kolunda, 1988). Despite these gains, Swedish family size stayed small; at its lowest point, in 1983, the average Swedish woman had 1.63 children (Ericsson and Jacobsson, 1985). Still, government policy in the 1930s and 1940s may have prevented the birth rate from declining even more dramatically. By 1986 a significant improvement in the birth rate became noticeable, with an increase of 12% between 1983 and 1986 (Jalakas, 1986). By 1989 the birth rate had risen to 2.0, one of the highest rates in Europe (Statistiska Centralbyrån, 1990; Swedish Institute, 1989d).

While early policies to promote childbearing were essentially failures, it was significant for later developments in that the Social Democratic government of Sweden, which has been in power for most of the last half century, has long had an official concern for the birth rate and the welfare of children. This concern for children remained a driving force behind Swedish welfare and family policy. Since the 1930s, several programs have been developed to ensure that children do not suffer because of inadequate family finances. The child's allowance, originally established around World War II, consists now of about $1100 per year until a child is sixteen years old or finishes school (Näsman and Falkenberg, 1990). This is paid for all children, regardless of economic status. Families with more than two children receive more than $1100 per extra child as a bonus. Parents may also receive additional financial assistance for home care and supervision of handicapped children or if one parent is deceased or unable to provide support payments. Housing subsidies are paid to about one-fourth of all Swedish families, to ensure that all families can afford to live in comfortable and spacious dwellings (Melsted, 1988). Such allowances are currently received by 315,000 families with 600,000 children (Ericsson and Jacobsson, 1985). Health care and education are virtually free. One reason parental leave was legislated in the 1970s was so that both parents could retain an attachment to the labor force, which could be seen as a supplement to these other programs designed to provide children with a more secure economic environment (Statens Offentliga Utredningar, 1982b).

Legislation passed since the 1930s has also secured considerable rights for Swedish children. At divorce, children are represented by a court-appointed attorney who looks after their best interests. Since 1977, all legal connotations of "illegitimacy" have been eliminated, so as not to stigmatize children born out of wedlock (Linnér, 1977). A child abuse law passed in 1979 states that corporal punishment (including spanking) and other forms of humiliating treatment are illegal (Adamo, 1980). Since 1978, Swedish children have an "ombudsman" at the national level, which no children in any other country have. This ombudsman

> mobilizes opinion and disseminates information concerning children's needs and works to strengthen children's rights . . . propose[s] and initiate[s] actions which can improve conditions for children . . . support[s] research about children . . . maintain[s] a telephone emergency service for the support and assistance of individual children in distress. (Adamo, 1980:4)

Since the 1970s, one of children's basic rights has also been the opportunity to have close relationships with both parents. Joint custody of children was made the rule for married and unmarried parents in 1983, to help children maintain ties with both parents after separation or divorce (Forsberg, 1984). One argument used for the original parental leave program and for its various extensions is that children need to spend intense time with both parents early in life in order to develop normally (Allen, 1988). A 1990 government-funded publication emphasized the importance of fathers' taking parental leave for the children's sake:

> When the father takes care of the child while the mother works, the groundwork is laid for a deeper relationship between father and child. (Falkenberg, 1990:2, my translation)

By 1990, the Swedish economy was plagued with high inflation and low productivity rates. This prompted a reconsideration of the welfare state model. Still strongly evident, however, was a general consensus that programs which promote children's well-being will remain intact. This is reflected in a statement by the deputy prime minister, who said, "The children . . . always come first" (Pettersson, 1990).

Backett (1982) maintains that a prerequisite for equal parenthood is a change in attitudes toward children. In the nineteenth century, change in attitudes toward children's needs and rights precipitated a major modification in the definition of motherhood in industrialized societies, with mothers put in charge of nurturance and child development. Changes in attitudes toward children occurring in twentieth century Sweden have led to children becoming regarded as precious national resources in need of economic security and nurturing by both parents. This attitude change may be a prerequisite for the development of equal parenthood.

NEED FOR WOMEN'S LABOR POWER

As discussed above, mothers' formal rights to employment were established early in Sweden, in the 1930s. Nevertheless, the pronatalist programs of the 1930s did nothing to stimulate mothers to take advantage of these newfound opportunities. The percentage of wives and mothers who were employed outside of the home stayed low for decades after their employment rights were assured (Scott, 1982). In 1950, only 15% of married women were employed (Hirdman, 1988). The "doctrine of separate spheres" for married men and women, whereby women were regarded as best suited for nurturing and homemaking and men for engaging in breadwinning through occupational pursuits outside of the home, dominated Swedish thinking. This sentiment was reflected in a bill introduced in the Swedish Parliament by conservatives which would have prohibited married women from seeking paid employment; the Social Democrats, however, opposed this bill and it was defeated (Adams and Winston, 1980).

Yet, except for formally ensuring wives' and mothers' employment rights and establishing maternity leave, the Social Democrats did not initiate special programs that would have improved women's job opportunities. For example, most of the public works jobs created by the government in the 1930s were physically arduous construction jobs intended for men (Adams and Winston, 1980). Although the Population Committee in the late 1930s recommended that the government fund day care centers, legislation to do so did not receive support in the Social Democratic–controlled Parliament.

It was not until the 1960s that a revolution in wives' and mothers' labor force participation rates occurred. During the 1960s the Swedish economy boomed; there was a shortage of male workers to fill positions created by expanding industry and the growing private and public service sectors. In the 1950s and early 1960s, some of the demand for labor was met by the importation of foreign workers, but the difficulties of assimilation eventually resulted in the government's deciding that native women were a better source of labor power (Adams and Winston, 1980). Swedish economists stated that it was no longer economically "efficient" for female talent to be wasted; one (Per Holmberg) claimed that the Swedish gross national product could be increased by 50% by allowing women to fill positions they were best suited for (Leijon, 1968). A projected continued shortage of male workers, a desire to increase the size of the public sector, and interest in increasing economic productivity prompted the Swedish government to start new programs to encourage more women—particularly mothers—to take jobs (Adams and Winston, 1980; Ruggie, 1984). The Social Democratic goal of full employment, upheld since the

1930s but generally applied only to men, was finally extended to women (Baude, 1979).

Several programs were instituted to increase women's qualifications for and interest in employment. One important program involved vocational training. Courses varied in length from a few weeks to two years, and trainees received the equivalent of an unskilled job's wage during the training period. Programs were expanded in the 1960s to include more housewives. These were a dramatic success: in 1960, only 14% of the people retrained were women, but by 1975 the figure was over 50% (Gustafsson and Lantz, 1985). The government also increased the number of study grants for higher education, which led to a great increase in the recruitment of females to colleges and universities (Wistrand, 1981). After 1980, student loans were made independent of spousal income, which increased married women's opportunities to acquire a second education (Gustafsson, 1983). A new national school curriculum in 1962 recommended "that girls with a leaning toward technical and scientific subjects be encouraged" (Sandlund, 1971). One hundred "activation inspectors" were employed by the National Labor Market Board (Arbetsmarknadsstyrelsen) to work in local employment offices for the special purpose of encouraging women to enter the labor force (Gustafsson, 1983). This agency also put out a considerable amount of advertising and held conferences to promote women's employment (Baude, 1979). All protective legislation limiting women's participation in certain jobs was abolished during the 1960s, generally by extending protections to all workers the protections originally intended for women only (Baude, 1979).

In 1972 the Advisory Council for Equality between Men and Women was established, which was a special panel (made up of Social Democrats) appointed by the national government and answerable to the Prime Minister (Adams and Winston, 1980). This council made recommendations to increase women's access to nontraditional jobs through government policies and programs. To combat sex segregation of jobs, the panel convinced the government to sponsor pilot programs to retrain women for nontraditional occupations, to institute financial subsidies for employers who hired women for nontraditional jobs, to place special counselors in schools and employment offices in order to encourage girls and women to consider nontraditional occupations, and to mandate that schoolchildren visit job sites in fields that were not traditional for their sex (Baude, 1979; Ruggie, 1984).

An important institutional restriction on Swedish women's abilities to enter employment in the 1950s and early 1960s was a tax policy whereby mates were forced to pool incomes for tax purposes. In Sweden's highly progressive income tax system, this had the effect of increasing the tax burden in families with two earners, thus discouraging women from entering the labor force. So in 1966 the tax laws were changed so that income taxes could be levied on individuals instead of on families. By 1971 the individual tax system was made obligatory (Gustafsson and Lantz, 1985). It was the Liberal Party which first advocated separate taxation; the Social Democrats apparently were not at first enthusiastic, because of a concern that the tax system would become somewhat less progressive in character (Eduards, 1988).

To encourage more mothers to work, the government decided in the 1960s to assume more responsibility for the provision of daycare centers. In 1975 new goals for daycare were established that involved specific target numbers and dates (Baude, 1979). The national government pays 50% of daycare costs and municipal governments pay 42%. Parents thus pay only 8% of actual costs (Gustafsson, 1983). These subsidies, as well as a commitment to expand the number of places, have led to a dramatic increase in the number of children using subsidized center- or family-based child care. In 1970 only 10% of preschool children (ages 0–6) were in government-subsidized center or home care (Gustafsson, 1983). By 1989, 55% of this group were in subsidized daycare centers or family daycare. An additional 29% of 7–12 year olds were cared for in government-subsidized after-school programs (Statistiska Centralbyrån, 1990).

Another measure that improved women's job opportunities was an increase in the supply of relief jobs in sectors where women had traditionally worked (e.g., hospitals). Relief jobs are created to maintain full employment, either by deliberate expansion of the public sector or by government subsidies to the private sector which cover 75% of a new employee's wages during the first six months. In 1973 only 12% of relief jobs went to women; by 1980, 41% did (Gustafsson, 1983). The increase in jobs made available to women demonstrated that the Swedish government was interested not just in exploitation of female labor power but also in the concept of full employment for women.

Starting in 1974, companies were encouraged to hire women workers by government subsidies to businesses which built or expanded facilities outside the three major metropolitan areas (Stockholm, Gothenburg, and Malmö). If at least 40% of the new hires were women, then a company could get location aid and subsidies for training new workers. American social scientists evaluating this program concluded that it was successful in improving employment opportunities for Swedish women (Brown and Wilcher, 1987).

In 1976 the Social Democrats lost control of the national government after a reign of nearly half a century. The loss appeared to be due not to any disagreement about existing welfare state policies or women's employment rights, but to other issues (including the Social Democrats' reluctance to ban nuclear power in the face of growing support for environmentalist causes). In his first statement of government policy to the Swedish Parliament, the new nonsocialist Prime Minister, Thorbjörn Fälldin, stated:

> The equality of men and women is one of the essential premises of government policy . . . and efforts to establish equality between men and women are to be speeded up. (McCrea, 1979:314)

The nonsocialist coalition which took power in 1976 made women's employment rights a top priority. The Advisory Council for Equality between the Sexes, formerly under the Prime Minister, was made into a standing committee with representatives from all political parties, under the auspices of the Ministry of Labor. The purpose of the committee was to propose and support equality policies and legislation (McCrea, 1979). Nonsocialists were particularly interested in an equal employment opportunity law for women, and this committee was instructed to draft such legislation. In 1977 the equal employment law was passed (to take effect in 1980). It banned sex discrimination in employment (both for equal work and work of equal value), requested employers to pursue efforts to promote workplace equality (i.e., affirmative action), and appointed an "equality ombudsman" to ensure compliance with the law (Gustafsson, 1983). The Social Democrats and the trade union federation (LO) that forms its main base of support originally opposed such legislation on the grounds that employment conditions and compensation should be negotiated in trade union agreements. After substantial initial opposition, however, the Social Democrats accepted the equal employment law as one tool of many which can be used to ensure gender equality in employment. In 1982 they made a campaign pledge to strengthen the equality act and its implementation (Ruggie, 1984).

Other employment reforms implemented by the nonsocialist coalition included fifty days of paid pregnancy leave, which became a benefit in 1980, completely separate from parental leave taken after the baby was born. In 1982, the government also set aside ten million Swedish crowns (almost $2 million) for a nationwide campaign, called "More Women for Industry," to recruit girls and women for nontraditional jobs. These funds financed special training for guidance counselors, teachers, and principals; provided schools with visiting role-models; organized field trips, weekend courses, and camps for interested girls; and furnished special computer literacy training for women already in the labor market (Ericsson and Jacobsson, 1985; Swedish Institute, 1989a). This campaign served as a model for a later one launched in 1985 by the Social Democrats. In that campaign, another fifteen million Swedish crowns (about $3 million) was used to acquaint preschool-aged girls with technology, to institute special technical courses for girls in the eighth and ninth grades, to establish support groups for women in postsecondary nontraditional education, and to develop models for training teachers, counselors, and principals in nontraditional education. At the workplace, women in nontraditional jobs were given special support, and supervisors received special training (Ericsson and Jacobsson, 1985).

While the government (both under Social Democratic and nonsocialist leadership) developed programs to promote women's equal employment opportunities, trade unions were also working toward this goal. The vast majority of Swedish employees (88%) belong to a trade union; local unions are organized into three large federations that include blue-collar, white-collar, and professional workers respectively. Women are almost half (47%) of all those who belong to unions (Statistiska Centralbyrån, 1987). Unions negotiate employment conditions and wages every three years with the Federation of Swedish Employers; wage policies have generally been developed through these negotiations rather than through legislation. Unions, because they represent such a large proportion of the adult Swedish population, are also often included as partners in the policy-making process within the government. For example, most of the employment programs and policies initiated in the 1960s to increase women's participation in the labor market were established upon the recommendation of the Joint Female Labor Council (originally founded in 1951), an advisory group composed of representatives from the federation of employers and the blue-collar trade union federation (LO).

The unions have had a history of general support for women's employment; however, this support has not always been as substantial as some feminists would like. As early as 1931, the blue-collar trade union federation (LO) rejected a proposal that would have prohibited married women from working in the state sector. At the same time, LO refused to take a stand against employment discrimination, an issue raised by women delegates (Scott, 1982). A women's council was created in 1947 to advise LO's leadership regarding women's employment issues; however, separate wage rates for women and men were still being written into wage contracts until 1960 (Scott, 1982).

It was not until 1977 that the blue collar (LO) and white-collar (TCO) union federations negotiated agreements with the employers' federation to promote equal employment opportunities for women. This agreement stipulated that

> women and men should have equal opportunities for employment, training, promotion and development at work . . . equal

> pay for equal work . . . [T]here should be more equal distribution between women and men in occupations where choice of vocation and recruitment have shown themselves to be biased against one of the sexes. (Ericsson and Jacobsson, 1985:25)

This agreement may have been at least partly motivated by a desire to prevent the nonsocialist government from involving itself in employment issues through the passage of an equal employment opportunity law (which was still passed in 1977). It also appears that unions were influenced by the 1970s women's movement in Sweden (Fredriksson, 1987).

Unions still tend to give equality between the sexes low priority, under that of securing rights for workers and leveling social class differences. For example, the program of the commercial workers' union states:

> We advocate equality between women and men, but only so long as it does not conflict with the union movement's other equality goals. (Fredriksson, 1987, my translation)

The most important union-initiated policy helping women's employment conditions was the "wage solidarity policy" initiated in the 1960s. This involved higher paid workers' foregoing as large raises as they might normally have obtained, in the interest of raising the wages of low-paid workers. This policy, however, was not explicitly motivated by a concern for women's wages. Wage solidarity policy advocates were waging a battle against social class differences, which were regarded as more important to eliminate than gender differences. Nevertheless, in the end, this policy helped women more than it did men, and it resulted in their receiving equal pay for comparable work.

All of these reforms and policies, instituted by the government and trade unions, were designed to increase women's employment opportunities and compensation. To help promote women's continued involvement in the labor market during the childbearing years, maternity leave policy was also modified. In 1963, legislation extended maternity leave to six months with full pay. Policymakers believed that maternity leaves would shorten the work interruption at childbirth, because a woman was allowed to keep her old job and did not need to seek a new one later (Gustafsson and Lantz, 1985).

Sweden was not the only country to have paid maternity leave as a conscious policy to keep women in the labor force. In 1960, 58 other countries had some form of provisions for paid maternity leaves; by 1980, this had increased to 72. These societies, like Sweden, were interested in providing maternity leave as a way to encourage women to retain an attachment to the labor market (Kamerman, 1989). But in 1963, with the establishment of a full six months of fully paid leave, Sweden took over the lead (which it still holds) in offering longer paid leaves than any other nation.

Efforts to recruit women into the labor force have been very successful. Swedish women are now almost as much a part of the labor force as men. In 1989, 85% of Swedish women ages 20–64 were employed, compared to 89% of men (Statistiska Centralbyrån, 1990). Unemployment rates for both sexes are essentially the same, hovering around 3% in the early 1980s and about 1% in the late 1980s (Statistiska Centralbyrån, 1987). In 1963 only 38% of mothers of preschool-aged children were employed; by 1989 the figure was 86% (Baude, 1979; Statistiska Centralbyrån, 1986a, 1990). Over 80% of women return to the labor force within one year of having a baby (Qvarfort, McCrae, and Kolunda, 1988).

The need for female labor power diminished for a period of time in the late 1970s and early 1980s with a weakening of the Swedish economy. Nevertheless, the concern for women's employment opportunities remained a permanent part of social policy during this time. Two incomes were seen as vital for a family's economic security, after real wages began to fall in the late 1970s (Hoem and Hoem, 1989). Women's economic independence is also seen as a prerequisite for sexual equality (Statens Offentliga Utredningar, 1982b). In this context, programs like parental leave were justified as ensuring women's continued equal access to employment.

While women, including mothers, are a permanent part of the labor force in Sweden, it is important to note that their status in the labor market still does not approximate men's. Almost half (43%) of women workers are employed less than thirty-five hours per week. They have taken job-sharing arrangements or permanent part-time jobs or have temporarily reduced their workday to six hours, which all parents of preschool-aged children are entitled to do by law. (The corresponding figure for men is only 7% [Nätti, 1990].) In 1989 the average number of work hours for women with preschool-aged children was 29.2, while the average for men was 42.5 (Statistiska Centralbyrån, 1990). Part-time jobs are more plentiful in Sweden than in many other societies, and Swedish women appear to prefer part-time work as the easiest way to combine the double role of mother and employee (Kalleberg and Rosenfeld, 1990; Kugelberg, 1987). Part-time work, however, usually consists of a thirty-hour work week, bringing women's average work week to thirty-two hours versus forty-one hours for men (Olofsson, 1986). Moreover, it is important to note that employees who work 17 hours or more a week are entitled to the same social welfare benefits and employment rights as full-time workers (Pettersson, 1989). A recent lowering of the tax rates might encourage more women to work full-time, since the high marginal tax rates of the past often discouraged workers from working as many hours as they could.

Because they so often work part-time, Swedish women draw only 41% of all wages paid to workers (Statistiska Centralbyrån, 1990). When they work full-time, Swedish women earn a fairly equitable wage, thanks to the wage solidarity policy promulgated by trade unions. In 1963 female industrial workers made (per hour) only 72% of what male workers did; by 1990 they made 90% (Gustafsson and Lantz, 1985; Hagberg and Johansson, 1986; Statistiska Centralbyrån, 1990). In 1973 women employed full-time by the national government made 80% of men's wages; by 1989 they made 89% (Hagberg and Johansson, 1986; Statistiska Centralbyrån, 1990). Slower progress has been made in the private white-collar sector, where women made 63% of what men earned in 1973, and 75% in 1989 (Hagberg and Johansson, 1986; Statistiska Centralbyrån, 1990). The latter wage difference reflects men's tendency to dominate the highly paid top-level positions in the private sector.

While these gains are impressive, it should be noted that no progress in wage rates is in evidence for the last half of the 1980s. There is even a hint that Swedish women's income gains are slipping. For example, in 1985 Swedish women industrial workers made 91% of the hourly wage of male workers; by 1990, this had slipped slightly to 90%. Female government workers made 91% of male government workers' wages in 1985, compared to 89% in 1989 (Gustafsson and Lantz, 1985; Hagberg and Johansson, 1986; Statistiska Centralbyrån, 1990). Legislation is currently being debated which would force employers to work harder on reducing wage differences in employment.

In terms of job placements, the Swedish labor market is still among the most sex-segregated in the industrial world (Ericsson and Jacobsson, 1985; Pettersson, 1989). Women and men tend to work in different sectors—women in the public and men in the private. Within these sectors they do different jobs. Only 7% of women and 6% of men work in jobs where the sexes are balanced, within a 40–60% range for each group (Statistiska Centralbyrån, 1990). Over half of all employed women are found in these ten jobs: secretaries and typists, nursing aides, shop assistants, cleaners, daycare workers, "home helpers" (assistants for the elderly or families with handicapped children), bookkeepers and office cashiers, nurses, elementary school teachers, and kitchen staff—in that order. On the other hand, about one-third of all men are employed in these jobs: machine fitters and assemblers, motor vehicle drivers, farmers and foresters, commercial travellers and buyers, mechanics, mechanical engineers, carpenters, construction engineers, electricians, and warehouse workers—in that order (Ericsson and Jacobsson, 1985).

Several explanations can be offered for the persistence of occupational sex segregation in Sweden. The relatively small pay differentials between women's and men's jobs may be one reason. The economic incentives which might encourage women to try to overcome barriers to their entry into male-dominated work settings are lacking. There has also been great demand for labor in the female-dominated occupations (e.g., clerical, sales, and caregiving work), making it unnecessary for women to enter male-dominated fields to seek employment (Kauppinen and Haavio-Mannila, 1989). Another explanation for the persistence of occupational segregation in Sweden suggests that traditional prejudices against women still operate to prevent them from pursuing a wide variety of occupational opportunities. In light of the strong legal, union, and cultural pressures to provide women with equal pay for equal *and* comparable work, limiting women's access to certain jobs remains a way to discriminate against women. One Swedish study of two companies uncovered ways in which informal rules and norms at the workplace discouraged women from remaining in nontraditional jobs (Lindgren, 1989). Socialization practices are also blamed for girls' occupational choices. Studies show that Swedish girls are still more comfortable when training for traditionally female jobs (Gustafsson, 1983).

There is some evidence that sex segregation in the labor market may decline in the future. More young people are choosing nontraditional subjects as majors in upper secondary school *(gymnasium).* Between 1977 and 1987, for example, the percentage of female students in the technical "line" increased from 12% to 23%. In 1989, 50% of all students majoring in business and economics were women. The percentage of male students in the clerical line rose from 10% to 18% between 1980 and 1987 (Rhoadie, 1989; Swedish Institute, 1989b).

In 1988 the Swedish government introduced a five-year plan for equality, largely designed to reduce sex segregation in the labor market. This plan calls for six new occupations to become entirely desegregated, more men working in the field of child care, and a reduction in the number of occupations where the minority sex is 10% or less from the present sixteen occupations to ten (Näsman and Falkenberg, 1990). The recent lowering of the tax rate might also encourage some women to enter male-dominated occupations as the financial incentives to do so will have risen.

Swedish women infrequently have access to positions of economic power, holding only 3% of the senior executive positions in businesses and public agencies (Ericsson and Jacobsson, 1985). Women also lack representation at the highest levels of trade unions. Women are 44% of the membership of the blue-collar trade union federation (LO) but only 7% of those at the top levels of leadership. Women fare only somewhat better in the white-collar trade union federation, making up 57% of the total membership and 18% of the leaders. Women have relatively more power in the leadership of the professionals' union, where they are 38% of the members and 20% of the leaders (Statistiska Centralbyrån, 1987).

Last but not least, the time women spend being employed has to be added to the time spent in domestic work. Adding in the latter, full-time working women have a 74-hour work week, in contrast to full-time working men, who have a 65-hour work week. Work loads between the sexes appear more equitable when women work part-time, which is probably why so many women work part-time. For example, in families with children under three years of age, mothers are employed an average of twenty-four hours per week and work thirty-eight hours in the home for a total of sixty-two, compared to men's average of forty-one paid and nineteen unpaid hours, for a total of sixty (Ericsson and Jacobsson, 1985).

Despite these remaining gaps between ideology and reality, some foreign observers have concluded that Swedish women have a stronger position in the labor force than do women in the rest of the world (Flanagan, 1987; Rhoadie, 1989; Ruggie, 1984). Full employment for women has become a tenet of labor market and family policy that is accepted by all political parties and trade unions. Swedes "hold sacred" everyone's right to work (Rollén, 1978) and entitlement to both the material rewards of employment and the opportunities for fulfillment and social contact. In recent years, Swedes have also adopted an ethic that holds sacred everyone's *obligation* to work, which is reflected in social policy as well. One policymaker stated:

> Women . . . must reject the housewife ideal and stop regarding the family as an institution for their own support. Women must consciously strive to make a career for themselves and to become socially and economically independent of men. (Leijon, 1968:40)

Even the laws governing the rights and obligations of married and cohabiting couples have been amended to state clearly that women should be economically independent (Swedish Institute, 1989a).

Beliefs about work were used to justify the development of the parental leave program in the early 1970s. Women's retention in the labor market was regarded as strengthened through parental leave policies. At the same time, since the programs were also made available to men, employers would be discouraged from discriminating against women who might go on leave. A 1990 government-funded publication emphasized the importance of fathers' right to parental leave for women's employment:

> It is worthwhile for the woman to keep contact with her job. Studies show that the longer the woman has been absent from her job the more difficult it is for her to come back to her old job. Today's women want as much as men to have a secure place at the workplace. Shortly said, it is a question of equality. . . . (Falkenberg, 1990:2–3, my translation)

DESIRE FOR MEN'S LIBERATION

During the 1950s and early 1960s, government leaders subscribed to the philosophy that women should have two roles—homemaker and breadwinner, a model first proposed by the Myrdals in the 1930s. As a rule, women did not engage in these roles simultaneously. Women were wage-earners before they had children and again after their children were school-aged.

This all changed in the mid-1960s as a result of an intensive public debate about gender roles. This debate was begun in 1961 by a feminist journalist, Eva Moberg, in an essay titled "Kvinnans villkorliga frigivning" ("The Conditional Emancipation of Women"), which was widely circulated in Swedish intellectual circles in an anthology titled *Unga liberaler (Young Liberals)* and later reprinted in popular magazines and in a book of essays published by Moberg in 1962. She argued that women would never achieve equal employment opportunities as long as it was assumed that women should adopt a double role of worker and housewife–mother. She saw no reason why women should be held primarily responsible for child care and housework:

> Actually there is no biological connection whatsoever between the function of giving birth to and nursing a child and the function of washing its clothes, preparing its food and trying to bring it up to be a good and harmonious person. . . . The

> concept of double roles can have an unhappy effect in the long run. It perpetuates the idea that woman has an inherent main task, the care and upbringing of children, homemaking and keeping the family together.... Both men and women have one main role, that of being human beings. (Moberg, 1962, my translation)

Moberg made specific recommendations about changing men's roles. She felt that men were too pressured to advance, compete, and raise the family's living standard. Swedes should lower their expectations regarding economic and social success and raise expectations regarding men's participation in domestic work and bringing up children.

Moberg's viewpoint on gender was provided with some scientific basis in a book by Swedish social scientists, titled *Kvinnors liv och arbete (Women's Lives and Work),* published in 1962. (An English edition appeared in 1971.) This book was widely reviewed and discussed, because the researchers involved had good contacts with the media (Scott, 1982). One of the articles in this anthology, written by a psychologist, claimed that there was no scientific basis for the opinion that maternal employment affected children adversely. In a message reminiscent of contemporary advice in American women's magazines, Tiller (1971) concluded that quality of mother–child interaction was more important than quantity. The editor of the anthology, sociologist Edmund Dahlström, described the radical position on sex roles as the only possible one. He stated:

> The concept of the 'two roles of women' is . . . untenable. Both men and women have *one* main role, that of human being. For both sexes, this role would include child care. (Dahlström, 1971:179)

The trade unions also began to advocate a more egalitarian sharing of child care. Reports in 1967 and 1976 from the blue-collar trade union federation (LO) and the white-collar federation (TCO) emphasized that men should be more responsible for child care (Landsorganisationen, 1976; Qvist, Acker, and Lorwin, 1984; Tjänstemännens Centralorganisation, 1976). In their 1977 agreement with the employers' federation, LO and TCO stipulated that "it should be possible for both men and women to combine employment with parental responsibilities" (Ericsson and Jacobsson, 1985). In the mid-1970s, the blue-collar trade union federation sponsored a traveling exhibition called "The Right to Be Human." According to Scott (1982:43):

> The exhibition's message was that imprisonment in the masculine role is at least as great a problem to men as conformity to a feminine ideal is to women; that a debate on liberation and equality must be about how men as well as women are forced to act out socially determined stereotypes.

The radical view advocating liberation for both men and women quickly gained acceptance by the government and its agencies. In Sweden, school curricula are nationally determined. When the basic school curriculum was revised in 1969, schools were told to play a more active role in promoting sexual equality. According to this curriculum, the school must

> promote equality between the sexes—in the family, in the labor market and in the community at large. This should be achieved partly by treating boys and girls the same at school, partly by working to counteract the traditional attitudes to sex roles and stimulating pupils to question the differences between men and women with respect to influence, work assignments and wages that exist in many sectors of society.... The schools should assume that men and women will play the same role in the future, that preparation for the parental role is just as important for boys as for girls, and that girls have reason to be just as interested in their careers as boys. (Baude, 1979:153)

In his 1972 charge to the Advisory Council for Equality Between Men and Women, Prime Minister Olof Palme stated:

> The demand for equality... involves changes not only in the conditions of women but also in the conditions of men. One purpose of such changes is to give women an increased opportunity for gainful employment and to give men an increased responsibility for care of the children. (Baude, 1979:151)

In 1977 the National Labor Market Board stated:

> Conditions of work must be altered so that in every job, men and women can combine gainful employment with domestic

> responsibilities. The right for men to take responsibility for their children on the same basis as women must be accepted and encouraged. (Arbetsmarknadsstyrelsen, 1977)

An extension of maternity benefits to men was seen early on as a way to symbolize the commitment to gender equality. In 1967 the Swedish Parliament appointed a family policy commission to investigate how the social insurance system could be changed to promote both women's employment and sexual equality. This committee presented reports in 1968 and 1969 recommending that maternity leave be converted into a parental leave system so that fathers also could have access to benefits (Familjepolitiska Kommittén, 1969). A 1969 report prepared by Alva Myrdal for the Social Democratic Party convention also advocated that parental leave be shared between mothers and fathers, as did reports prepared by the two largest trade union federations (Landsorganisationen, 1976; Qvist, Acker, and Lorwin, 1984).

In 1974, on the vote of Parliament, maternity leave policy was replaced with a parental insurance system which allowed fathers as well as mothers to take time off with pay after the birth of a child. Couples had six months of leave to share. They would be compensated at 90% of their usual salary and be granted their original job or an equivalent position upon their return to work. In 1975 the leave time was extended to seven months.

Additional legislation was passed that would encourage men to take on a more active parenting role. A 1974 law granted men ten days off with pay, to be taken within the first month following childbirth (usually when mother and baby return home). They were also allowed to share with mothers ten paid days off per year to care for a sick child or to care for a child when its caregiver is ill.

When the nonsocialist parties took power in 1976, efforts to promote gender equality continued. In the first year of the nonsocialists' reign, the most conservative political party involved in the coalition put forth a motion in Parliament which expressed its commitment to "increase responsibility on the part of men for home and children" (Eduards, 1988:7). Paid parental leave was extended twice, to nine months in 1978 and to twelve months in 1980 (with nine months fully paid). In 1977, the number of paid days off from work to care for a sick child was increased to 12–18, depending on the number of children in the family; in 1980, the number of days was again increased to sixty in order to help parents manage a child's catastrophic or chronic illness.

In 1978 both fathers and mothers were granted the right to take unpaid leave from their jobs until their children were eighteen months old, as well as the right to reduce their workday (without compensation) to six hours (Baude, 1979). In 1979 family law was changed to say explicitly that spouses should share breadwinning, housework, and child care roles (Statens Offentliga Utredningar, 1982b). A 1979 law offered voluntary parent education (with time off from work with pay) for ten hours before childbirth and ten hours after. One of the motivations for the law was to give men the opportunity to learn how to do child care. In 1981, the Ministry of Social Affairs sent out new directives to promote the involvement of the father in prenatal care and at childbirth; a man's need for support during his partner's pregnancy was also emphasized (Sellström and Swedin, 1987).

In 1982 the Social Democrats returned to power, and governmental efforts to promote men's liberation and equal parenthood continued. In 1983 the Swedish government was the first in the world to appoint a commission to study men's roles. This group conducted seminars and research studies. It published several books advocating men's liberation that received considerable publicity in the mass media (Arbetsgruppen, 1985; Jalmert, 1983; Jalmert, 1984). One of the major recommendations of the group was that the government provide stronger encouragement for men to share child care. By 1985 a report for the Third United Nations Women's Conference stated that

> the Government has concentrated its attention on two main aspects of equal opportunities: strengthening the position of women in the labor market and strengthening the position of men above all as parents. (Ericsson and Jacobsson, 1985:5)

In 1986 the first government-sponsored men's crisis center in the Nordic countries opened in Gothenburg, to help men cope with some of the problems brought on by the traditional male role. Two additional centers were established in 1988 in Stockholm and Östersund. Services are provided free. In 1987 the government agency assigned to sponsor and encourage research on gender issues was instructed to promote research programs on men (Bengtsson and Frykman, 1987).

Independent initiatives in regard to men's liberation have also taken place in Sweden. In 1975, a book was published with interviews of fifty men who spoke of their "right to be human" (Paulsen, Andersson, and Sessler, 1975). In May of 1989, an idea fair on "The Man of the Future" opened in Uppsala, with researchers, union and business leaders, government officials, sports figures, and church leaders participating.

In 1986 changes were made in the parental leave policy to allow fathers to take leave even if their mates were not eligible. In 1988 parents became eligible for an additional three months of parental leave, raising the number of nearly fully paid months to twelve, with an additional minimally paid three months of leave (Swedish Institute, 1989a). This last extension followed an election campaign, where the Social Democrats lauded extending parental leave and subsidized daycare as solutions to combining work and family, while nonsocialist parties wanted to enact a caregiver's allowance as a form of payment to the parent staying home. This latter proposal seemed to reflect a preference for the traditional gender-based division of labor with the mother at home, while the Social Democratic promoted the involvement of both parents, as well as the state, in childrearing. Soon after the Social Democrats won the 1988 election, parental leave was quickly extended by three months, following what appeared to be an electoral mandate for equal parenthood.

Parental leave is an expensive social program, now costing about $1 billion a year (Riksförsäkringsverket, 1989a). In 1989 the Swedish government embarked upon a series of economic programs and cutbacks designed to reduce inflation and improve productivity. While there has been no move to reduce or eliminate current parental leave benefits, the three-month extension of benefits passed by Parliament for 1990 was postponed, pending an improvement in the national economy.

While interest in changing men's roles remains high, there is considerable evidence that Swedish men are far from "whole human beings" when it comes to participation in employment, housework, child care, and, as will be discussed in the next chapter, in usage of parental leave benefits. Few men elect to work part-time while their children are young (Statistiska Centralbyrån, 1987). Even at the national level, where equality rhetoric is high, the Moderate Party leader was ousted in 1986 partly because of criticism by male party regulars that he left too many meetings early to care for his preschool-aged children. A 1983 study of five thousand men revealed the widespread existence of the "in-principle man." Swedish men thought that men ought *in principle* to devote themselves to housework and take care of children, but for them personally it was difficult to do this (Trost, 1983a). Other studies of the Swedish domestic division of labor have also found complete equality to be lacking, although it appears that Swedish men are more involved in domestic work and child care than are men in other parts of the world (Haas, 1981, 1982; Konsumentverket, 1982; Liljeström, Svensson, and Mellström, 1976; Näsman, Nordström, and Hammarström, 1983; Sandqvist, 1987b; Statens Offentliga Utredningar, 1982b; Statistiska Centralbyrån, 1980; Trost, 1983b).

Parental leave had the support of Swedish political parties, trade unions, and influential social scientists. The policy fitted in well with the concern for the low birth rate, an interest in promoting women's employment opportunities, and a new concern for men's liberation. There are, however, some additional reasons why parental leave was legislated so easily—reasons that relate to the political, economic and social climate of Sweden.

POLITICAL FACTORS FAVORING PARENTAL LEAVE

One important political reason for the development of parental leave may have been that by 1974, the year parental leave was made into law, women made up 21% of the membership of the Swedish Parliament. At that time, this was the highest level of female representation in the legislative body of any democracy or socialist state (Hedvall, 1975). Currently, 33% of the members of the Swedish Parliament are women. Women also hold one-third of the cabinet seats in the government (Swedish Institute, 1989a). According to Rhoadie (1989:31), Sweden is one of only three countries in the world (along with Norway and Iceland) where there is a "constantly expanding and sustained high level of participation by women in representative politics." Most of these women have taken advantage of their unusual political clout to advocate equal participation of mothers and fathers in child care. Women's relatively high representation in Parliament reflects both the history of the feminist movement in Sweden and the type of political system Sweden has.

Most Swedish feminists have chosen to work within the confines of the women's sections of the major political parties, rather than in autonomous women's groups. In 1970, for example, 198,000 Swedish women belonged to the women's auxiliaries of the four main political parties, while only eleven thousand belonged to the autonomous feminist organization, the Fredrika Bremer Society, and only one thousand belonged to the radical women's liberation organization called Group 8 (Adams and Winston, 1980; Lyle and Qvist, 1974).

The first women's section of a political party was established by the Social Democrats in 1882; the remaining four parties developed sections by the mid-1930s (Adams and Winston, 1980). In the beginning, women's sections had subordinate positions within the party hierarchy. As time passed, women's sections generated considerable debate regarding family and labor policies within the party and sensitized male leaders to the importance of women's holding high-level decisionmaking positions. The members of women's sections have typically been the more radical women in the party, considerably more radical than the predominantly male party leadership (Eduards, 1988; Hernes, 1987; Qvist, 1980).

Swedish feminists have chosen legislative politics as a route to power because they believe the solutions for women's problems lie in changes in family and labor market policies. While other European and North American feminists, particularly in the 1960s, have concentrated on raising women's consciousness of oppression through the establishment of support groups, Swedish feminists have sought solutions at the societal, rather than the individual, level. According to Adams and Winston:

> Swedish feminists express little faith in the possibility of changing social conditions by changing individual consciousness. Consciousness raising seems to them to be a completely backward approach: It is not a woman's consciousness that determines her social circumstances; rather her circumstances determine her consciousness. (1980:137)

Accordingly, Swedish feminists regard government policy as an essential tool for the liberation of women. Since government policy is necessary, it is essential for them to be involved directly in the political process, and there is no better way to do this than active involvement in the political parties themselves.

Nordic feminists in general have sought political office because they want to change the content of dominant social ideology. Their major ideological aim has been to define women's interests as "general" interests, rather than as "special" interests. The concerns that women have traditionally espoused—particularly children's welfare, equal employment opportunity for women, and family stability and security—are defined by feminists as appropriate concerns for the entire society to have. To a considerable extent, this ideological aim has been realized (Hernes, 1987).

The type of political system that exists in Sweden has also made it possible for women to exert influence over social policy. Sweden's political system is based on proportional representation. Voters do not register support for individual candidates, which can work to the disadvantage of candidates (like women) who could be victims of social stereotyping. An individual candidate wins office based on the size of the popular vote for the *party* which the electorate has given as well as on that candidate's *ranking* on the party list. Women became politically astute and experienced through work in women's sections and gradually worked their way up through the party hierarchies. This meant that they were moved up further on the party slates and eventually elected to Parliament.

Women's involvement in traditional party politics and their election to office in record numbers has undoubtedly had an effect on the direction and pace of Swedish family and labor market policy. Nevertheless, it seems unlikely that women would have been able to have much influence if the objective (economic) circumstances that called for changes in government policy did not exist, namely concern for the welfare of the next generation and the need for women's labor power.

While most women interested in effecting radical change in social institutions work through women's sections of political parties, there are autonomous women's organizations in Sweden which have exerted pressure on women in the political establishment. Indeed, Eva Moberg, who started the debate about men's roles, was active in one such organization, the Frederika Bremer Society, as the editor of its bimonthly publication. Frederika Bremer herself was a model of a woman who worked outside established channels for women's rights. She was a 19th century feminist who campaigned for single women's economic and civil rights and for women's suffrage (Oakley, 1966).

Another political reason for the development of parental leave concerns the proportional representation system. When voters vote for parties which gain representation in Parliament in the same proportion as the popular vote obtained, there is considerable competition between parties for voters. In Sweden this seems to make parties more responsive to voters' interests. While the Social Democrats have ruled alone or in a coalition for most of the time since 1932, their control of the government has been tenuous, and was even lost for a six-year period just after the advent of parental leave (1976–1982). To attract new voters and members among women (and liberal-minded men), most parties have made promises designed to help individuals combine work and family roles (Eduards, 1988). When one party put women high on the ballot, other parties followed suit (Selbyg, 1989).

An additional facet of the Swedish political system that has contributed to the development of parental leave policy is the extent of centralized coordination involved in developing social policy. Cabinet members, who are leading members of the ruling party or coalition, draft legislation in response to particular circumstances and public concerns (like a concern for a declining birth rate, a need for women's labor power, and a desire for men's liberation). These drafts directly reflect campaign promises, the recommendations of government commissions specially appointed to study specific policy issues, and the opinions of relevant administrative agencies. In the case of parental leave, legislation was drafted based on the 1968 and 1969 recommendations of a government commission, appointed in the wake of the debate started in 1962 regarding men's and women's appropriate roles. Once legislation is drafted, it undergoes a lengthy and extensive process (called *remiss*) that allows for feedback from local level administrative agencies, trade unions, political parties, study circles (a unique form of cooperative adult education), and individuals. Extensive debate in the mass media also ensues. The legislation may be redrafted to incorporate the concerns emerging in this *remiss* process. According to American political scientists Adams and Winston:

> The emphasis is on consensus formation and coalition building before the final legislation is drafted thus assuring the widest possible support base for the legislation. (1980:12)

This process paves the wave for general agreement on proposals that may at first have seemed too "radical and innovative" (Childs, 1980). By the time parental leave became law in 1974, the vast majority of Swedish organizations and individuals supported the concept. Once established, a Swedish law is not very susceptible to repeal, because a broad base of support for it had previously been generated through the *remiss* process.

The remarkable period of political continuity that has existed in Sweden with the long reign of the Social Democrats is also a factor here. This stability has helped policy to develop consistently toward specific goals, goals which are based on an evolutionary brand of socialist ideology. Sweden has basically a capitalist economy, as 90% of business is privately owned. Nevertheless, the Social Democrats have always espoused socialist ideals regarding full employment and social equality. As early as 1889, they expressed support for the Second International's directives that women should have the right to vote, to work, and to receive equal pay (Qvist, 1980). Since the late 1960s they have strongly supported the adoption of the idea of gender equality.

The Social Democrats' political competitors, the nonsocialist parties, now also heartily support the concept of equal parenthood and under their leadership parental leave benefits have been extended. However, it seems unlikely that the nonsocialists would have been as enthusiastic about gender equality if they weren't locked in a close race with the Social Democrats for voters and members.

Social Democrats have also played a crucial role in the development of supportive attitudes amongst employers toward equal parenthood. Swedish employers have become important cooperating partners with unions and political parties in efforts to improve the status of Swedish women in the labor market and in developing programs designed to help men, as well as women, combine work and family roles. Employers have generally responded positively because they have been convinced by Social Democrats that it is in their best economic interests to do so. While Swedish employers operate within a market economy and are therefore as concerned as employers in the rest of the world about making a profit, they have been persuaded to view corporate success as hinging more on long-term rather than on short-term economic planning. The Social Democrats have encouraged this view through the maintenance of voluntary economic planning organizations and investment funds, which are designed to help Swedish companies weather temporary fluctuations in domestic and world markets (Ruggie, 1984). From a long-term perspective on economic productivity, parental leave seems relatively unthreatening to Swedish employers. (The support Swedish employers give to men interested in taking parental leave will be taken up in more detail in Chapter 4.)

Although the temporary absence of a worker staying home to care for children might be an inconvenience and the payment for such a program also has to be figured into corporate costs, the long-term benefits of parental leave to individual companies and to the Swedish economy are generally recognized. The welfare of the next generation of workers (now babies) becomes a relevant part of the equation when calculating long-term benefits associated with parental leave. A representative of the employers' federation stated:

> Some people might think it too costly, but there's no question we need it . . . there's no way to measure all the benefits to the next generation. (Allen, 1988:254)

Parental leave also helps women retain a lifelong attachment to the workforce, and the savings in recruitment and training costs are important (Gustafsson, 1983). Employers also recognize that productivity levels of workers might be low if they worry about child care. A Swedish banker said, "[The leaves are] good for the fathers and mothers and that *must* be good for the bank" (Allen, 1988:255). No figures on the cost effectiveness of parental leave in Sweden are available, but calculations have been made for government subsidies for daycare, another costly social program. Swedish economists have calculated that women who work at least ten years, at least half-time, increase the gross national product *twice* the cost of two daycare places for children (ages 1–6) (Gustafsson, 1983).

From the discussion presented above, we can see that Sweden has developed a social structure with considerable overlap and permeability between government, market, and family spheres (Hernes, 1988). Such permeability is regarded as necessary if social equality and welfare are to be enhanced. It is also probably a prerequisite for the development of policies, like parental leave, which help individuals combine work and family roles.

This reflects the high level of trust Swedes have in their government and their readiness to support social policy as a way to prevent and solve social problems. The government is generally regarded by citizens as a "constructive instrument of social change rather than as an intrusive and constraining force" (Moen, 1989:29). According to the Swedish political scientist Maud Eduards, "faith in the benevolence, capability and responsibility of the state is an old tradition in Sweden" (1988:3).

This faith may have historical roots in preindustrial Sweden. Most people were free—not oppressed by a feudal system, the church, or the national government. Kings and peasantry actually formed alliances against the aristocracy, in an effort to curb the latter's influence. When the enclosure movement began (with the centralization of landholdings), the central government played an important role in preventing strife and ensuring individual rights (Eduards, 1988). Because Swedes generally trust government, they are comfortable with efforts government makes to promote social change.

ECONOMIC REASONS FOR THE DEVELOPMENT OF PARENTAL LEAVE

Besides the need for women's labor power, there are some additional economic reasons why Sweden developed such a radical viewpoint on gender roles. One reason concerns the development of the welfare state. When the government assumed primary responsibility for families' economic well-being through welfare programs, it took this responsibility away from men. Families with no income earners receive direct assistance, generally in the form of cash payments and free services. Even in families with gainfully employed adults, the government plays a prominent role in family economics through heavy taxation and (in exchange thereof) the provision of general social benefits (health insurance, housing subsidies, child allowances, etc.). Swedish welfare state policies have been enormously successful. In 1981, the Overseas Development Council ranked Sweden as having the highest quality of life amongst the twelve industrial nations studied, because of its low infant mortality rate, high life expectancy, and high literacy rate (Qvarfort, McCrae, and Kolunda, 1988). As the government has become a crucial contributor to the standard of living in Swedish families, the economic function of the latter has waned; in its place the role of families as caretakers of the next generation is much more emphasized (Adams and Winston, 1980). It thus may seem logical that since men no longer have so much economic responsibility for children, they should share emotional responsibility for children (Eduards, 1988).

Another economic reason for parental leave relates to the changing labor market structure. As women gained more employment opportunities, through special government programs and increased demand in the ever-growing service sector, fewer women were content with being private domestic workers. When domestic workers were in plentiful supply, middle class women relied upon them to help them manage the double role of worker and housewife–mother. Thus, middle class women (who dominated the 1960s debate about changing gender roles) became more interested in changing men's responsibility for housework and child care than they may have been if they had still been able to purchase help (Sandqvist, 1987b).

A final characteristic of Swedish society which seems to have had implications for the development of parental leave is pacifism. The Swedish government has not been involved in warfare for almost two hundred years, although it keeps a strong defense establishment and contributes personnel for the United Nations' peacekeeping forces. Sweden remained neutral during World War I, even in the face of invasion threats. Consequently, defense expenditures were relatively low and money was available for the social welfare and educational programs introduced after the war (Verney, 1972). Neutrality during World War II left Sweden with its industrial base intact, in an excellent market position on the war-damaged European continent. This along with Sweden's abundance of natural resources (especially timber and minerals) contributed to postwar economic expansion, which in turn led to the need for women's labor power (Eduards, 1988). In Sweden, social welfare programs like parental leave have not had to compete with an aggressive military establishment for funding. The absence of war and male war heroes not only may have helped save money for welfare spending, but also may have made male dominance and traditional male worldviews appear less legitimate. This may have helped women gain positions of political power in Sweden and contributed to the ascendancy of the equality model which emphasizes the value of nurturing children (Sandqvist, 1989).

IDEOLOGICAL REASONS FOR PARENTAL LEAVE

As suggested above, ideology has been an important motivating force behind the development of parental leave, through interest in *jämställdhet* and the liberation of both women and men. Support for the welfare of children, belief in full employment for women, support for socialist principles, and trust in government are all aspects of ideology that have already been discussed as having important influences.

An additional ideological reason for the development of parental leave policy in Sweden is the lack of support for organizations which support traditional roles of men and women. There are organizations which express strong disagreement with government policy regarding the human being model. For example, the Swedish Communist Party and the women's liberation organization, Group 8, frequently express discontent with Social Democratic policies which they feel do not go far enough to eliminate class differences, a classic Marxist prerequisite for equality between the sexes. But these groups do not disagree with the model itself, only in the route used to achieve it.

In some societies, the religious climate would serve as an important impediment to interest in equal parenthood. In Sweden, however, religious sentiment is not strong. Christianity came late to Sweden and seems never to have become a deeply rooted force. During the Enlightenment, rationalist ideas from England and France were able to compete easily with fundamentalist religious teachings. Today, virtually all Swedes (92%) officially belong and pay tithes to the state-supported Lutheran Church. (Children automatically become members at birth if their parents are members.) Yet church attendance is very low, with less than 5% attending church each week (Swedish Institute, 1989c). Swedes do not report religion to be a significant factor influencing their values or conduct. Lack of religious fervor has been cited as a reason for the high incidence of premarital sex, cohabitation, and out-of-wedlock births in Sweden (Popenoe, 1988). The types of religious attitudes that might also lead to strong adherence to traditional gender roles (and thus oppose women and men sharing traditional roles of nurturer and breadwinner) are therefore absent in Sweden.

Another ideological factor that has been mentioned as a contributing factor in the development of Swedish social policy regarding gender is the historical status of Swedish women. Some have contended that Swedish women have always enjoyed a relatively high status (e.g., Bernheim, 1970; Mitchell, 1971). The current support for the equality model might be a reflection of this high regard.

There is some evidence that particularly in preindustrial Sweden, women enjoyed a relatively high status. During medieval times, women "held an influential and responsible place in the house," and daughters were given the right to inherit (Grimberg, 1935). In northern Sweden, where men typically were sailors, artisans, or hunters, women generally managed and ran farms alone. In southern Sweden, women typically made up 10–20% of the labor force in mines and stores, and owned one-third of the businesses. When industrialization came in the late 1800s, women made up a significant proportion of factory workers (20%). Swedish women also won many legal rights during the nineteenth century that women in other parts of the world did not. These included the establishment of coeducation (1842), equal inheritance rights (1845), equal rights to seek employment (1846), the right to take over the husband's business or trade at his death (1846), the right to vote for town and county councils (1862), abolition of male guardianship over single women (1858), married women's right to own property (1874), and equal rights to university education (1873) (Liljeström, Mellström, and Svensson, 1975; Löfgren, 1976; Myrdal, 1938; Rössel, 1970).

Still, researchers have concluded that preindustrial Sweden was basically patriarchal (Liljeström, Mellström, and Svensson, 1975; Myrdal, 1938; Ruggie, 1984; Skard and Haavio-Mannila, 1984). Women had as little access to formal power as women in other countries (Selbyg, 1989). Daughters received only half an inheritance until the mid-nineteenth century, and men still "reigned supreme" even over households they seldom visited. Women owned only the smaller businesses, and women workers typically earned only two-thirds of men's wages for the same work. The legal reforms enacted in the 1800s were apparently not aimed at improving the status of women as much as they were designed to pave the way for industrialization. An industrialized society needed educated workers, available land (made possible by diluting landowners' authority through equal inheritance by males and females), and access to working capital which employed or landed women or men could provide (Qvist, 1980; Widerberg, 1978).

There is no evidence that women held a particularly strong position in the family. Historians have stated: "Marriage was based upon the two being united into one—the one being the man" (Frykman and Löfgren, 1987:101). The roles of father and mother were also quite distinct. Swedish fathers were respected from a distance. They spent limited time with their children; what time was spent was devoted to play, reading, or instruction, not caretaking. Fathers were seen as the family's link with the outside world and psychologically preoccupied with their occupations even when physically present at home. Mothers, on the other hand, were viewed as warm, loving, and serving as mediators between husbands and children. They were primarily responsible for all the direct care of children (Frykman and Löfgren, 1987). With industrialization, the "culture of motherhood" arrived in Sweden, much as it did in other North American and Western European nations (Widerberg, 1978). Moberg's 1961 essay promoting equal roles for men and women suggests that the culture of motherhood was still well entrenched at that time, helping to keep women restricted to the domestic sphere.

There is no evidence, then, that Swedish society has always held an ideology of equality between the sexes, which could be an explanation for advocacy of equal parenthood in today's Sweden. On the other hand, Swedish women now clearly enjoy a high status compared to women in the rest of the world. A 1988 study of ninety-nine countries representing 92% of the world's population found that equality between women and men was highest in Sweden (Haavio-Mannila and Kaupinnen, 1990). This high status achieved by Swedish women, particularly in politics and as wage-earners, undoubtedly serves as a contemporary factor in maintaining and extending social policies designed to bring about complete gender equality.

CONCLUSION

Historically, mothers have been more responsible for and involved in the direct care of small children than fathers have. This pattern has had important implications for both women's and men's involvement in productive activities and for the structure of power in society. Sweden is the only society that has a longstanding commitment to the abolition of gender equality, including elimination of the division of labor that calls for women to be responsible for child care. Sweden's unique stance on the issue of equal parenthood is best exemplified by its parental leave policy. With their jobs guaranteed, both fathers and mothers can take a generous amount of time off from their jobs with nearly full pay to care for their babies. The aim of this policy is to promote both parents' involvement in parenting and in the labor force, so that equality between the sexes can be realized.

The Swedish parental leave policy developed in response to three social concerns. The first of these is a concern about a low birth rate. The Swedish economy has been weakened by an aging population. Swedes also tend to have a high regard for children, and they view childbearing as something to be encouraged. Parental leave is seen as improving couples' chances of having children by helping individuals combine parenting and employment roles. Parental leave, along with other work-family policies like subsidized child care, seems to have had the desired result. Sweden's present birth rate is now among the highest in Western Europe.

The second concern relates to a need for women's labor power. A low birth rate and a booming economy have combined to force Swedish employers to turn to women as a labor resource. Programs like parental leave encourage women to remain attached to the labor force, even during their childbearing years, since their jobs are guaranteed. Not surprisingly, Swedish women now have a labor force participation rate that is among the highest in the world, and very close to that of Swedish men.

Lastly, the ideological debate in Sweden has focused on the need to change men's as well as women's traditional roles. Maternity leave was extended to fathers in 1974 partly in order to liberate men from traditional gender stereotypes. While Swedish men clearly fall short of the officially promoted image of the liberated man, research suggests they share more in child care than fathers elsewhere in the world.

The presence of these concerns, however, is probably not sufficient for the development of a parental leave policy. Findings from Sweden suggest that a number of factors associated with the political, economic, and ideological climate of a country play important roles in the development of social programs designed to result in gender equality.

In terms of political factors, the extent and nature of women's political influence appears important. In Sweden, women make up an unusually high proportion of legislators, and the nature of the electoral process has led to party competition for women's votes. As a result of Swedes' traditional trust in government, women have regarded government policy as an essential tool for the liberation of women. Sweden also is characterized by a legislative process that stresses achievement of certain broadly held social goals such as equality and a willingness to infringe upon the private sector in order to promote family well-being. These characteristics seem conducive to the development of egalitarian family and work policies in other countries as well.

Parental leave policy seems to be partly a consequence of the type of economic system which exists in Sweden. In this welfare state, parental leave fits in well with other programs designed to promote family well-being. Because of policies aimed at levelling social class differences, there is no underclass of potential servants to take on women's traditional domestic responsibilities as they move into the labor force in increasing numbers. A pacifist stance has also left sufficient economic resources to launch costly social programs like parental leave.

Ideological forces have helped to bring about parental leave in Sweden. Swedes hold a high regard for children's welfare and a belief that all citizens are responsible for it. This is an important prerequisite for work-family policies, like parental leave, since parents alone cannot be expected to foot the huge costs such programs incur. Right-wing organizations generally advocate a return to the traditional gender-based division of labor and resent government involvement in family life. The absence of such organizations as major players in policy debates in Sweden seems to have helped work-family programs gain a strong foothold.

Clearly, social policy of the sort generated in Sweden to promote gender equality is a result of a unique combination of immediate social concerns, the nature of political and economic institutions, and the ideological climate. It is highly unlikely that many other societies will experience this exact combination. Nevertheless, this study of the circumstances under which Sweden came to develop parental leave policy can provide valuable leads that can be used to study the evolution of social policy aimed at promoting equal parenthood in other societies.

3

PARTICIPATION OF SWEDISH FATHERS IN PARENTAL LEAVE

Sweden's parental leave program is the oldest, most generous, and most flexible of its kind in the world. It is designed to allow both mothers and fathers time off from work with pay, so that both parents can develop a close bond with their new offspring while simultaneously retaining an attachment to the labor force. Will fathers take advantage of a program which allows them to stay home to take care of their babies? The long-established Swedish program allows us to answer that question.

The main purpose of this chapter is to describe Swedish fathers' rates and patterns of participation in the parental leave program over time. Swedish fathers' participation in parental leave will be compared to mothers' participation and with their usage of other parental benefits designed to increase their involvement with small children. Policy changes designed to improve men's participation in parental leave will also be described.

A second purpose of the chapter is to look at parental leave in terms of public acceptance of and interest in the program. The 1986 Gothenburg study of new parents contained several questions designed to explore the extent of Swedes' approval of the concept and identify which types of parents are more supportive.

FATHERS' PARTICIPATION IN PARENTAL LEAVE OVER TIME

Swedish fathers gained the right to stay home to take care of their new babies in 1974. Fathers were entitled to share any of the six months of paid leave previously granted only to mothers, if the mothers of their children had been employed nine months or more just before childbirth (or twelve months in the previous two years). Parents on leave generally received 90% of their usual pay in compensation and were assured of their original jobs of the equivalent upon return to work.

Less than 3% of eligible fathers took parental leave the first year it was available, while virtually all (98%) of new mothers did (see table 3.1). This stark initial contrast is not surprising. The program was new, and the fathers who took part the first year were engaged in a dramatic social experiment. In 1975 parental leave was extended to seven months, and fathers' participation began to increase. By 1977, 10% of eligible fathers took some parental leave, which represented a tripling of the original percentage three years earlier.

In 1978 the parental leave program was lengthened by two additional months. This extension resulted in a substantial increase in the percentage of fathers who took parental leave. In 1978, 21% of all eligible fathers took parental leave, and in 1979, 23% did. The 1978 extension also involved a change in the types of benefits offered. Two types of parental leave were distinguished: six months of *regular leave* (taken typically at the beginning of a child's life) and three months of *special leave* (which could be taken anytime until the child turned eight years old). Two months of the special parental leave were paid at a level of 90% of an eligible parent's salary; the remaining month was paid at a low "guarantee" level of 32 crowns (approximately $5) a day.

In 1980 the length of parental leave was extended once more, to twelve months (six months of regular leave and six months of special leave). The last three months were paid at the low level (raised to 37 crowns or $6 a day). Despite these enhancements in the program, fathers' participation in parental leave remained at the pre-1980 level, at 22–24% between 1980 and 1987 (see table 3.1).

For children born in 1989, parents could share 12 months of almost fully paid leave and three months of lowly paid. A significant improvement in fathers' participation in parental leave seems to have resulted from this lengthening of leave. Looking only at married fathers with employed wives, we find that forty-

Table 3.1
Swedish Fathers' Participation in Parental Leave

Year*	Months of leave offered at 90% pay	Months of leave offered at low level	Percent of eligible fathers who took leave in first year	Average number of days taken by fathers who took leave	Average number of days taken by mothers who took leave	Percent of leave days taken by men who took leave	Percent of leave days taken by all fathers
1974	6	0	3	26	122	15	**
1975	7	0	5	33	139	18	**
1976	7	0	8	40	138	22	**
1977	7	0	10	42	140	23	**
1978	8	1	21	43	233	16	**
1979	8	1	23	42	234	15	**
1980	9	3	23	47	263	15	5.2
1981	9	3	22	47	265	15	4.9
1982	9	3	22	45	262	15	5.1
1983	9	3	22	44	258	15	5.2
1984	9	3	22	**	**	**	5.1
1985	9	3	22	47	**	**	5.5
1986	9	3	23	**	**	16	6.2
1987	9	3	24	**	**	**	7.5

* Year refers to the year of the child's birth or adoption.

** Statistics not available.

Sources: Falkenberg, 1989; Lamb and Levine, 1983; National Social Insurance Board, 1989; Pleck, 1988; Riksförsäkringsverket, 1984, 1985, 1989a; Röcklinger, 1987; Statistiska Centralbyrån, 1988, 1990.

four percent of fathers whose children were born in January and February of that year took leave during the child's first year (Riksförsäkringsverket, 1990).

National statistics indicate that there are regional variations in fathers' levels of participation in parental leave. For children born in 1985, 35–39% of fathers took leave within the child's first two years in northern Sweden (which is more rural), while 21–24% of fathers took leave in southern Sweden (which is more industrialized). This pattern of regional differences is also found for fathers' taking leave to care for sick children (Riksförsäkringsverket, 1989b). Röcklinger (1987) speculates that such regional variations can be due to variation in the strength of the efforts made to encourage men to question the traditional father role and to take parental leave. Other possible reasons could be offered. The north has traditionally been a hotbed of socialism, and therefore potentially more receptive to Social Democratic programs such as parental leave. The jobs in mining and forestry, which are common in the North, are among the most strenuous occupations in all of Sweden and might therefore be more tempting to leave for a time.

Swedish parents are allowed to use parental leave anytime until their children enter school, at age seven. (In 1982 this age limit was lowered to age four, but it was changed back to school entrance age in 1985.) Statistics indicate that 86% of all parental leave days are used during the child's first year (Riksförsäkringsverket, 1989a). However, men are more likely than women to take leave after the first year. If the time span examined is extended to the child's second birthday, instead of the child's first birthday, we find that fathers' participation in parental leave has been somewhat higher than previously noted. For example, in 1985, 29% of all eligible fathers took leave during the child's first two years, in contrast to the 22% of fathers who took leave in the child's first year (Röcklinger, 1987).

Fathers' usage of the program appears even higher if only the highly paid portion of the leave is considered. In 1985, for example, 49% of fathers took leave in those families where only the nine months of nearly fully paid leave was taken (Riksförsäkringsverket, 1985; Röcklinger, 1987).

Swedish fathers' levels of participation in parental leave appear to be greater than those of fathers using other paid parental leave programs in the world, based on the small amount of data that are available on this topic from other Nordic countries. Finland appears to have the next highest rate, where 13% of fathers take advantage of some of the thirty-one weeks of paid leave, for an average of fifteen days. In Iceland, men can share twelve weeks of the paid leave, but only 3% do. Danish fathers can share ten weeks of paid leave with mothers; only 2% do. Norwegian fathers have twenty-four weeks of paid leave they can take, but only 1% take any of it (Kaul and Brandth, 1988; Nordic Council of Ministers, 1988).

While a sizable proportion of Swedish fathers now take parental leave, the number of days taken remains rather small. In 1974 the average father on leave took about one month (twenty-six days), out of a total possible leave of six months (see table 3.1). By 1978 this figure had increased substantially to forty-three days, but it has not increased much since, with the latest figure (for children born in 1989) standing at forty-three.

Fathers' participation in parental leave can also be compared to mothers'. Since statistics show that most couples (80%) do not take advantage of all leave days available to them (Riksförsäkringsverket, 1985), it is important to compare fathers' usage to mothers' actual usage. Amongst families where the father has taken parental leave, national statistics show that since the late 1970s, fathers have taken about 14–16% of all parental leave days taken by the couple. If all fathers who may or may not have taken leave are considered, it appears that men took only 5–8% of all parental leave days taken.

National statistics do not state what percentage of couples share parental leave equally. When picking a sample for the 1986 survey of new parents in Gothenburg, it was possible to record the number of days of parental leave taken by individuals and match that with those taken by their mates. This allowed me to calculate what percentage of couples shared parental leave equally, among the 728 couples who obtained benefits from two particular local social insurance offices for children born in 1984. (See Appendix A for more information.) This group in Gothenburg shares parental leave less often than is true for Swedes nationally, but the results are consistent with the lower averages for southern Sweden where the offices are located. (For example, fathers took only 12% of all days taken when couples shared parental leave, compared to 15% nationally.) Equal sharing of parental leave was considered to have occurred when the father took between 40% and 60% of all days taken by the couple. Looking only at couples where men took at least some leave, 6% had taken an equal share; an additional 1% had taken more than 60% of the days. Looking at the entire group of fathers including those who had not taken leave, only 1% had shared parental leave equitably with their babies' mothers.

PATTERNS OF FATHERS' LEAVETAKING

There are distinct patterns in fathers' usage of parental leave benefits. The most important one concerns timing. Fathers seldom take leave during the child's first six months. For example, in 1983, 28% of fathers took special parental leave (after the child was six months old), compared to only 6% of fathers who took regular parental leave (before the child was six months old) (Riksförsäkringsverket, 1984).

Fathers' usage of regular parental leave during the child's first six months has been limited to some degree by the common tendency for Swedish women to take advantage of a rule that allows them to use some of the regular parental leave during the last month of pregnancy. In 1983, for example, over three-fourths (76%) of Swedish mothers took parental leave early, for an average of eighteen working days (Riksförsäkringsverket, 1985). Swedish women are entitled to fifty days of paid pregnancy leave, but only in cases where they experience pregnancy complications, or where their jobs would pose a hazard to their pregnancy (and they cannot be transferred to a temporary job in the same facility). Because of these restrictions, relatively few women (21% in 1986) actually take pregnancy leave (Riksförsäkringsverket, 1989a).

Swedish fathers are also discouraged from taking parental leave during the first six months after birth by a strong interest among women to breastfeed children for their first five or six months. (The medical establishment also now supports this practice.) If breastfeeding is not successful, it is almost impossible for fathers to arrange to stay home sooner, since employers must be notified at least two months before leavetaking is to begin.

Table 3.2
Participation in Different Types of Parental Leave in Two Districts of Gothenburg, 1984
(N=738 Couples)*

	Mothers	Fathers
Regular parental leave		
Percentage who took leave	100	6
Average number of days taken by those who took such leave	77 (N=737)	34 (N=46)
Highly paid special leave		
Percentage who took leave	84	16
Average number of days taken by those who took such leave	78 (N=620)	32 (N=122)
Lowly paid special leave		
Percentage who took leave	57	5
Average number of days taken by those who took such leave	61 (N=424)	24 (N=39)
All types of leave		
Percentage who took any type of leave	100	22
Average number of days taken by those who took such leave	277 (N=738)	39 (N=165)

* Original group included 740 couples, but data were missing for two.

The 1986 study of records on 738 couples from two local social insurance offices in Gothenburg also showed how fathers were unlikely to stay home during the regular leave in comparison to special leave (see table 3.2). These records, moreover, allowed a closer look at fathers' usage of the two types of special leave—the highly paid portion (usually taken when the child is between six and nine months of age) and the lowly paid portion, which for children born in 1985 had been raised to 48 crowns (or $8) a day. Fathers were found to be much more likely to take the highly paid part of special leave than they were the lowly paid special leave, with 16% of fathers taking the former type of leave and 5% of fathers taking the latter. (Mothers were also less likely to take minimum guarantee days than highly paid special leave days, but over one-half (57%) still took the lowly paid days.) When mothers and fathers *both* took some days of the highly paid special leave (which happened in 11% of the cases) the father took one-third of all such days taken by the couple (fifty-six). When mothers and fathers both took some lowly paid special leave days (which happened in only 3% of the cases), the man took 25% of all such days taken by the couple.

In considering patterns of leavetaking for Swedish fathers, let us examine whether or not they have taken advantage of the flexibility of the system which allows them to take leave in full, half, or quarter days. The intention of this flexibility was to offer parents the opportunity to work part-time with full pay for an extended period of time. National statistics indicate that parents are unlikely to take out parental leave in less than full days; 84% of all leave time taken is taken out in whole days (Riksförsäkringsverket, 1989a). However, fathers are more likely than mothers to take out their leave in less than full days, usually in half rather than quarter days. For example, in 1986, 16% of the leave time taken by fathers was in the form of half or quarter days, compared to only 7% for mothers (Riksförsäkringsverket, 1989a). Social insurance rules also allow parents to take parental leave out intermittently. Three interruptions of leave are allowed—weekends and vacations do not count as interruptions. All indications are, however, that parents of both sexes tend to take leave days out in a single stretch (Arbetsgruppen, 1985).

FATHERS' USAGE OF OTHER PARENTAL BENEFITS

Swedish fathers' participation in parental leave is less than their usage of other social programs designed to increase their involvement in child care. One such program grants fathers ten days off with pay after childbirth (twenty days off in the event of twins). In its first year of operation (1976), almost two-thirds (64%) of Swedish fathers took these "daddy days," staying home an average of 7.5 days (Lamb and Levine, 1983). By 1980, 85% of fathers used the program, for an average of 8.5 days. In 1986 it appeared that about the same percentage of fathers took advantage of this short-term after-birth program, with a slight increase in the average amount of time to 9.4 days

(Pleck, 1988; Riksförsäkringsverket, 1989a; Statens Offentliga Utredningar, 1982b).

Another program designed to help both working mothers and fathers cope with child care responsibilities is time off from work with pay to care for a sick child (or to care for a healthy child when the regular caretaker is ill). Swedes refer to this as "temporary parental leave for child care"; it is completely separated from workers' own sick leave benefits. A doctor's note is needed only after seven straight days of illness. Parents cannot use this benefit, however, in the first three months immediately following childbirth, because one parent is presumed to be home already during that time. In 1989, 41% of fathers had taken days off to care for sick children. This figure has stayed fairly constant since 1980. Fathers took 35% of all such days taken by couples (Riksförsäkringsverket, 1989b). This latter figure has ranged from 33% to 37% since 1980.

A third policy designed to involve men in child care is the six-hour workday, which all parents of children less than seven years old have been able to take since 1979. (Government employees can take advantage of this policy until the child is twelve.) If they choose to take advantage of this policy, parents must manage with a corresponding reduction in pay. It is impossible to know exactly how many fathers take advantage of this policy, since no official recordkeeping on this topic could be located. It is, on the other hand, possible to extrapolate from statistics on part-time work how rare it must be for fathers to work part-time for child care purposes. A study of the Nordic countries found that in 1987, 7% of Swedish men worked part-time (less than thirty-five hours per week), compared to 43% of women. Of this relatively small proportion of men, only 5% said they worked part-time for the reasons of "child or home care". In contrast, 29% of women reported working part-time for this reason (Nätti, 1990). From these numbers, we can assume that few men are likely to be taking advantage of the six hour work day. However, statistics also indicate that the number of men engaged in part-time employment in Sweden has increased 93% between 1976 to 1988, while women's has increased only 26%.

The most recent social program designed to help working parents is "contact days," established in 1986. Parents share access to two days per child per year, for children ages four through eleven, usually in order to visit their child care setting or school. In 1987 fathers used 32% of all the contact days taken (Riksförsäkringsverket, 1989b; Statistiska Centralbyrån, 1990).

There are some noteworthy patterns in the types of parental programs Swedish fathers use. First, fathers take advantage of benefits more often when they do not lead to a significant loss of income. Consequently, they are highly unlikely to take unpaid parental leave or to reduce their work week to thirty hours, which would result in a loss of pay. Second, they take advantage of programs that do not involve competition with the mother for time with the child. Thus, popular daddy days go only to fathers, and the generous amount of days available for sick child care keeps parents from competing for time off.

Third, Swedish fathers participate more in programs that do not challenge so much the traditional gender-based division of labor for child care. Sandqvist (1987b) has suggested that fathers participate less in parental leave than they do in the other parental insurance programs because staying home on parental leave implies a more radical restructuring of the traditional division of labor in the family. The other parental benefits do not challenge the age-old gender-based division of labor in quite the same way—fathers are responsible for child care only a day or so at a time or are home simultaneously with mothers (as during daddy days). When a man takes parental leave, he is home by himself taking care of his child while his partner returns to work, because social insurance rules do not pay two parents to stay home simultaneously after daddy days are over. A father in this situation is not just "helping out" with child care or "babysitting." He becomes the parent solely responsible for the baby's care and well-being for a good part of the day, as well as for general maintenance of the home, cooking, shopping, etc. Such "solo" responsibility for child care has historically been the province of women. Couples who share parental leave are thus embarking upon a dramatic break with social tradition; both mothers and fathers may feel uncomfortable with this. It is thus probably not surprising that fewer couples share parental leave than other parental benefits. A more detailed examination of the barriers to fathers' taking parental leave will be undertaken in Chapter 4.

EFFORTS TO BOOST MEN'S PARTICIPATION IN PARENTAL LEAVE

Swedish policymakers have never been satisfied with the extent of fathers' participation in the parental leave program. Soon after the establishment of the program in 1974, a nationwide campaign was launched to bring attention to men's new right to take parental leave. Masculine-looking sports figures were featured in social insurance brochures and on posters holding babies, declaring that taking parental leave was "right" for men to do (see figure 3.1). Changes in the law were also designed to encourage men to take parental leave. The duration was extended to nine months in order to increase men's access to leave, once the period of breastfeeding was over. To encourage men to consider taking special parental leave, half of the special leave (forty-five days) was designated for the father, and half for the mother. One parent could take the other's leave only if the latter relinquished it by signing a specific form (Ministry of Health and Social Affairs, 1979). All these efforts culminated in an increase in men's participation in parental leave.

By the mid-1980s it was obvious that the percentage of men taking parental leave was still not substantial and was no longer increasing. With the extension of leave to twelve months, the amount specifically designated to each parent increased to ninety days. In 1986 a second information campaign was launched. This campaign involved the showing of four television spots (public information announcements are the only types of "commercials" on Swedish public television), a twenty-minute promotional video that could be shown to parents at local social insurance offices, and a new brochure—this time featuring a decidedly nonathletic-looking, slightly balding middle-aged dad holding a baby (see figure 3.2).

In 1986, changes in the law were enacted to make parental leave more attractive to men. The father's eligibility would no longer depend on the mother's eligibility; this had the potential of improving men's participation in parental leave in cases where their partners were not eligible for leave (e.g., where the women were students, recent entrants into the labor force, or unpaid workers in the family farm or business). The distinction between regular benefits and special benefits was also elimi-

Figure 3.1

Figure 3.2

Figure 3.3

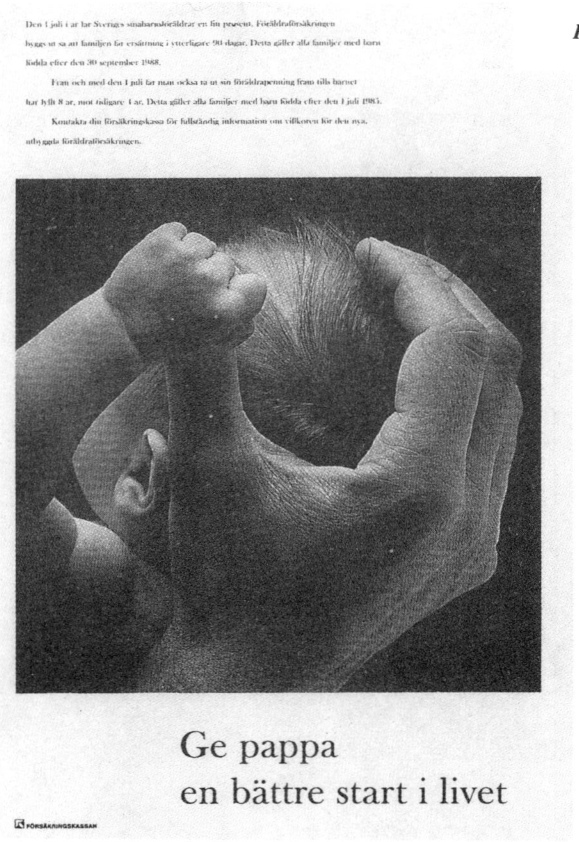

Den 1 juli i år får Sveriges småbarnsföräldrar en fin present. Föräldraförsäkringen byggs ut så att familjen får ersättning i ytterligare 90 dagar. Detta gäller alla familjer med barn födda efter den 30 september 1988.
Från och med den 1 juli får man också ta ut sin föräldrapenning fram tills barnet har fyllt 8 år, mot tidigare 4 år. Detta gäller alla familjer med barn födda efter den 1 juli 1985.
Kontakta din försäkringskassa för fullständig information om villkoren för den nya, utbyggda föräldraförsäkringen.
Ge pappa
en bättre start i livet
FÖRSÄKRINGSKASSAN

Give Dad a better start in life!

Nu kan du ge barnet
i dig en chans
Den 1 juli i år får Sveriges småbarnsföräldrar en fin present. Föräldraförsäkringen byggs ut så att familjen får ersättning i ytterligare 90 dagar. Detta gäller alla familjer med barn födda efter den 30 september 1988.
Från och med den 1 juli får man också ta ut sin föräldrapenning fram tills barnet har fyllt 8 år, mot tidigare 4 år. Detta gäller alla familjer med barn födda efter den 1 juli 1985.
Kontakta din försäkringskassa för fullständig information om villkoren för den nya, utbyggda föräldraförsäkringen.
FÖRSÄKRINGSKASSAN

Now you can give the child in you a chance

nated at this time (Försäkringskassan, 1987), in the hope that this would make administration easier and encourage men to take more leave.

While men technically had had the right to take the regular parental benefit since 1974, in practice they seldom did so. Indeed, an inspection of two local social insurance offices' records in 1986 showed that even the authorities did not expect men to take regular parental leave. A man's usage of the regular parental leave benefit was filed under his *partner's* name, while his usage of special parental benefits was recorded under his own name.

The latest attempt to increase fathers' participation in parental leave is the 1989 extension of parental leave to fifteen months (twelve months nearly fully paid), in the hope that men will take half a year off after the mother takes half a year to breastfeed (Falkenberg, 1989). This has been accompanied by a third media campaign, initiated and financed by the Ministry of Social Affairs at two million crowns ($0.3 million) (Näsman and Falkenberg, 1990). One aspect of the campaign was the wide distribution of bumper stickers saying "*Pappa kom hem*" ("Daddy come home"). Posters showing cute babies declared "Give Dad a better start in life" (see figure 3.3). For the first time, unions were drawn into the advertising effort, by government funds which subsidized unions' production of informational pamphlets and posters. One poster produced by the blue-collar LO federation depicts a dad sitting in an armchair holding a baby and says that the world's best papa takes parental leave. A white-collar union federation (TCO) pamphlet on fathers' taking parental leave has the title "100% father". The cover of the January 1990 issue of the construction workers' union magazine depicted a muscular father (shirtless) holding a naked baby. The headline read: "Stand up for yourself and take leave! For the children's sake, for your own sake, and for women's sake!" A five-page article inside was titled "Dare to be a dad!" A thirty-second public affair spot for TV showed a father with his baby and said, "See a little more of your baby—Contact the social insurance office." A second spot said, "Up to now, no man has regretted taking parental leave. Those who take leave are never quite the same again." The changes in the law since 1986 and the information campaigns seem to have had a substantial impact on men's participation in parental leave, since the percentage using the benefit has dramatically increased from 22% in 1985 to 44% in 1989 (Riksförsäkringsverket, 1990).

Up to now, information campaigns and modifications in the law have been used to increase men's interest in parental leave. Over the years, a more radical approach to increasing fathers' participation in parental leave has also been considered but never taken. Proposals have been made which would offer families strong financial incentives to share parental leave or even require fathers to take parental leave. The first such proposal came from a government-appointed commission on family assistance that was established in 1974 to consider further modifications of parental leave. To give men an equal chance at parental leave, the commission proposed that parental leave be extended from seven to eight months, and that neither parent be allowed to take more than seven months of the leave. The Ministry of Social Affairs used this suggestion to draft legislation in 1976, but the measure failed to pass in Parliament. In 1982 a government commission proposed encouraging men to share parental leave by giving couples 100% compensation if they shared leave (Statens Offentliga Utredningar, 1982a). This proposal was also introduced by the task force on men's roles in 1986. Organizations such as the Swedish Communist Party and the Fredrika Bremer Society (an autonomous feminist organization) have proposed that fathers be obligated to take at least some parental leave. In 1988 the Social Democratic Minister of Equality recommended in a policy statement the same type of proposal, to limit women's usage of the entire leave (Eduards, 1988).

The lack of progress in enacting proposals to pressure men to take parental leave appears to be due to the lack of public support for such an idea. The 1986 survey of 319 sets of new parents in Gothenburg (Appendix B) contained some questions about parents' interest in these more radical types of reforms. Respondents were asked how important they considered it to be for certain parental leave reforms to be carried through in the near future. Less than half of the respondents were in favor of a proposal which would lengthen parental leave for those couples where the parents took turns staying home; men were even less supportive of this proposal than women (see table 3.3). When asked what they thought of a proposal to require obligatory equal sharing of parental leave between the parents, even more were opposed, with only 8% of mothers and 6% of fathers saying it was a "very important" reform to enact. (Women were no more likely than men to recommend this.)

Table 3.3
Attitudes toward Reforms in Parental Leave

	Percentage responding:	
	Mothers (N=319)	Fathers (N=319)
"How important is it to lengthen parental leave for those couples where the woman and man take turns staying home?"		
very important	28	22
somewhat important	24	21
uncertain	8	11
not very important	20	22
not at all important	20	24
	100	100
"How important is it to change parental leave so that both parents are obligated to take it?"		
very important	8	6
somewhat important	10	6
uncertain	7	10
not very important	23	22
not at all important	53	55
	101	99

Note: Percentages may not add up to 100% due to rounding. Differences in the means of mothers' and fathers' responses were significant for the first item only according to a two-tailed t-test on differences in means (p ≤ 05, t=-.2.63).

ATTITUDES TOWARD PARENTAL LEAVE

Information campaigns and legislative changes have dramatically boosted fathers' actual participation in parental leave; such measures also appear to have influenced Swedes' support for the policy. In a 1982 study of a nationally representative sample of over four thousand Swedish men, 75% felt fathers' taking parental leave was the "right" thing to do; almost half were very positive toward the idea (Jalmert, 1983; Statens Offentliga Utredningar, 1982a). A regional study of over four hundred prospective fathers conducted in 1987 in the northern region of Jämtland also found that about three-fourths of men were positively predisposed toward parental leave, with one-third being very positive toward the idea (Sellström and Swedin, 1987). A 1981 national study of five hundred parents of children born in 1980 investigated men's regrets regarding their failure to take parental leave. It found that almost two-thirds (63%) of fathers who had not taken leave wished they had, and half of the latter wished they had shared the leave fifty–fifty (Statens Offentliga Utredningar, 1982b).

Women's attitudes toward sharing parental leave have also been found to be positive. In the Jämtland study of prospective parents, a majority of women were found to favor the idea of their mates taking parental leave. However, national studies have also indicated that the vast majority of mothers are *not* interested in sharing parental leave *equally* with their mates (Statens Offentliga Utredningar, 1979, 1982b). The role women play in their partners' taking of parental leave will be examined in Chapter 4.

The 1986 mail survey of new parents in Gothenburg contained four questions which measured attitudes toward fathers' taking parental leave. The first question measured respondents' general attitudes about this, by asking their extent of agreement with this statement: "A father ought to take paid parental leave in order to care for his child." While the vast majority of both sexes were positive toward the idea, only about one-third of both sexes expressed a great amount of enthusiasm for the idea (by answering "agree absolutely"). The level of high support for the concept found in this regional study was very similar to that

Table 3.4
Attitudes toward Men's Participation in Parental Leave

	Percentage responding:	
	Mothers (N=319)	Fathers (N=319)
"A father ought to take parent leave in order to take care of his child."		
agree absolutely	38	33
agree partly	53	49
unsure	4	13
disagree partly	2	3
disagree completely	2	2
	99	100
"If you were to have another baby, would you choose to take parental leave?"		
yes	91	51
unsure	7	35
no	2	14
	100	100

Note: Percentages may not add up to 100% because of rounding. Mothers' and fathers' responses were significantly different for both items in two-tailed t-tests on differences between means ($p \leq .05$; $t=2.70$, 11.97 respectively).

found in the 1987 regional study of another area and in past national studies (Statens Offentliga Utredningar, 1982b; Sellström and Swedin, 1987); the percentage of parents expressing lukewarm support for the idea, however, is higher than that noticed in the previous studies (see table 3.4).

A second question attempted to measure how much of the egalitarian rhetoric had been internalized. Fathers in the study were asked if they would take parental leave in the future, should they have another child. Substantially fewer fathers said they would actually stay home than agreed with the general statement that fathers should take parental leave. Only half of fathers said they would take parental leave, compared to the 82% who said it was a good thing for fathers to do (see table

3.4). This suggests that some men may feel social pressure to say they would consider taking leave when their attitudes are still somewhat traditional on the subject.

Another question measured attitudes toward mothers and fathers *equally* sharing the amount of parental leave available. Only about half of the parents studied agreed with this statement: "Parental leave ought to be shared evenly between fathers and mothers." Their levels of enthusiasm were markedly less than for the general idea that men should take some parental leave (see table 3.5).

The last question addressed parents' feelings about their recent decision to share parental leave when their last child was

Table 3.5
Attitudes toward Men's Equal Sharing of Parental Leave

	Percentage responding:	
	Mothers (N=319)	Fathers (N=319)
"Parental leave ought to be shared equally between fathers and mothers."		
agree absolutely	13	12
agree partly	45	34
unsure	7	13
disagree partly	17	18
disagree completely	18	23
	100	100
"Do you wish you and your partner had shared parental leave equally [for the child that was born in 1984]?"		
yes	13	17
unsure	31	37
no	56	46
	100	100

Note: Fathers were significantly more likely than mothers to say they wished parental leave had actually been shared in the their families the last time, in two-tailed t-test on differences in means ($p \leq .05$, $t=2.95$). Mothers were significantly more likely than fathers to agree that leave ought to be shared ($p \leq .05$, $t=2.86$).

born (1–2 years before the study was conducted) (see table 3.5). Few individuals regretted not sharing parental leave equally: less than one-fifth of both sexes said they wished they had shared equally with their mates. (In many of the latter cases, the couple had actually shared leave equitably, and were thus merely affirming this decision.) Fathers were significantly more likely than mothers to regret that the leave was not more shared.

Why some parents were more supportive of fathers' taking parental leave was explored. More positive attitudes about fathers taking parental leave were expected to occur:

1. ***when individuals held nontraditional gender role attitudes.*** Three measures of attitudes were examined: a three-item scale measuring attitudes toward gender-based parenting abilities (items F1, F3, F4 in Appendix B); a three-item scale measuring attitudes toward sharing traditional roles (items F2, F5, F6); and attitude toward sharing breadwinning in their own household (item F8).
2. ***when individuals had been exposed to the idea of men's taking parental leave.*** Three measures of exposure were investigated. The first was whether or not they knew other men who had taken parental leave. The second was the level of their attentiveness to the media debate about fathers' taking parental leave (item B2 in Appendix B). The third was whether or not they worked in the public sector, where employees received additional incentives to take parental leave and where the propaganda level is higher than it is in the private sector.
3. ***when individuals' work orientation and jobs made sharing parental leave attractive.*** For men, this was assumed to occur when they felt work was less important (item E2 in Appendix B), when they did not hold a professional or managerial job, and when they earned less income. For women, this was assumed to occur when they felt work was more important, when they held a professional or managerial job, and when they earned more income.

Stepwise regression analyses were conducted to ascertain which of these factors had the strongest effects on attitudes, independent of the effects of other variables. Seven measures of attitudes were examined. For women, these included attitudes toward fathers in general taking parental leave, toward fathers in general taking an equal portion of the leave, and their feelings of regret about their partners not taking an equal portion of parental leave in the past. Men were asked about their attitudes toward fathers' taking leave and toward fathers' taking an equal portion of leave, whether they would take leave in the future, and if they regretted that they had not shared leave equally with their partners in the past. A standard level of .05 was accepted as the standard for statistical significance. Table 3.6 lists the results for these calculations.

The results indicate that women's attitudes toward sharing parental leave were related mostly to their holding egalitarian gender role attitudes, and (to a lesser extent) to their attentiveness to the parental leave debate and their labor market opportunities (in the form of holding a high status job). The variables examined were much more likely to be related to men's attitudes, however. Men's attitudes were positively and almost equally affected by egalitarian gender role attitudes, exposure to the idea of men's taking leave (through the debate and through knowing other men), and work variables (particularly holding a nonprofessional or managerial job and, to some extent, having less work commitment).

These results suggest that Swedish officials' efforts to promote parental leave through education and informational campaigns have generated public support for the program. Increased efforts in this area might pay off in terms of greater usage of parental leave benefits as well. Nevertheless, Swedes are far from being avid supporters of fathers' participating in parental leave on the same level as mothers. Public approval of equal parenthood therefore lags behind the rhetoric of social policymakers.

IMPLICATIONS

The Swedish experience suggests that it takes a long time to involve men in a parental leave program. The Swedish program

Table 3.6
Stepwise Multiple Regression Results for Relationships between Attitudes toward Fathers' Equally Sharing Parental Leave and Selected Independent Variables
(Significant beta coefficients only)

	Agree fathers should take leave		Agree couples should share leave equally		Wished father had shared leave equally		Would like to take leave
	Mothers	Fathers	Mothers	Fathers	Mothers	Fathers	Fathers
Gender attitudes							
Negative attitudes toward gender-based skills	.13	.18				.15	
Positive attitudes toward role sharing	.17	.12				.18	.14
Shared breadwinning orientation	.17				.21		
Exposure to idea							
Knowing men who had taken leave						.14	.32
Attention to media debate		.24	.15	.20		.16	.14
Public sector employment							
Work							
Work commitment				-.17			
Professional/managerial job		-.13		-.22	.15	-.12	-.12
Income							
R^2	.10	.17	.02	.12	.07	.10	.18

Note: All R^2s were statistically significant, at the .05 level.

originated in 1974; now almost half of fathers take advantage of the program. However, those who take leave take only about one and one-half months of the twelve months available to the couple; very few Swedish fathers (less than 10% of those who take leave) share parental leave equally with mothers.

In order to raise participation to the current level, the Swedish government changed the program in important ways, notably by extending the time available and making fathers' eligibility for highly paid leave independent of their partners' participation in the labor force. Extensive information campaigns have also been designed to convince fathers to take leave. These efforts to encourage men to take parental leave have been based on a strong national commitment to the concept of equal parenthood.

Extension of parental leave well beyond the time prescribed for breastfeeding (six months) had the effect of increasing Swedish fathers' participation in parental leave. Swedish fathers were also found to be more likely to use that portion of the leave available after six months which is highly compensated at nearly normal wage rates. We might therefore predict that efforts to increase the length of highly paid parental leave will result in parental leave becoming more attractive to Swedish fathers.

Survey results indicate that while Swedes are generally supportive of the idea that men should take parental leave, the majority are opposed to the idea that men should take the same amount of parental leave as women. Even when Swedes support this idea in principle, few indicate that they would like this to happen in their own families. This reluctance is even noted in women. The Swedish system of parental leave makes women and men potential competitors for the leave available, since only one parent at a time can stay home. Such a system may actually reinforce the traditional gender-based division of labor, since it forces couples to choose between extremes and does not give them the option of staying home together to share leave time simultaneously.

Results of this analysis of fathers' participation in parental leave in Sweden paint a somewhat pessimistic picture with regard to the potential of social policy as an instrument to promote sexual equality. The next chapter considers why more Swedish fathers do not take more advantage of the parental leave program.

4

DETERMINANTS OF FATHERS' PARTICIPATION IN PARENTAL LEAVE

Why don't more Swedish fathers take advantage of parental leave? When Swedish fathers do take parental leave, why do so few take an amount equal to that taken by mothers? By law, an employer must allow both fathers and mothers to take the leave. The leave is paid, generally at a high level. An employee is guaranteed the same or an equivalent job upon return. In other words, obvious structural obstacles to men's leaving work to do child care are not present in Sweden. We have also seen that Swedish policymakers and parents alike approve the idea that fathers should take parental leave. Lack of acceptance of the policy on the part of government officials or the public therefore appears not to be a major obstacle to men's participation in the program.

What, then, inhibits Swedish fathers' participation in parental leave? This chapter reviews previous research on fathers' participation in child care and presents findings from the 1986 survey of Gothenburg parents. One purpose of this survey was to investigate the circumstances under which men elected to take parental leave and chose to take a large portion in comparison with mothers. Nine couples responding to the survey were later interviewed in person; in each case the man had taken at least two months of parental leave. Quotes from these interviews are presented in this chapter in order to give additional insight into some of the barriers couples face in sharing parental leave. (See Appendix A for more details on the survey and these interviews.)

Past studies of fathers' participation in parental leave in Sweden have looked at factors associated with men's taking parental leave (Hamrin, Nilsson, and Sörman, 1983; Hwang, Eldén, and Fransson, 1984; Statens Offentliga Utredningar, 1978, 1982b). The study reported here is an attempt to improve upon these previous efforts in several ways. It involves a larger and more representative sample than those used in two of the three previous studies (Hamrin, Nilsson, and Sörman, 1983; Hwang, Eldén, and Fransson, 1984). It also looks at a wider range of potential barriers. In addition to looking at fathers' backgrounds, attitudes, and employment situations, this study examines how *mothers'* backgrounds, attitudes, and employment situations influence the pattern of leavetaking within families. The role played by social support is also investigated. Finally, this study examines the circumstances under which couples choose to share the leave more equitably, once fathers have decided to take leave. Previous studies have not examined the factors associated with fathers' taking a more equal portion of the leave. Since the goal of Swedish social policy is equal parenthood, this is very important to measure, if we are to evaluate the effectiveness of the program.

As discussed in Chapter 1, women's responsibility for young children has up to now been a cultural universal. Research suggests that social factors are more likely to be determinants of the division of labor for child care than are biological predeterminants. In this chapter, three categories of social forces are examined for their impact on fathers' participation in parental leave: social psychological factors, social structural factors, and family context.

SOCIAL PSYCHOLOGICAL BARRIERS AFFECTING MEN

Much of the literature on gender differences in parenting behavior attributes the division of labor to men and women having different personality traits and internalizing traditional gender role expectations (Risman, 1989). Men are seen as employment-oriented, unemotional, tough, and competitive, while women are seen as people-oriented, tender, and nurturing (Benokraitis, 1985; Giveans and Robinson, 1985). These different sets of personality traits are considered to be a consequence of gender role socialization (mainly in childhood) and are generally regarded as immutable. Fathers are thus seen as lacking specific skills and abilities that would enable them to participate actively in child care. Their motivation to be equal parents would also be assumed to be low because of low self-confidence in the nurturing role, a learned devaluation of domestic activities, and internalization of traditional gender role attitudes (Cohen, 1987; Coverman, 1985; Hamrin, Nilsson and Sörman, 1983; Hwang, 1985; Pleck, 1986). According to this perspective, we should not be surprised that less than half of Swedish fathers take parental leave, given the pervasiveness of traditional gender role socialization practices, and we would expect fathers to participate more in parental leave only when they somehow escaped typical gender role socialization and had come to adopt nontraditional attitudes toward women's and men's domestic roles.

Childhood Socialization

Social psychological theories stress the importance of modeling after one's parents as an aspect of childhood gender socialization (cf. Herzog and Bachman, 1982). The lack of nontraditional role models in childhood has been named a major obstacle to men's sharing child care (Hamrin, Nilsson, and Sörman, 1983; Hwang, 1985; Pleck, 1986; Russell and Radin, 1983). According to a social psychological perspective, men exposed to mothers who worked outside the home and fathers who participated in child care would be more likely to participate in parental leave. Participation in parental leave would seem to require a certain feeling of comfort with the idea that men can do child care and the idea that mothers can be employed (since the mother returns to work while the father stays home on leave).

Over half (51%) of the men in the survey had grown up having mothers who had worked outside the home, although most of these mothers (75%) had worked part-time. Men had generally experienced a traditional division of labor for child care, with over half (57%) reporting that their mothers had been primarily responsible for their care and upbringing. Less than 10%

reported that their mothers and fathers shared child care equally. (The remainder—33%—reported some sharing of child care, with mothers still being more involved than fathers.)

The impact of these and other variables on fathers' participation in parental leave was investigated in two separate ways. These variables were correlated first with a variable that measured whether or not the father took leave and then with the father's share of all days taken by the couple. This last measure ranged from 1% to 67% with a mean of 19% and represented the extent to which couples equally shared the leave. Pearson product moment correlation coefficients were calculated. A conventional .05 significance level for a one-tailed test was applied as the standard for determining noteworthy results.

Survey results showed that having a working mother had no bearing on men's participation in parental leave (see table 4.1). Findings regarding their fathers' participation in child care also did not support the social psychological perspective; men were not any more likely to take leave when their fathers had participated in child care. On the contrary, a tendency in the opposite direction was found; men were somewhat more likely to take a higher portion of parental leave if their own fathers had been *uninvolved* in their care. When asked why he decided to take parental leave, a computer consultant at a Volvo auto factory who had taken four months of parental leave said, with some bitterness, "I never saw *my* dad except at bedtime." A father who was a psychiatric nurse said, "I *didn't* follow my father's model—he couldn't even boil water." These findings suggest that contemporary influences and situations have caused men to question the division of labor practiced in their families of orientation rather than to emulate it.

Lacking the appropriate skills to take care of infants might be a substantial barrier to a father's choosing to stay home alone to take care of his new baby (Hwang, 1985; Pleck, 1986). Such skills could come from caring for siblings or babysitting. Men in the study were asked if they had previous experience with child care before they became a parent (a lot, some, or none). Only 18% of the men in the study reported having a lot of previous child care experience; the majority (58%) reported none. Previous experience with child care, however, proved not to influence men's participation in parental leave.

Table 4.1
Social Psychological Correlates of Fathers' Participation in Parental Leave
(Pearson's *r* coefficients)

	Father took leave (0=no/1=yes) (N=319)	Father's percentage of couple's (total) leave (N=85)
MEN		
Childhood socialization		
Mother's employment (1=none/2=part-time/3=full-time)	.04	.16
Parental sharing of child care (1=mother most/2=mother more/3=shared/ 4=father more/5=father most)	-.11	-.22*
Previous experience with child care (1=none/2=some/3=a lot)	.01	.11
Gender attitudes		
Nontraditional attitudes toward gender-based parenting ability (1=traditional...3=nontraditional)	.14*	.08
Positive attitudes toward role sharing (1=traditional...3=nontraditional)	.21*	.28*
Shared breadwinning orientation (Who is responsible for breadwinning: 1=man mostly/2=man a little more/3=shared)	.09	.10
Positive reaction to partner's taking leave (1=negative...3=positive)	-.15*	.03
WOMEN		
Childhood socialization		
Mother's employment	.14*	.32*
Parental sharing of child care	.08	.25*
Previous experience with child care	.02	.02
Woman's experience compared to partner's (1=less/2=same/3=more)	.00	.12
Gender attitudes		
Nontraditional attitudes toward gender-based parenting ability	.07	.20*
Positive attitudes toward role sharing	.21*	.09
Shared breadwinning orientation	.05	.17
Positive reaction to partner's taking leave	.18*	.19*

* Significant at the .05 level in one-tailed test

Attitudes toward Gender Roles

Another test of the social psychological perspective is to measure the impact that men's attitudes toward gender roles had on their propensity to take parental leave. Three types of attitudes were examined.

The first type concerned men's beliefs regarding men's and women's interest in and ability to nurture. Three questions asked about women's interest in employment over child care, men's ability to be emotionally close to children, and men's capacity for child care. (See the top half of table 4.2 for the word-

Table 4.2
Attitudes toward Gender Roles

	Percentage responding nontraditionally #		
	Fathers (N=319)		Mothers (N=319)
Attitudes toward gender-based parenting capabilities			
"Women can be as interested in employment as in children."	69		70
"A father can be as close emotionally to his child as a mother."	81	*	88
"A man can become as capable as a woman at child care if he has the chance to learn."	77	*	91
Attitudes toward role sharing			
"If the woman works full-time, the man and the woman ought to share equally in child care."	65	*	85
"The man is the one who should be the family's primary breadwinner."	23	*	43
"Success on the job ought to be a man's main goal in life."	34	*	46

For the first four items, "nontraditional" includes those who "agreed completely." For the last two items, "nontraditional" includes those who "disagreed completely."

* Women's scores were significantly less traditional than men's for these items, according to one-tailed t-tests on differences between means ($p \leq .05$; $t=3.51$, 5.58, 6.21, 5.95, 4.65 respectively).

ing of the items and a breakdown of responses.) The vast majority of fathers in the study rejected the idea that women were more interested in child care than employment; even more felt that men were capable of being close to children and performing child care tasks. Responses to these three attitude items were averaged to form a scale (hereafter called the scale for attitudes toward gender-based parenting ability), which was in turn treated as a single measure. (Responses scaled with a reproducibility coefficient, Cronbach's alpha, of .81.) This procedure resulted in a measure with greater variability in responses than any of the individual items had; for example, only 44% of fathers expressed strong agreement with all three items.

Fathers' attitudes toward men's and women's parenting capabilities were significantly correlated with their tendency to take parental leave. The less fathers believed in gender differences in capabilities, the more likely they were to take parental leave (see table 4.1). Biological differences between the sexes probably do not keep fathers from participating in early child care, but when men think such differences exist they are less likely to take parental leave.

The second type of attitudes examined concerned individuals' beliefs regarding appropriate roles for the sexes. The first item asked about the desirability of equal parenthood in dual-earner families, the second asked if men should be their families' primary breadwinners, and the third examined if they thought success was men's main goal in life. (See the bottom half of table 4.2 for the wording of the items.) Fathers' responses to these items were not uniform. (The coefficient of reproducibility, alpha, was quite low at .18.) They thought men should participate equally in child care, yet they had difficulty giving up the ideas that men should be primary breadwinners and that men should define occupational achievement as their main goal in life. These fathers appeared to subscribe to the "role expansionist" view of gender role change. Just as the women tend to have dual roles (worker and mother), they seemed to feel that men should also have two roles (breadwinner and nurturing father). This tendency has also been noticed for American men (Haas, 1988; Robinson and Barret, 1986). Responses to these three items were added together and averaged to form a scale (hereafter called the role-sharing attitude scale), which was treated as a single measure for analytic purposes. Men with more egalitarian attitudes toward role-sharing were significantly more likely to take leave and, once having taken leave, to take proportionately more of it.

The third type of attitude considered as having a possible influence on men's sharing parental leave was their assumption of personal responsibility for the breadwinning role. Men who felt primarily responsible for earning their family's income were expected to be unwilling to take parental leave because it would take them away from their provider role. Men were asked, "Who had the most responsibility for your family's income, before the baby was born—you mostly, you a little more, you and your partner equally, your partner a little more, or your partner mostly?" A majority of the men said they were mostly (23%) or a little more (35%) responsible for securing family income, despite the fact that their partners were employed. Feeling responsible for breadwinning, however, was not associated with men's participation in parental leave. Since the leave is paid, staying home may not detract from men's sense of being their families' providers. On the other hand, men may be interested in role expansion more than they are in giving up one role to take on another.

The final attitude item concerned men's reactions to their partners' taking parental leave. Women were asked about the reaction of their male partners to their taking parental leave—whether it was positive, negative, or both. It was assumed that men who supported their partner's leavetaking more enthusiastically would take leave less often themselves. When a man strongly supported his partner's leavetaking, he was significantly less likely to take leave himself (see table 4.1).

Men in the study were asked point-blank if their lack of ability was a reason why they did not share parental leave equally with their partners. Almost all fathers rejected this idea (see table 4.3). The survey also found no evidence that lack of ability was a factor in men's reluctance to take parental leave.

Almost all fathers also rejected the notion that their lack of interest played a role in their pattern of leavetaking. However, as noted earlier (table 4.2), traditional gender role attitudes and

Table 4.3
Perceived Obstacles to Men's Taking Parental Leave

	Percentage responding affirmatively		
	Fathers (N=319)		Mothers (N=319)
"In most families, the mother uses all the parental leave or more days than the father. If this happened in your case, what were the most important reasons for this? (Check in front of each suitable answer)."			
—the man's work situation	47		51
—the man could not manage caring for an infant	4		4
—the family income	36		39
—breastfeeding of the child	29	*	44
—the man was not interested	5		6
—the mother wanted to stay home	40	*	48

* Significant difference between men's and women's answers ($p \leq .05$ in χ^2 test).

strong support for the mother's taking leave were significantly associated with a lack of participation in parental leave on the part of fathers. It is possible to reconcile these two apparently conflicting findings. Attitudes were measured after parental leave was over, and men's attitudes may have changed as a result of the leavetaking experience. If we assume that attitudes are amenable to change in a short period of time, such attitudes might better be regarded as a consequence rather than a determinant of leavetaking.

On the other hand, it is possible that fathers in the study did not want to admit readily their opposition to leavetaking, especially in a society such as Sweden where equal parenthood is lauded. If this were the case, then men's attitudes may have indeed played an influential role in their participation in the parental leave program. Support for this interpretation comes from the interviews with couples who shared parental leave fairly equitably. In a discussion about why so few Swedish men take parental leave, the *first* thing mentioned by *everyone* of these fathers was the role played by traditional values. A teacher said,

"We are still raised after old values, even those who are younger." A psychiatric nurse claimed, "It's male values. Men are afraid of being soft, of taking care of children." An architect said, "Traditional attitudes are strongly embedded. One feels pressed into the old pattern despite all the discussion and debate."

Summary

In general, the results suggest that contemporary experiences are likely to be more important than childhood situations for determining men's likelihood of participating in parental leave. Men in the study were not found to model themselves after the division of labor practiced by their parents. This conclusion seems to be in agreement with another study of changing gender roles by Gerson (1985:37). She concluded that people tend to continue to act, not on the basis of models, attitudes and values acquired in childhood, but upon "motives, goals, and capacities [which] develop as they move through a series of life stages and confront a series of choices in which they must make consequential life commitments."

SOCIAL PSYCHOLOGICAL BARRIERS AFFECTING WOMEN

Parental leave is a benefit that applies to couples rather than to individuals. When a child is born or adopted, couples are given a year of paid leave to take. However, only one parent at a time can take leave; this means that negotiation and discussion must occur between partners. While it is theoretically possible for a mother to take the leave without discussing the option of sharing it with her partner, anecdotal evidence suggests that this rarely occurs in Sweden, where considerable publicity is given to fathers' rights (and responsibility) to take parental leave. At the time of the study, forty-five days of the leave were specifically earmarked for each parent. The mother could not take all of the leave without the father signing over his rights on a special form available from the social insurance office.

Given that fathers' leavetaking behavior is likely to be the outcome of discussion and negotiation between partners, it is important to examine the role played by mothers in this process. Swedish and Norwegian researchers have suggested that women serve as "gatekeepers" to men participating in parental leave. Previous qualitative studies suggest that mothers have trouble giving up traditional authority for child care, feel guilty about relinquishing child care to their partners, believe men cannot manage alone, and fear a loss of self-respect if they do not make motherhood their primary role (Brandth and Kvande, 1989; Hamrin, Nilsson, and Sörman, 1983; Uddenberg, 1982). In a recent study of 1,410 Stockholm men, women's monopolization of the leave was identified as an important barrier to their taking of leave (Von Hall, 1989). An editorial appearing in Stockholm's largest daily newspaper describes women's gatekeeper role:

> For years, there has been crying and nagging about men who don't want to take responsibility for the children. But many women allow their feelings to take over after the child's birth and monopolize, more or less unconsciously, the care of the child. The woman has therefore chosen for the man. There rests a big responsibility on the woman if the man should enjoy his right to take parental leave. She must dare to let go of the child and allow the man to form his own way of caring for it.... (Von Hall, 1989, p. A2, my translation)

In asking parents in the survey what they thought were the most important barriers to their sharing parental leave, almost half of each sex said mothers' desire to stay home played an important role (see table 4.3). Additional evidence concerning mothers' lack of enthusiasm about men's taking parental leave was described in Chapter 3. Just one-third of mothers expressed strong agreement with the idea that men should take parental leave. Only about one in ten strongly supported the notion that fathers should take an equal portion of the leave, and only about one in ten were sorry that they had not shared parental leave equally with their mates the last time around.

The interviews conducted with nine couples who shared parental leave hinted at some of the bargaining and negotiation processes involved in men's decisions to take parental leave and the important role played by the mothers' attitudes. Couples were asked how the decision for the man to take parental leave was reached. In four of the nine cases, sharing parental leave seemed clearly to be initiated and pressed for by the mother. Here is how two women described how their partners came to take parental leave:

> *Woman:* "It was an easy decision. [The man nods in agreement.] I made up my mind not to stay home the whole time. I was more interested in my job than he was." [The man nods again.]

> *Woman:* "I asked if he wanted to stay home, we talked about it. I was glad he was willing; I thought it was important."

When the decision seemed more mutual, the important role played by the mother was still evident. She seemed to be the gatekeeper—without her approval, her partner might not have taken leave. Here is how one couple described the decision-making process:

> *Man:* "I was home because I wanted to see what it was like, wanted to develop a good relationship with the baby, wanted [the mother] to get to be out in 'real' life. It was *obvious* that I would be home."

> *Woman:* "I liked being at home but I wanted him to build a relationship with the child and not miss out on that important time."

> Another couple explained their decision:

> *Man:* "There was no dispute or even discussion. We were completely agreed. Both of us wanted it."

> *Man:* "We had decided to share the leave equally, out of ideological reasons. There is no biological reason I shouldn't share child care. It seems natural to our generation. Neither of us wanted it more."

> *Woman:* "We divided household tasks, it was natural to extend this to child care. I would have been very surprised and unpleasantly shocked if you hadn't wanted to stay home."

The role played by the mother in the man's decision to take parental leave in the group of nine couples who were interviewed in person is obvious. It was more difficult to ascertain the role played by the mother in the larger quantitative study of 319 couples. The measures of mothers' attitudes toward fathers' taking parental leave used in Chapter 3 were obtained after the couple had completed their stint at taking parental leave. Because parental leave is such a new program, it seemed likely that attitudes toward it are in a state of flux for most people, likely to be significantly affected by recent personal experiences. Consequently, these attitudes may very well be a *consequence* of the pattern of leavetaking chosen by the couple, rather than a *determinant* of it. Therefore, these attitude items were not considered in the analysis of possible barriers to father taking parental leave. These attitudes toward sharing parental leave, however, were found to be highly correlated with fathers' leavetaking behavior. Mothers' agreement with the statement that fathers should take parental leave was significantly correlated with their partners' leavetaking ($r = .24$). Mothers' agreement with the statement that fathers should take an equal portion of leave was also correlated with their partners' taking a higher portion of the leave ($r = .37$), as was their report that they wished their partners had shared leave equally ($r = .41$).

It seemed likely that aspects of women's socialization and gender role attitudes might affect their partners' likelihood of participating in parental leave. The same variables examined for fathers were examined for mothers.

Childhood Socialization

Women's socialization experiences were examined to see if these were related to their likelihood of sharing parental leave with their partners. Compared with the men, the percentage of women in the sample who had had working mothers was the same (51%). Their fathers were similarly unlikely to have participated in their care, with almost three-fifths of the women and men saying their mothers had been the ones responsible for child care. The woman's having a working mother was found to be associated with her partner's taking parental leave, and the leave was more equitably shared if the woman had a working mother or a nurturing father. Apparently, women are more likely to model themselves after their parents than men are prone to do. Having parents who practiced a traditional division of labor seems to discourage women from considering a more egalitarian one in their own families.

In terms of prior experience with child care, women reported having more prior experience than did their partners. One-third of women reported a lot of experience, in comparison to only 18% of men. A comparison measure for experience was also developed. Over two-fifths (43%) of women had more experience than their partners, 43% had the same amount, and 14% had less. Neither women's absolute nor relative amount of prior experience with child care before becoming a parent, however, was related to their likelihood of sharing parental leave with their partners. Gender differences in nurturing experiences prior to actual parenthood do not appear to explain women's monopolization of parental leave.

Gender Role Attitudes

Women's responses to the attitude questions tended to be significantly less nontraditional than their partners' (see table 4.2). The vast majority of women rejected the idea that gender-based parenting capabilities existed. There was some variation in responses, however, since only 65% of the sample consistently responded in the most nontraditional way for all three such items. These items were formed into a scale, with a coefficient of reproducibility of .61. Women who rejected the idea that gender-based parenting abilities existed were found to be more likely to share parental leave equally with their partners ($r = .20$).

Despite their belief in non-sex-typed parenting abilities, women hesitated to endorse role-sharing. While less traditional than men in this regard, over half of the women still believed that men should orient themselves primarily to occupational roles. Responses to the three role-sharing items were averaged to form a scale, with a coefficient of reproducibility of .50.

Women with higher scores on this scale, indicating attitudes favorable to role-sharing, were more likely to have partners who took parental leave (r = .21).

About the same proportion of women as men (56% vs. 57%) believed that the man was more responsible than the woman for breadwinning in their own households. As with men, no significant association existed between women's views on this and their actual sharing of parental leave.

The last measure of mothers' attitudes toward sharing parental leave was obtained by asking men whether their partners supported their taking parental leave. Almost three-fourths (72%) of men reported their partners to be positive. (Most of the remainder presumed their partners were neutral.) Men who reported their partners were positive were more likely to take parental leave and to share leave more equally (r = .15 and .19 respectively). Some 87% of the men who took leave had positive partners, compared to 68% of the men who did not take leave.

The results suggest that men will make little headway in participating equally in parental leave as long as their partners are not really that interested in sharing. Several characteristics of the women correlated significantly with the men's participation in parental leave. Women who had been exposed to nontraditional gender models in childhood were more likely to have partners who elected to take parental leave and to share leave more equitably. When women held less traditional attitudes, they were also more likely to share parental leave.

Several surveys have shown that wives' characteristics correlate more with husbands' level of participation in child care than husbands' own characteristics (Barnett and Baruch, 1987; Feldman, Nash, and Aschenbrenner, 1983; Grossman, Pollack, and Golding, 1988; Haas, 1988; Hiller and Philliber, 1986; McHale and Huston, 1984; Palkovitz, 1984; Radin, 1988; Sandqvist, 1987b; Yogman, Cooley, and Kindlon, 1988). How women come to support a more egalitarian sharing of child care in their own households appears likely to be a complicated process, not discernible from the cross-sectional data analyzed here. The findings of this study lend support for the microstructural perspective on gender role change, which presumes that the division of labor for child care is the result of "ongoing roles and relationships [within the family], where individuals negotiate more or less satisfactory arrangements" (Ferree, 1988:10). Social scientists who have looked at parenting arrangements from this perspective include Backett (1982), Hochschild (1989), Hood (1983), LaRossa and LaRossa (1981) and Risman (1989). Within this approach, it is assumed that "definitions of masculinity are historically reactive to changing definitions of femininity" (Kimmel, 1987:12) and that women are the ones who must push for change in traditional roles and relationships if equality is to develop (Ferree, 1988). Studies on the division of labor for child care in the United States have also noticed that, despite popular rhetoric, women typically exhibit little interest in the concept of equal parenthood and that they have difficulty giving up responsibility for child care (Benokraitis, 1985; Genevie and Margolies, 1987; Haas, 1980; Heath, 1976; Jump and Haas, 1987; Yogev, 1981).

SOCIAL STRUCTURAL BARRIERS AFFECTING MEN

In addition to the partner's own characteristics and background, another set of possible barriers to men's participation in child care involves the larger social structure beyond their household. These potential impediments include opposition at the father's workplace and the lack of social support for fathers' participation in parental leave.

Work-related Barriers

Men's jobs are widely regarded as the most important obstacle to men's participation in both child care (Lamb, Russell, and Sagi, 1983; Pleck, 1986) and parental leave (Statens Offentliga Utredningar 1978, 1982b; Von Hall, 1989). Parents in the 1986 study also named the man's job as the most important obstacle more often than any other barrier (see table 4.3). Employers are assumed to view male employees as indispensable, more so than female employees, who are in key positions less often and whose staying at home for child care purposes is taken for granted more.

In Sweden, employers' opposition to men's particip parental leave seems likely to be much weaker than in othe cieties. The parental leave law obligates employers to permit fathers to take parental leave. Although no direct study of Swedish employers' attitudes toward parental leave could be found, the public discussion about parental leave suggests that employers are less upset about the parental leave law than they are about other Social Democratic initiatives such as the laws granting workers considerable decisionmaking power and a control of a portion of corporate profits. Studies have shown that at any given time only 1.4% of all workers are off work due to parental leave (Hamrin, Nilsson, and Sörman, 1983). This small percentage seems to pose little threat to Swedish productivity.

Employers and supervisors might not see parental leave as threatening, but it cannot be said that they are enthusiastic about the prospect of male employees taking off for child care as female employees have traditionally done. While it is difficult to establish with certainty what Swedish employers' attitudes toward parental leave actually are, survey results suggest that men *perceive* a lack of positive support from their workplace. Survey respondents were asked how specific people at their workplace reacted to the possibility of their taking parental leave, including employers, immediate supervisors, male co-workers, and female co-workers. These replies were then correlated with men's participation in parental leave. People at men's workplaces were reported to be generally neutral toward their taking parental leave (see table 4.4). A high-level government administrator's description of workplace reactions demonstrates how unsupportive a so-called neutral response can be:

> My local boss grumbled, expressed worry about what would happen with this or that project, but was not actually negative. These bosses are old, had *their* kids in the 1940s, and see the law as a little silly. As for my workmates, it depended on their ages. The older ones found it difficult to understand really, thought it was a little silly. Those who were my age, or at least younger than 50, thought it is natural for fathers to participate in child care but not go so far as to stay home full-time for three months! The ones I worked closest with acted a little surprised that I would want to stay home when I had such an interesting, stimulating job. They expressed no nega-

Table 4.4

…tions toward Leavetaking

	Percentage responding:	
	Fathers (N=319)	Mothers (N=319)
"…ving people react when you … al leave? If you did not take parenta… , how do you believe the people mentioned below would have reacted if you had taken leave?"		
your employer		
positive	13	40
neutral	62	54
negative	25	6
your supervisor		
positive	16	47
neutral	58	46
negative	25	7
your male co-workers		
positive	27	50
neutral	60	49
negative	13	1
your female co-workers		
positive	41	76
neutral	53	23
negative	5	1
your friends		
positive	45	87
neutral	53	13
negative	2	0
your mother		
positive	41	89
neutral	52	11
negative	6	0
your father		
postive	27	81
neutral	65	20
negative	8	0

Note: Percentages may not add up to 100% due to rounding. All differences between mothers' and fathers' responses were statistically significant, according to one-tailed t-tests on differences in means ($p \leq .05$; t=9.89, 10.23, 7.75, 9.51, 12.80, 14.26, 16.11 respectively).

> tive attitudes though, and, as team members should be, expressed solidarity by helping to do my job while I was away.

Female co-workers were found to be the most positive toward men's taking parental leave. (Women apparently are more positive toward other women's partners' taking leave than they are toward their own partners'!) A gym teacher reported on his female co-workers' reactions:

> The reactions from co-workers varied by sex. Women thought it was good. I was considered to be a good role model for the teenage boys I taught. A man could be tough and take care of a small baby, too, Men gave no direct response—they might have felt funny, realizing that they could also have stayed home.

It may be that workplace attitudes are becoming more positive over time. An earlier study of Swedish fathers found similar levels of employer support but less positive responses from co-workers (Hwang, Eldén, and Fransson, 1984). A more recent study in the northern province of Jämtland found somewhat more support from supervisors than I found and substantially more from co-workers (Sellström and Swedin, 1987).

The four measures of workplace attitudes were collapsed into a single scale (with a coefficient of reproducibility of .74). When men received more positive support from the workplace, they were more likely to take leave and, once taking leave, to take more leave (see table 4.5).

Swedish men who work in the public sector have been found in other studies to be significantly more likely than men in the private sector to take parental leave (Hamrin, Nilsson, and Sörman, 1983; Hwang, 1987; Hwang, Eldén, and Fransson, 1984; Török, 1990). The assumption has been that employers, supervisors, and co-workers in the public sector are more exposed to, and therefore positively influenced by, official rhetoric regarding equal parenthood. The government administrator quoted above, in explaining workplace reactions to his taking leave, stated:

> I work for the state and I feel they adhere more than the private sector to the law. Men who work in the private sector have a harder time taking leave. The law exists, but is seen as a pain.... [The private sector] is a different world— one must

Table 4.5
Social Structural Correlates of Fathers' Participation in Parental Leave
(Pearson's *r* coefficients)

	Father took leave (0=no/1=yes) (N=319)	Father's percentage of couple's (total) leave (N=85)
MEN		
Work-related		
Positive workplace attitudes (1=negative/2=neutral/3=positive)	.24*	.28*
Public sector employment (1=no/2=yes)	.21*	.11
Professional/managerial job (1=no/2=yes)	.14*	.06
Years of education	.16*	.22*
Nontraditional job (1=no/2=yes)	.09	.19*
Income	.07	.24*
Social support		
Support from significant others (1=negative/2=neutral/3=positive)	.26*	.18
Knowing men who had taken leave	.29*	.12
Attention to parental leave debate (1=not/2=some/3=a lot)	.18*	.25*
WOMEN		
Work-related		
Positive workplace attitudes	.03	.03
Public sector employment	.06	.07
Professional/managerial job	.18*	.17
Years of education	.22*	.15
Nontraditional job	.16*	.04
Income	.12*	.13
Income relative to partner's (1=above/2=same/3=1 category below/ 4=2 categories below/5=3 categories below/ 6=4 categories below)	-.17*	-.13
Social support		
Support from significant others	.02	-.12
Knowing men who had taken leave	.26*	.26*
Attention to parental leave debate	.11*	.10

* Significant at the .05 level in one-tailed test

> choose between career and family. And if you choose career, you must have a wife who stays home and takes care of things for you.

In the Gothenburg survey, men who worked in the public sector were significantly more likely to take parental leave than those in the private sector. Moreover, public sector employees reported less workplace opposition than did private sector workers (r = .20).

Another reason men working in the public sector might take parental leave more often relates to economics. Reflecting the high support for parental leave in the public sector, government employees generally receive 100% of their pay when they are on parental leave, compared to 90% for private sector employees. Because tax rates have historically been so progressive and high, the increase from 90% to 100% of one's income may not seem like a significant incentive. Nevertheless, men in the private sector were significantly more likely to name economic barriers to their taking parental leave than those employed in the public sector (r = .11).

The types of jobs men hold might make a difference in their ability to take parental leave. For example, men who hold professional or managerial positions might be seen as less dispensable at the workplace and thus find it harder to take parental leave. Practically the only time controversy about men's taking parental leave has emerged in the public discussion about parental leave in Sweden is when high-level men take the leave; such men are regarded as particularly indispensable. Ove Rainer, Sweden's former postmaster general, is perhaps the highest level employee to have taken parental leave he stayed home one month each time with his two children. Rainer reported:

> My attackers asked why, as leader of 63,000 workers, I should take care of one child instead of sitting in my office. I told [them] that no leader is indispensable. We are only indispensable to our children (Pogrebin, 1982:70).

About the same time as Rainer made this statement (1981), the Stockholm daily newspaper, *Dagens Nyheter*, was the setting for a typical exchange on the issue between two economists. One blamed Sweden's 1981 recession on the growing tendency for key male personnel to take parental leave. He stated:

> It is a shame that good resources—in a time when they are most needed—shall be home looking after children . . . Foreign contacts have extreme difficulty understanding our social ambitions [like equal parenthood] . . . it can in certain cases lead to difficulty when certain personnel for "this and that" reason are not on the job. (Wahlström, 1981, my translation)

The economist in favor of parental leave (who happened to be home on leave for the second time) defended parental leave as an important measure for children's optimal development (which he felt in the long term would build up human capital) and as a policy designed to level gender differences in working involvement and achievement. He suggested these effects would raise the total production of the economy (Eidem, 1981).

Criticisms about men taking parental leave may have centered on the issue of key professional and managerial men staying home as this is precisely the group most likely to take parental leave, according to other studies (Brandth and Kvande, 1989; Grönvik, Sellström, and Swedin, 1988; Hwang, Eldén, and Fransson, 1984; Török, 1990). Such men were also found to be more likely to take parental leave in the 1986 study of Gothenburg parents (see table 4.5).

Why do men who are professionals and managers share parental leave with their mates more often? One reason may be that they have considerable autonomy and flexibility at the workplace. The government administrator quoted above explained his ability to withstand pressure as follows: "I had some informal power of my own and I could say to hell with what you want." Other men who were interviewed pointed out that they were able to plan ahead to take leave, since their projects often lasted months and even years. Some took work home during the leave or remained available by telephone.

Another possible reason professional and managerial men might take leave more often is that they were more educated, and education tends to make people less apt to follow traditional lifestyles blindly. The professional and managerial men in the study did tend to hold less traditional attitudes about women's and men's parenting ability ($r = .18$), and they were more educated ($r = .47$). More educated men were also likely to share parental leave with their partners, but not because of any liberal attitudes on the gender-role scales (see table 4.5).

The real reason professional and managerial men take parental leave more often might be their tendency to have high-status women as partners. Almost two-thirds (63%) of the professional and managerial men were living with women in similar occupations ($r = .43$). As we will soon see, women's job status was significantly related to their mates' leavetaking.

Another aspect of his occupation that might affect a man's tendency to take parental leave is whether the job he holds is a traditionally "feminine" occupation, where 70% or more of the workers are women. Traditionally, women's jobs might be easier for men to leave, since employers are accustomed to women's taking time off for child care purposes. Only 11% of the fathers in the survey held female-dominated jobs. However, those who did were more likely to share parental leave ($r = .19$).

The last work-related barrier considered in the study was men's income. Since Swedish men on the average make more money than women do, the family loses more money when he stays home than when she does. While both are compensated generally at 90% of their usual salary, the 10% forfeited by the man can amount to considerably more actual money than the 10% forfeited by the woman. This forfeiture can be the most serious for the highest income groups, where the income gap between the mates can be wider.

There is another respect in which men earning high income might be discouraged from taking parental leave. Insurance regulations contain a ceiling for income compensation, now standing at approximately $37,000. People who earn above that level will receive only compensation up to the ceiling. If a man earns considerably more than the ceiling, he will lose a bigger proportion of his income by staying home. Previous studies have reported mixed results on this topic. Some have found that higher earning men are less likely to take parental leave (Hamrin, Nilsson, and Sörman, 1983; Statens Offentliga Utredningar, 1982b); others have found the opposite (Brandth and Kvande, 1990; Török, 1990). In this study, men's income level was not associated with whether they took leave or not, but higher earning men did tend to take a smaller portion of leave than did lower earning men. A high-level government administrator explained why he was home only three months:

> I earn more than she does, so I was home less. The time I was home was a compromise between two conflicting goals—my desire to be at home and the family's economy.

Social Support

Another potential barrier to fathers' participation in child care is lack of support from friends and acquaintances. Since child care has traditionally been regarded as women's responsibility, people may dissuade new fathers from active involvement in their care. Anecdotal evidence suggests that Swedish men often feel they lack social support for the decision to take parental leave (Hamrin, Nilsson, and Sörman, 1983). One very early statement about this appeared as an anonymous letter in *Dagens Nyheter* in 1976, soon after parental leave for fathers was offered. Because of its eloquence it is quoted at length:

> The whole society has created expectations for the man to provide for his family, to put up a good front, to be strong and smart, to play soccer with the kids, to boast of feminine conquests, to be able to know more than women about many subjects, to make a career. During his whole upbringing a man has been indoctrinated with this.
>
> Breaking with this role demands a strong person. I have, in spirit and heart, become convinced of the flaws in this traditional male role. It is bad for the woman, it is bad for the children, it is bad for the society, and it is bad for the man. But one must disregard demands from society (and one's parents!) for a nice material environment, with career and house and car and color TV and instead concentrate on one's family. But this is difficult.
>
> One must be a strong person to manage it. It is hard to meet old school friends who have all the material things, a good job, and, at least on the surface, a typical harmonious family and answer the question, "What do you do nowadays then?" Certainly one can look them straight in the eye and say "I have in fact done nothing the last year. I have looked after

> the children and house and between these studied a little and worked now and then half-time or less so that my wife could get a good start in worklife while we had small children." Perhaps one ought to be proud to answer so. But I can't...
>
> Women have, mostly through the women's movement, received the strength they need to be able to stand up against pressure from society. Men must up to now stand alone. It is hard (my translation).

Encouragement from others can provide needed emotional support and validation, as well as concrete resources and help (Hamrin, Nilsson, and Sörmon, 1983; Pleck, 1986; Uddenberg, 1982). Men who receive support from others to participate in child care have been found to do so more often (Lein, 1979; Pleck, 1986). The Gothenburg study included some questions about the reactions of friends and parents toward the possibility of a father taking parental leave. Most men in the sample did not receive positive support from their friends and parents; their own fathers were particularly unsupportive (see table 4.4).

The reactions of mothers, fathers, and friends to the possibility of their taking leave was made into a three-item scale, with a coefficient of reproducibility of .77. Men who reported positive reaction from significant others were significantly more likely to take parental leave than those with less support (see table 4.5).

Another measure of social support was obtained by asking the fathers in the Gothenburg study how many men they knew personally who had taken parental leave. Knowing other men who had already taken leave could be of considerable importance to men contemplating the same, as acquaintances could provide inspiration and guidance. Almost three-quarters of the men in the study knew at least one other man who had taken parental leave. Knowing someone who had taken parental leave turned out to be positively related to men's tendency to take leave ($r = .29$). Some 94% of the men who took leave knew other men who had, compared to only 65% of non-leavetakers.

Men were also asked about their attentiveness to the media discussion about parental leave. Since parental leave was established in Sweden, positive models of men who have taken leave have been displayed and discussed in the mass media. In general, this publicity has been positive and might help to make men feel that society supports their choosing to take parental leave. One such article appeared in the daily newspaper *Aftonbladet* on 3 June 1984, taking up a whole page. It had the headline "I became a new man—and got a new chance!" and featured the case of a metalworker (depicted hugging his ten month old baby) who had not stayed home on parental leave for his first two children but who had decided to take parental leave for his third child after joining a men's liberation group. In the Gothenburg study, respondents' attentiveness to this type of publicity was measured by asking how much attention they had paid to the discussion about parental leave in the mass media (a lot, a little, or none). The majority of men (72%) had paid at least some attention to this discussion, although only 15% had paid a lot of attention. Attention to the media discussion about parental leave was found to be related significantly to men's tendency to take parental leave, as well as to their inclination to share this leave equally with their partners (see Table 4.5).

In summary, findings from the study suggest that social factors are important determinants of fathers' participation in parental leave in Sweden. Workplace opposition, particularly in the private sector, keeps men from participating in the parental leave program. The current involvement of unions as agents of publicity about the program might help to make workplace attitudes toward men's taking leave more positive.

Men appear to need social support for their leavetaking. Whenever people break from tradition, it is helpful to know others who also have done this and to have supportive friends and family. The pioneering men who now take leave in Sweden undoubtedly serve as important role models for those who will come later.

Lastly, the income ceiling on parental leave appears to play a role in keeping men who are otherwise inclined to take leave from taking as much as they would desire. The cost of the program would rise significantly if high-income earning parents could draw 90% of their full salary while on leave. Given the prevailing economic climate, it is doubtful that the Swedish economy could absorb such an increase in cost as such benefits would bring, and therefore it seems likely that the income ceiling will remain as a barrier to some fathers sharing parental leave.

SOCIAL STRUCTURAL BARRIERS AFFECTING WOMEN

Work-related Barriers

In investigating determinants of fathers' participation in parental leave, it is important to consider how mothers' position in the labor market influences their willingness to share leave. The same work-related factors thought to influence men's leavetaking behavior were investigated for mothers' leavesharing behavior.

First, the impact of workplace attitudes on women's share of the leave was examined. As table 4.4 shows, women reported significantly less negative reactions from employers, supervisors, and co-workers than their male partners did, although a majority of them still did not receive positive support from employers and supervisors. The three workplace attitude items were formed into a scale (with a coefficient of reproducibility of .79). Workplace attitudes, however, did not affect women's likelihood of sharing parental leave with partners.

Women were significantly more likely than men to work in the public sector (70% vs. 41%). This reflects the fact that women, who entered at the same time as the public sector grew, are more recent entrants into the Swedish labor market. Many of women's traditional jobs, such as teaching, nursing, and social work, are also found in the government sector. In general, propaganda regarding men's taking parental leave is more often directed toward government workers, so we might expect women working in the public sector to be more likely to encourage their partners to take leave. On the other hand, as public employees, women might have an easier time taking off from work without arousing resentment. If this were true, women who worked in the public sector might be more likely to monopolize the leave.

Neither of these hypotheses were supported; there was no significant relationship between women's employment sector and their sharing of leave. Perhaps both forces were operating, and canceling each other out, causing no distinct pattern of relationship to emerge. Interestingly, women working in the public sector reported no more workplace support for leavetaking than did women working in the private sector. (Male workers who worked in the public sector did report more support than private sector workers.) Perhaps women are so determined to take parental leave that the lack of workplace support makes no difference.

The nature of the woman's job and her occupational potential seemed likely to be important factors in determining her willingness to share parental leave with her mate. Stimulating, well-paid jobs seem likely to lead women to feel that employment is an important part of their lives, while monotonous and low-paid work would leave women content with seeing themselves first and foremost as housewives and mothers (Fagerström, 1976). A nurse who was interviewed, whose own husband had taken a substantial amount of parental leave, told me that more Swedish fathers don't take parental leave because

> Women won't let them. Most think that staying home with a baby is their real purpose in life. And no wonder they want to stay home—most have boring, routine jobs that are not much to go back to.

On the other hand, challenging professional or managerial types of jobs can be difficult to combine with childrearing. Career-oriented mothers may want their partners to get an early start in sharing responsibility for child care so that after parental leave is over, this responsibility would remain shared, enabling them to devote more time to their careers.

Previous research on Swedish and Norwegian fathers' likelihood of taking parental leave supports this idea that women's job type has an important impact here. Couples are more likely to share parental leave when women have high-status jobs (Brandth and Kvande, 1989; Grönvik, Sellström, and Swedin, 1988; Hamrin, Nilsson, and Sörman, 1983; Hwang, Eldén, and Fransson, 1984; Schönnesson, 1986; Statens Offentliga Utredningar, 1978, 1982b). Studies on men's participation in child care in Sweden and the U.S. have also found that men whose wives had white-collar jobs or professional careers were more likely to share child care (Bird, Bird, and Scruggs, 1984; Hwang, Eldén, and Fransson, 1984).

A high percentage (41%) of women in the sample held jobs in the professional and managerial category, which reflects the sampling strategy of choosing parents from one middle-class social insurance district and one working-class district (see Appendix A). Women in professional and managerial jobs were more likely to have partners who took parental leave (see table 4.5). Women with such jobs were also likely to be highly educated (r = .57), which in turn was related to their partners' likelihood of taking leave.

Whether or not women held a traditionally female job was also investigated as a possible influence on the tendency to share parental leave with their partners. Women in jobs not dominated by their own sex might be more likely to share leave because their workplaces would be less tolerant of any employees going on leave, not having had considerable experience with this. Such women might also have had to cross many hurdles to enter their fields, and not want to jeopardize their position by taking an extended time off. Only about one-fourth (27%) of the women in the survey held nontraditional jobs. Women who held such jobs were more likely both to have partners who took leave (r = .16) and to work in places where there was less tolerance of leavetaking (r = .11).

The last work-related factor examined for women was their income. This has been previously found to affect their partners' tendency to take parental leave. The Swedish National Social Insurance Board reports that one-half of Swedish men take an even proportion of the leave when their partners' incomes fall in the highest categories (Riksförsäkringsverket, 1985). Other Swedish and Norwegian studies also found men's tendency to take leave enhanced by their partners' income levels (Brandth and Kvande, 1989; Statens Offentliga Utredningar, 1978, 1982b). Women typically do not earn as much as men, so it may appear to a couple to be less expensive for her to stay home for child care purposes that it would be for him if each of them would be entitled to receive only 90% of their regular income level as compensation for taking parental leave. (It may actually be *more* expensive in the long run if the woman stays out of the labor force for an extended period of time, since this could hurt her long-term opportunities for promotion and higher pay more than it would for both partners to be out half of the time.) Higher income women might also have more power in the family, and thus be more in a position to "convince" their mates to stay home for child care purposes than women who have less financial power as a resource. In the analysis, the absolute level of the woman's income before the baby was born was considered as a potential factor influencing men's participation in parental leave. Their income relative to that of their partners' was also examined, for other researchers have suggested that the power balance changes and men become more active in child care when women's income approximates or exceeds their mates (Brandth and Kvande, 1989; Hood, 1983; Hunt and Hunt, 1987). Income was measured in terms of intervals. The relative income variable had categories that compared a woman's income interval to that of her partner's.

Income differences between mothers and fathers were dramatic. Over half (58%) of the mothers in the study had incomes in the lowest category ($900 or less a month), while only 17% of fathers did—a significant difference. Women earned about as much or more than their mates in only one-third of the families studied. Findings showed that women with higher incomes (both absolutely and relative to their mates') were more likely to have partners who took parental leave.

Women's occupational position before the baby was born was also correlated with their attitudes toward their partners' taking leave and toward men's absorption in the breadwinning role. For example, women in professional or managerial jobs and women who earned more (in absolute as well as relative terms) were more likely to express support for their partners' leavetaking than were women in less advantaged circumstances ($r = .20$, .14 and .19, respectively).

Social Support

Women's experiences with social support were also investigated for their impact on leavesharing behavior. As table 4.4 shows, women reported more support from friends and family than men did. However, this had no influence on women's tendency to monopolize the leave.

Women's exposure to alternative models of parenting was examined as a potential influence on their tendency to share parental leave. Such exposure was found to positively affect leave sharing. Women were asked if they knew other men who had taken parental leave. The average (or mean) number of men known was four, but the range was enormous—from one to ninety. This yielded a modal value of one and a median value of three. The women's knowledge of other men who had taken leave was significantly associated with both measures of their partners' participation in parental leave.

The vast majority of women (85%) had paid attention to the public debate in the mass media about men taking parental leave. Women were significantly more attentive than men to this debate, but still only one-fourth of women reported that they had paid a lot of notice. Women's attentiveness to the discussion on parental leave was significantly correlated with their partner's tendency to divide parental leave more equally ($r = .11$).

In summary, women were found to be more likely to share parental leave with their partners when they held high-status, nontraditional, and well-paying jobs and when they had been exposed to contemporary models of equal parenthood. As women come to experience better job opportunities, we might expect that sharing of parental leave will become more commonplace. Propaganda aimed at convincing women that men should take parental leave seems also to be a promising way to end Swedish women's monopolization of parental leave, since results showed that women's learning about men who take leave is associated with greater sharing of leave.

These results underscore the important role mothers play in fathers' likelihood of taking parental leave. Policymakers interested in promoting sharing of parental leave by mothers and fathers may need to pay more attention to women's economic opportunities and attitudes if they wish to realize the goal of equal parenthood.

THE FAMILY CONTEXT

The primary purpose of the study was to analyze the relative impacts of social psychological and social structural variables associated with men and women on fathers' participation in parental leave. There is, however, another set of variables that might have an influence on fathers' participation in parental leave that relates to the family context.

Cohabitation

In Sweden, the nuclear family is still the most common family type, but in many cases it is not based on marriage. Cohabitation has become increasingly common. At the time of the study one in five Swedish couples were not married. (The impending abolition of an old law about widows' benefits prompted a record number of Swedish couples to marry in 1989 before the law was phased out. It is too soon to know if this high rate of marriage will continue.) Cohabitation is especially common among young people, and unmarried couples do not hesitate to have children. In 1987, for example, 50% of all Swedish children were born out of wedlock (Swedish Institute, 1989d). In the Gothenburg survey, 13% of couples were cohabiting. (This figure reflects the fact that over two-thirds of the couples had more than one child, a situation that prompts many Swedish couples to marry.)

It is possible that marital status might have an impact on couples' sharing of parental leave. On the one hand, fathers might feel less of an obligation to be involved with their children if they are not married to the children's mother. On the other hand, cohabiting couples may maintain a more egalitarian arrangement, which could lead to fathers' being more responsible for child care. Marital status turned out, however, not to have a significant association with fathers' participation in parental leave (see table 4.6). This might be due to the lack of variation in marital status.

Delayed Parenthood

Swedes tend to delay parenting. The average woman has her first child at the age of 27 (Swedish Institute, 1989d). Since men are on the average two years older than their partners, men are often close to thirty years old before they become fathers.

Table 4.6
Family Contextual Correlates of Fathers' Participation in Parental Leave
(Pearson's *r* coefficients)

	Father took leave (0=no/1=yes) (N=319)	Father's percentage of couple's (total) leave (N=85)
Marital status (1=married/2=cohabiting)	.00	.14
Father's age	.04	.04
Presence of other children (1=no/2=yes)	.12*	.11
Months of full-time breastfeeding	.01	.27*
Months of part-time breastfeeding	.02	.05
Total months of breastfeeding	.02	.16

* Significant at the .05 level in one-tailed test

The age of fathers might have some influence on the tendency to share parental leave. On one hand, individuals who elect to delay childbearing might be more likely to share parental leave because of the novelty of caring for children and because they feel well-established, even bored with their regular employment. On the other hand, younger fathers might be more inclined to share parental leave because younger people have been exposed to egalitarian ideals for a greater portion of their lives. The father's age, however, turned out not to have a significant relationship with taking leave or the proportion of leave taken (see table 4.6), or with measures of gender role attitudes, for that matter.

Number of Siblings

Until recently, Swedish family size was small, with couples having only one or two children. This has changed dramatically in the past few years, with the Swedish birth rate now being one of the highest in the industrial world. As family size increases, it is interesting to speculate on what effects this might have on fathers' taking parental leave.

Swedish couples tend to space their children close together. This is partly a function of delayed parenting, but also due to parental leave eligibility rules. These allow couples to take parental leave with full pay for a new child even if the woman has not returned to the labor force after taking leave for an earlier child, as long as the two children are born within two years of one another. Parents who take parental leave often have more than one small child to care for at home. Anecdotal evidence suggests that couples reduce an older child's involvement in daycare when they are home on parental leave in order to spend more time together.

Having more than one child might discourage fathers from taking leave if they are a little nervous about their child care abilities. On the other hand, fathers might be more inclined to take parental leave if it means getting to spend some time with an older child who would be much more interesting to talk and play with than a new baby.

Sixty percent of the couples in the study had more than one child. Most of these (62%) had two children. Having at least one other sibling at home to care for increased the likelihood of fathers' taking parental leave (see table 4.6). We might expect, then, that the rising birth rate in Sweden will not serve as a brake to men's participation in the parental leave program.

Breastfeeding

As discussed in Chapter 1, perhaps the only real, established biological difference between the sexes which is relevant to the division of labor for child care is women's unique ability to breastfeed. While modern technology allows parents to feed babies breastmilk without the mother's continual presence, many couples might reasonably decide that it would be more convenient for the mother to be home full-time when the baby is young so that breastfeeding can proceed smoothly. As mentioned in Chapter 3, Swedish men rarely take parental leave during the baby's first six months. Some Swedish studies have found that parents believe breastfeeding is a barrier to fathers' participation in infant care (Hamrin, Nilsson, and Sörman, 1983;

Hwang, 1985; Statens Offentliga Utredningar, 1978). Respondents in the 1986 survey of new parents in Gothenburg also often named breastfeeding as a barrier to the father's taking parental leave in their families (see table 4.3).

The survey allowed a more objective evaluation of the impact of breastfeeding on leavetaking. Respondents were asked about the number of months mothers had breastfed the child born in 1984, and these answers were correlated with fathers' participation in parental leave. In line with a strong societal emphasis regarding the importance of breastfeeding, 90% of the Swedish mothers in the study reported breastfeeding their infants. Those who had nursed their babies did so for an average of ten months, half of this on a part-time basis. The number of months the mother breastfed (full-time, part-time, and altogether) was not related to her partner's decision to take leave. However, the number of months she breastfed full-time was negatively associated with the proportion of the leave taken by her partner (see table 4.6).

In summary, a number of factors associated with the family were considered as having a possible influence on fathers' participation in parental leave. Marital status and the age of the father were found to have no significant impact on fathers' taking leave. Swedes are unusual in their high rate of cohabitation and the delayed age of parenthood, but these factors do not seem to encourage or discourage fathers' participation in parental leave.

It was found that when there was already another child at home, fathers were more likely to take leave. This suggests that fathers are willing to rise to the challenge of caring for more than one child at a time while they are home on leave and that they are interested in increasing their care of earlier children.

Breastfeeding was reported to be a significant barrier by a sizeable number of Swedish parents. The longer mothers nursed full-time, the less leave fathers took. Breastfeeding, however, promises to be less a barrier to fathers' participation in early child care as the length of parental leave increases. The changes made in the law in 1988 (extending the leave to twelve months of almost fully paid leave, with three additional months of partly paid leave) may increase the number of fathers who take a more equitable portion of the leave. It seems unlikely that such an extension would merely encourage women to breastfeed full-time for a longer period, since the Swedish medical establishment insists that babies be fed additional foods from six months of age.

MULTIVARIATE ANALYSIS

Hierarchical multiple regression analysis was used to assess the relative utility of different groups of variables, such as social psychological and social structural variables, in explaining leavetaking behavior.

The potential for multicollinearity (i.e., high intercorrelation between variables) seemed great because of the number of related independent variables involved. A method suggested by Lewis-Beck (1980) was used to test for instances of multicollinearity, and two cases were found: men's experience with child care compared to their partners' was too highly correlated with their absolute level of experience, and women's income relative to men was too highly correlated with men's absolute income. It was decided, therefore, to drop the variables measuring relative standing from the multivariate analyses.

Another problem occurred due to the large number of independent variables that had been considered in the zero-order analysis. Multivariate estimates can become misleading if too many independent variables are entered into the equation; a good rule of thumb is no more than one independent variable for every ten cases (DiLeonardi and Curtis, 1988). To reduce the number of variables when examining determinants of fathers' taking leave, family context variables unrelated to fathers' taking leave were dropped from the analyses. A more drastic reduction was necessary when it was time to analyze the determinants of fathers' percentage of leave taken, since the sample size was reduced to the eighty-five fathers who had taken leave. A decision was made to include only variables which had significant zero-order correlations with percentage of leave taken.

In seeking determinants of fathers' taking of parental leave, variables were entered into the equation as groups in three steps. In the first step, family context variables were introduced. In the second step, social psychological variables were entered. In the last step, social structural variables were entered. F tests were conducted at each step to evaluate the significance of the contribution of each group of variables to the predictability of fathers' participation in parental leave.

To assess the relative importance of mother- and father-related variables, a second type of hierarchical multiple regression analysis was conducted. Here, variables associated with fathers were introduced in the first step, and then variables associated with mothers were introduced in the second step. Amount of time breastfeeding was considered a variable associated with mothers.

Tables 4.7 and 4.8 present the results of the hierarchical multiple regression analyses. The variables that had the strongest independent relationships with fathers' participation in parental leave are indicated. The results support conclusions drawn from the zero-order correlations presented earlier. Family context, social psychological variables, and social structural variables all have some utility in explaining why some fathers take parental leave and why some take a greater portion of the leave. The amount of variance explained in the dependent variables significantly increases when each group of variables is entered into the equation.

The results also underscore the important role played by mothers in fathers' leavetaking decisions (see tables 4.9 and 4.10). Variables associated with mothers were associated with the two measures of fathers' participation in parental leave more often than the fathers' own characteristics and circumstances. Adding the group of variables associated with women also increased significantly the amount of variation explained. The model explained about one-third of the variance in whether or not fathers took leave and about half of the variance in the proportion of leave taken by fathers. These amounts suggest that the determinants examined here are likely to be important factors associated with sharing of early child care; at the same time, it is clear that more research needs to be done to uncover barriers to sharing of early child care.

Table 4.7
Hierarchical Regression
Predicting Fathers' Taking of Parental Leave
(N=319)

	Standardized Beta Coefficients		
	Step 1: Family context variables added	Step 2: Social psychological variables added	Step 3: Social structural variables
Family context			
Presence of other children	.12*	.17*	.15*
Men's social psychological variables			
Mother's employment		.07	.03
Parental sharing of child care		.10	.08
Previous experience with child care		.09	.07
Nontraditional attitudes toward gender-based parenting ability		.05	.04
Positive attitudes toward role-sharing		.10	.05
Shared breadwinning orientation		.05	.00
Positive reaction to partner's leavetaking		-.15*	-.16*
Women's social psychological variables			
Mother's employment		.11*	.09*
Parental sharing of child care		.07	.08
Previous experience with child care		.05	.04
Nontraditional attitudes toward gender-based parenting ability		.00	.02
Positive attitudes toward role sharing		.14*	.11*
Shared breadwinning orientation		.02	.13
Positive reaction to partner's leavetaking		.11*	.00

A FRAMEWORK FOR UNDERSTANDING THE GENDER-BASED DIVISION OF LABOR FOR CHILD CARE

Nowhere in the world are fathers equally involved in the care of small children or regularly left solely responsible for their care on a regular basis. The eighty-five thousand Swedish men who take parental leave every year (Riksförsäkringsverket, 1989a) are therefore engaged in a radical departure from social

Table 4.7 (Cont.)

	Standardized Beta Coefficients		
	Step 1: Family context variables added	Step 2: Social psychological variables added	Step 3: Social structural variables
Men's social structural variables			
Positive workplace attitudes			.06
Public sector employment			.15*
Professional/managerial job			.04
Years of education			.02
Nontraditional job			.04
Income			-.11*
Support from significant others			.11*
Knowing men who had taken leave			.13*
Attention to parental leave debate			.07
Women's social structural variables			
Positive workplace attitudes			-.02
Public sector employment			.01
Professional/managerial job			.00
Years of education			.05
Nontraditional job			.13*
Income			.09
Support from significant others			.05
Knowing men who had taken leave			.13*
Attention to parental leave debate			.02
R^2	.01*	** .16*	** .31*

*Significant at the .05 level according to one-tailed F-test
**Significant increase in variance explained according to one-tailed F-test

tradition. Why some make the decision to share parental leave with their partners while others do not has been the subject of this chapter.

Many different variables were considered as having a potential influence on men's participation in parental leave. These variables were considered under three major categories, each representing different theoretical perspectives on the bases of the traditional division of labor for child care. It was discovered

Table 4.8
Hierarchical Regression
Predicting Fathers' Proportion of Parental Leave
(N=85)

	Standardized Beta Coefficients		
	Step 1: Family context variables	Step 2: Social psycho-logical variables added	Step 3: Social structural variables added
Family context variables			
Months of full-time breastfeeding	.27*	.30*	.30*
Men's social psychological variables			
Parental sharing of child care		-.07	-.07
Positive attitudes toward role sharing		.35*	.33*
Women's social psychological variables			
Mother's employment		.26*	.24*
Parental sharing of child care		.20*	.17*
Nontraditional attitudes toward gender-based parenting ability		.19*	.19*
Positive reaction to partner's leavetaking		.17*	.22*
Men's social structural variables			
Positive workplace attitudes			.02
Education			.32*
Nontraditional job			.09
Income			-.13
Attention to parental leave debate			.04
Women's social structural variables			
Knowing men who took leave			.02
R^2	.07* **	.40* **	.51*

* Significant at the .05 level according to one-tailed F test
** Increase in variance explained was significant according to one-tailed F test

Table 4.9
Hierarchical Regression
Predicting Fathers' Taking of Parental Leave
(N=319)

	Standardized Beta Coefficients		
	Step 1: Family context variables	Step 2: Father variables added	Step 3: Mother variables added
Family context			
Presence of other children	.12*	.16*	.15*
Men's social psychological variables			
Mother's employment		.02	.03
Parental sharing of child care		.11*	.08
Previous experience with child care		.07	.07
Nontraditional attitudes toward gender-based parenting ability		.03	.04
Positive attitudes toward role-sharing		.09	.05
Shared breadwinning orientation		.01	.00
Positive reaction to partner's leavetaking		.13*	.16*
Men's structural variables			
Positive workplace attitudes		.07	.06
Public sector employment		.13*	.15*
Professional/managerial jjob		.10	.04
Years of education		.05	.02
Nontraditional job		.02	.03
Income		.08	-.11
Support from significant others		.13*	.11*
Knowing men who had taken leave		.19*	.13*
Attention to parental leave debate		.07	.07

that all perspectives had some merit in improving our understanding of why women dominate child care.

A social psychological perspective on gender assumes that people are socialized into specific static roles early on in childhood through their exposure to, and rewards for, sex-typed behaviors. Such socialization would presumably limit individuals' behavioral repertoire, making the crossing of gender role lines in adulthood more unthinkable and difficult. The measures that were included in the Gothenburg survey suggested that child-

Table 4.9 (Cont.)

	Standardized Beta Coefficients				
	Step 1: Family context variables		Step 2: Father variables added		Step 3: Mother variables added
Women's social psychological variables					
Mother's employment					.09*
Parental sharing of child care			.08		
Previous experience with child care			.04		
Nontraditional attitudes toward gender-based parenting ability					.02
Positive attitudes toward role sharing					.11*
Shared breadwinning orientation					.13
Positive reaction to partner's leavetaking					.00
Women's social structural variables					
Positive workplace attitudes					-.02
Public sector employment					.01
Professional/managerial job					.00
Years of education					.05
Nontraditional job					.13*
Income					.09
Support from significant others					.05
Knowing men who had taken leave					.13*
Attention to parental leave debate					.02
R^2	.01	**	.25*	**	.31*

* Significant at the .05 level according to one-tailed F test
** Significant increase in variance explained according to one-tailed F test

hood socialization experiences probably do not prevent men from assuming a more androgynous lifestyle in adulthood. Contemporary influences and circumstances seem much more important. On the other hand, childhood experiences appeared to have an impact on *women's* predisposition to share early child care. When women experienced more androgynous childhood models, they were more likely to share parental leave with their partners.

Traditional thinking about gender roles persisted among some of the parents in the survey. When men believed in innate

Table 4.10
Hierarchical Regression
Predicting Fathers' Proportion of Parental Leave
(N=85)

	Standardized Beta Coefficients		
	Step 1: Father variables added		Step 2: Mother variables added
Father variables			
Parental sharing of child care	-.17*		-.07
Positive attitudes toward role sharing	.18		.33*
Positive workplace attitudes	.10		.02
Years of education	.27*		.32*
Nontraditional job	.12		.09
Income	-.17		-.13
Attention to the parental leave debate	.16		.04
Mother variables			
Months of full-time breastfeeding			.30*
Mother's employment			.24*
Parental sharing of child care			.17*
Nontraditional attitudes toward gender-based parenting ability			.19*
Positive reaction to partner's leavetaking			.22*
Knowing men who had taken parental leave			.02
R^2	.28*	**	.51*

* Significant at the .05 level according to one-tailed F test
** Increase in variance explained was significant according to one-tailed F test

differences in parenting ability, they were less likely to take parental leave. When women believed that traditional domestic responsibilities should not be shared by both sexes, then they were less likely to share parental leave with their partners. These attitudes may have been developed in childhood; on the other hand, they may have been reinforced by adult experiences, including awareness of sex differences in occupational opportunities.

Mothers were found to be generally lukewarm toward the prospect of their partners' being responsible for early child care; they were negatively disposed toward equally sharing parental leave. When women were less positive about sharing parental leave, fathers took less leave. Further research is needed to uncover the negotiation and bargaining processes involved in couples' decisions to share or not share early child care.

While social psychological explanations for the persistence of the gender-based division of labor for child care seem apt to some degree, findings from this investigation suggest that a structural perspective is also useful. While fathers' lack of participation in parental leave was related to their partners' lack of willingness to share, it is important to consider how structural factors lying outside the family may have conditioned women's interest. In particular, a gender-segregated labor market, in which women work for less pay at less attractive jobs, may lead women to resign themselves to focus on domestic activities as a source of self-esteem. Women's access to high status, nontraditional, and better paying jobs appears to be a prerequisite for the equal sharing of early child care by women and men.

Other types of structural factors should also be considered as potential barriers to equal parenthood. One is the opposition men encounter in the workplace. While Swedish employers cannot prevent men from taking parental leave (and strong unions exist to back up workers' rights in this regard), men often perceive a lack of support from employers, supervisors, and coworkers. When this is their impression, they participate less in parental leave. The public sector seems to adhere more to government rhetoric about equality, so men are more likely to experience support there.

Another structural factor impeding progress toward parents' sharing early child care in Sweden may be the design of the program itself, particularly the rules regarding compensation for parental leave. Higher paid men take a lower percentage of leave days, probably because they would be compensated only to a certain amount. Public employees' greater inclination to take leave might be due to the fact that they typically get 100% of their pay during leave while private employees get 90%.

The last structural factor which appeared likely to be a catalyst for equal parenthood was social support. It is difficult to swim against the current of tradition and social opinion. Knowing or hearing of others who have deviated from the typical pattern can make it much easier for an individual to adopt a new lifestyle. We tend to think that men are self-confident and independent and that the regard of others, and even of society, would perhaps be less important to them when trying a new social arrangement than it would be for women. Yet this study shows that men depend on contemporary role models and the emotional support of those close to them for encouragement to adopt a new parenting arrangement. Women, too, were more likely to share leave when exposed to contemporary models of equal parenting.

An analysis of several family-related variables indicated that cohabitation and age of parenting are neither barriers nor facilitators of equal parenting arrangements. Having more than one child to care for seemed to make parental leave more attractive to men. The mothers' tendency to breastfeed did not affect fathers' decision to take leave, but it did tend to reduce the amount of time fathers took. This points to the need to make leaves last well beyond the period of full-time breastfeeding, if men are to be given a chance to take the leave.

What do these results suggest will be the future of fathers' participation in parental leave in Sweden? Some of the factors found to be positively related to fathers' taking parental leave seem likely to become more common. For example, family size is increasing; and since fathers seem to take parental leave more often when there are other children to care for, we might expect fathers to take leave more often. When mothers had egalitarian role models in their own families of origin, they were more likely to relinquish their monopoly on parental leave; we would expect that more and more of these role models will exist. In a similar fashion, the importance of knowing other men who have taken leave was discovered in the study. As the number of men who have taken parental leave grows, we would expect a snowball phenomenon to occur, with more and more men feeling comfortable taking leave and more of their partners accepting this arrangement. The government's recent efforts to publicize the virtues of fathers' taking parental leave may have positive effects on workplace attitudes, removing this as a barrier to leavetaking, especially in the private sector. Last but not least, as Swedish women's job opportunities improve, we would expect a greater number of mothers to step aside to allow their partners to take leave.

5

DADDIES AND MOMMIES AT HOME: PARENTS' EXPERIENCES WITH LEAVE

Fathers who stay home on parental leave are involved in a dramatic departure from social tradition. Taking on so much responsibility for an infant's care is unusual for men. What is it like for fathers to stay home with their babies while the mothers return to work? Why do some men have more positive experiences on leave than others in such a situation? In what ways do fathers experience parental leave differently than mothers? To investigate how men evaluate the experience, this chapter focuses on the 85 (of 319) fathers in the Gothenburg mail survey who had taken parental leave. To help interpret the quantitative findings, quotes from interviews with nine couples where the man took two or more months of parental leave are included.

FATHERS' EXPERIENCES

Since staying home to care for a baby has traditionally not been something fathers have done, it is not surprising that even men who enthusiastically support the idea and decide to take parental leave might be apprehensive at the outset. Below is a poem written by a father on his first day of parental leave:

> Now we are here
> You and I
> left to each other.
> I have prepared myself for a long time
> on weekends, evenings yet
> Will it work?
> The door has just closed after your mommy

> who with a mixture of gladness and worry has gone
> to her first day at work . . .
> Now shall we have days, nights, time
> together.
> I have worked hard the last few days
> on the job.
> Now comes something completely different
> You and me.
> Will I understand you
> be able to give you what you ask for
> Will you accept me?
> (Hamrin, Nilsson, and Sörman, 1983:138,
> my translation)

In this section, how fathers actually fared while on parental leave will be described.

Over-all Evaluation of the Leave

Over three-fourths of the fathers in the study (77%) reported that they "got along well" with being at home to care for their babies (see table 5.1). This figure is somewhat higher than that found in a 1981 study of fifty Swedish fathers who took parental leave, where only two-thirds of fathers (68%) reported their leaves as basically positive (Hwang, Eldén, and Fransson, 1984). Perhaps in the intervening five years fathers' participation in parental leave has become more acceptable, leading to more fathers experiencing it positively.

Over one-quarter (29%) of the fathers in the survey indicated that they got along very well while on leave. The 1981 study of men who had taken parental leave also found that about 30% of fathers described the parental leave as one of the best experiences in their lives. The stability of this level of extreme satisfaction over time suggests that we cannot expect all fathers to experience leave in an intensely positive way, although the vast majority will be satisfied that they took leave.

Fathers who had taken leave were asked if they would take parental leave again, should the opportunity arise. The vast majority (80%) said they would; most of the remainder (18%) were unsure. Only 2% said they would not take parental leave again.

Table 5.1
Fathers' Experiences with Parental Leave
(N=85)

Over-all Evaluation

"How well did you get along in general when you were home caring for the child?"

29%	very well
48%	rather well
21%	neither well nor badly
1%	rather badly
0%	very badly

"If you were to have another baby, would you choose to take parental leave?"

80%	yes
18%	unsure
2%	no

* * *

Specific Problems with Leavetaking

"What were the consequences for your workplace when you went on parental leave?"

22%	no difficulties at the workplace
47%	problem-free for the most part
27%	some difficulties
4%	great problems occurred

"Was your family's income affected adversely by your being at home on parental leave?"

9%	yes, a lot
52%	yes, a little
39%	no

"Indicate whether the following statements applied to your leave."

	Very true	Rather true	No opinion	Not especially true	Not at all true
"I felt lonely."	2%	20%	18%	33%	27%
"I liked caring for the child."	55%	26%	18%	1%	0%
"It was boring."	1%	6%	18%	26%	49%
"It felt good not to be working for awhile."	33%	21%	18%	15%	13%
"It was hard work and stressful."	6%	21%	18%	29%	26%

Problems Experienced by Men on Parental Leave

Previous studies have asked fathers about their experiences while on leave, generally with open-ended questions (Hamrin, Nilsson, and Sörman, 1983; Hwang, Eldén, and Fransson, 1984; Kjellman and Wizelius, 1983). These studies have discovered that while on leave, some fathers reported difficulties at their workplace, and some mentioned that their family income suffered. Fathers often volunteered that they had problems with loneliness, disliked caretaking activities, felt bored, missed their jobs, and found being home full-time to be burdensome and stressful. Specific questions were developed for this study to investigate the extent to which fathers experienced each particular problem. The wordings of the items and the distributions of responses are given in table 5.1.

Of the specific problems investigated, the most common one reported by men who had taken leave was that their family income had suffered. Three-fifths of fathers said this was the case, although only 9% reported that the effects were major.

The next most common problem reported by the men who had taken leave was that their temporary absence had caused problems at their workplace. Over three-fourths of fathers reported some problems; for example, a government administrator said in an interview that he was pressured to take work home. However, relatively few fathers (4%) reported that major problems had occurred. This percentage of fathers who reported major problems was similar to that found in a more recent study of parents who took leave in Sweden (Török, 1990). In that study, the biggest problem men reported was that it was difficult to find substitutes with the same background or specialty. Most men, however, were not on leave long, and their work tasks tended to be redistributed among co-workers.

The next most common problem experienced by fathers on leave was missing their jobs. A physician was reported by his wife to be "very achievement-oriented. He didn't feel like he achieved anything by staying home—at least nothing that was easily measured. . . ." However, only about one-quarter of the fathers who took leave said this was a problem. Most Swedish men do not become fathers until some years after their first entrance into the labor market. It is probably therefore not surprising that the majority perceived leave as a welcome respite from the demands and routine of employment. A gym teacher said, "I was very happy at home. My boss had said I would be bored and miss work, but I wasn't."

Only about one quarter of fathers who took leave found it to be "a lot of work and stressful." The interviews suggest that men sometimes reduced stress levels by neglecting housework chores in favor of child care. This sometimes caused difficulties with partners. In an interview with two gym teachers, the woman reported several arguments concerning her partner's neglect of housework. She said:

> We had different priorities regarding domestic work. I expected that the laundry would be done, the dishes washed, things picked up when I got home. When I was on leave I felt I had to get those things done, as well as child care. He would spend more time with Amanda, leaving chores until last. I felt I couldn't let myself play with Amanda if other things needed to be done.

Experiences with the difficulties involved in doing child care made some fathers more understanding of the plight of the typical mother at home. A computer consultant at Volvo said:

> I know what it's like to be home. . . . I am more sympathetic to my wife when she's home—I don't place demands on her.

Problems with loneliness were reported by less than one-fourth of leavetaking fathers, and most of these said such problems were minor. Fathers seemed to have coped with loneliness by developing more contacts over time or arranging out-of-home events when their partners returned home. As one father in the interviews described it:

> I sometimes missed adult contact. I was the only guy at the sandbox; others there thought it was strange. But they began talking to me after a while.

A teacher admitted:

> I looked forward to [my wife's] coming home so I'd have someone to talk to. I signed up for an evening course to get out of the house once a week.

An architect said:

> If she came home late I was disappointed. I now know how the classic housewife felt. You need contact with other adults. We lived in the country and we eventually met a nice family we could keep company with.

Men on leave who felt isolated may have been so because they did not know other men in similar circumstances. A physician reported on her husband's experiences with parental leave:

> When I was home on leave I could visit friends and have them over. He didn't know any men at home. His relationships with friends were based on activity—like sports—which doesn't combine well with child care anyway.

In a book of interviews with fathers on parental leave, another reason for feeling isolated was noted: men home on leave did not feel comfortable developing relationships with women on leave. A crane operator stated:

> There are no other fathers on leave here in the neighborhood, only some mothers. Certainly we ought to have a lot to talk about and we could help each other with babysitting, but this has not happened. One of the mothers has invited me into her home for ten minutes at a time. I would rather not go there. I don't know what her husband thinks. . . . I don't want to risk some gossip. Someone might say, "The young ones are crying in the living room and the leavetakers are together in the bedroom." (Kjellman and Wizelius, 1983:17, my translation)

Boredom was not a problem for most of the fathers in the study. The interviews suggest that the need to continually adjust to the child's rhythm, as well as cope with the demands of household and child care, left little time for boredom. Many men expected that being on parental leave would give them leisure to pursue other activities that they enjoyed, such as home and car repairs, independent research, hobbies like woodworking. A computer consultant said:

> The time went so fast, I couldn't get enough done. I thought I would have time to do home repairs, but I didn't.

A gym teacher said, "It's not just a time for relaxation like a lot of guys think."

Only one father out of eighty-five reported problems with disliking child care. The vast majority expressed their enjoyment in the strongest terms. One reason fathers seemed to enjoy caregiving was because it provided them with interesting learning experiences. One teacher reported, "I gained insight into what goes into child care that I never had and could get no other way." Others tied in enjoyment of caregiving with the opportunity that it gave them to know and develop a relationship with their child. A teacher said, "I learned to know her as a person, what she liked." An assembly-line worker said, "The leave gave me a much better relationship with the child and made me a real parent."

Correlates of Fathers' Experiences with Parental Leave

An exploratory effort was undertaken to see what factors were associated with men's reactions to parental leave. There is little literature on fathers' experiences as full-time caretakers of infants. There are accounts of househusbands (e.g., Beer, 1983; Lutwin and Siperstein, 1985; Russell, 1987), but in these cases the children involved are rarely infants and the men are usually home involuntarily because of unemployment. These accounts also tend to focus more on men's difficulties with housework than they do on problems with child care.

In identifying correlates of fathers' experiences with parental leave, three dependent variables were considered: over-all evaluation of the leave (how well he "got along"), interest in taking leave again, and a seven-item scale made up of all the other experience items measured above (hereafter called the "problem scale," which had a coefficient of reproducibility of .46). The average score on the problem scale was 2.83, where five indicated a lot of problems and one indicated no problems. These three variables were significantly intercorrelated, with r − values in the .32–.64 range.

Among the variables considered in the search for potential correlates of fathers' experiences with parental leave were the factors discussed in Chapter 4 as possible hindrances to men's taking leave in the first place. In the first category were social psychological barriers such as aspects of the division of labor practiced in the man's family while he was growing up and his previous experience with child care. Fathers with nontraditional role models and previous child care experience might have an easier time staying home to take care of a small child because the experience would not seem so odd. Gender role attitudes were also included in this category; men with less traditional attitudes toward men's parenting capabilities and the male role might feel more comfortable pursuing the nontraditional role of baby's primary caretaker. The women's socialization and gender role attitudes were also examined as having a potential influence on men's experiences with parental leave.

The second category of factors examined were social structural obstacles related to the man's job and level of social support. Men who received more support from their workplace for taking the leave might feel more relaxed at home than those who left behind angry feelings and resentment. The type of job a man held might also affect his experiences with leavetaking. For instance, men working in the public sector might have a better leave because they would be receiving 100% compensation and would thus not be so worried about the financial picture. Finally, men who received support from significant others and knew other men taking leave seemed likely to be happier staying at home, for such people could provide them with emotional support and concrete assistance when they needed it. Factors associated with the women's workplace, job, and support systems were also examined as having a potential impact on men's evaluation of parental leave.

The third set of variables concerned the family context. Here, marital status and father's age (as a measure of delayed childbearing) were examined as having possible influences on men's experiences with leave. Cohabiting fathers might have perceived themselves in a more precarious family role and thus not enjoy parental leave as much. Older fathers might enjoy parental leave more if they waited to have children; on the other hand, younger fathers might find it easier to adapt to the stresses and strains of childrearing.

The effect of the presence of other children was also investigated. While fathers on parental leave are technically paid to stay home and care only for the newborn, in reality a father cares for the baby's siblings as well, if there are any. Taking care of more than one child might prove such a challenge that it would cause a father to experience his leavetaking more negatively than if he had only one child to care for. On the other hand, having an older child present might give men more company and assistance; the opportunity to have closer contact with the older child might also enhance the benefits of parental leave.

The amount of time mothers breastfed was also investigated as having a possible influence on men's evaluation of parental leave. The longer the period of breastfeeding, the more likely it is for the baby to become more accustomed to the mother's care and emotionally closer to the mother. This could make it difficult for the father to win acceptance as a substitute caretaker.

A fourth set of variables examined in this exploratory search for correlates of satisfactory leavetaking concerned the length of the leave. Parents are supposed to inform the social insurance offices and their employers in advance of their plans for sharing parental leave. So a father is committed to following through on his original plan of leave length, even if the leave proves unsatisfactory. Since fathers' being primarily responsible for babies is still rare in contemporary industrial societies, it could be that the generally unprepared fathers who took more days of leave would experience the leave more negatively than the men who took fewer days. The latter did not have as much time to get frustrated with their lack of preparation or to tire of the novelty of caring for an infant. Staying home longer might also have more serious repercussions for the workplace and the family budget than staying home only a short time. On the other hand, men who took longer leaves might ultimately exhibit more adjustment, for they might become more accustomed to managing the demands of child care the longer they were home. The older the child became, the more interesting a person they would be to be around. Consequently, the effects of leave length were examined but not predicted to exert an influence in any particular direction.

The length of the woman's leave was also considered. It seemed likely that men would have more difficulty adjusting to parental leave when their babies had had a longer period to train their mommies how best to respond to their demands. Their partners might also develop and display more of a "know-it-all" attitude about child care when they were home longer, which could undermine the men's self-confidence and sense of accomplishment as caretakers.

Finally, all the specific problems examined as part of the problem scale were considered as possible correlates of the first two variables, men's over-all evaluation of the leave and men's inclination to take leave again. These included encountering opposition at the workplace, worrying about family income, feeling lonely, being bored, missing work, disliking caretaking, and feeling the leave was hard work and stressful. Ideas for problems to consider came from an examination of three past studies of Swedish men taking parental leave (Hamrin, Nilsson, and Sörman, 1983; Hwang, Eldén, and Fransson, 1984; Kjellman and Wizelius, 1983). The salience, or importance, of these problems for men's satisfaction with parental leave, however, has never been ascertained.

Zero-order correlation coefficients were calculated to establish which variables had significant associations with the measures of men's experiences with parental leave. Of all the variables considered as having possible influences on how well men got along while on leave, the only ones which had significant correlations were those which measured specific problems encountered while on leave. Men reported their leaves as more satisfactory when they caused fewer problems with the workplace and the family income ($r = -.21, -.22$), when they experienced less loneliness and boredom ($r = -.29, -.55$), when they perceived the leave as a respite from work, and when they enjoyed caregiving activities ($r = .28, .73$). Perceiving the leave to be difficult and stressful, however, did not keep men from reporting the leave as a positive experience.

Men were more likely to say they would take leave again if they had gotten along well on leave ($r = .51$), if they enjoyed caretaking ($r = .52$), and if they had not felt bored ($r = -.28$). Men were also likely to say they would take leave again if they held more egalitarian attitudes toward role-sharing, if they had known other men who had taken leave, and if they had been attentive to the debate about parental leave ($r = .29, .31, .33$). In addition, men were likely to say they would take leave again if their partners had taken shorter leaves and if their partners had known other men who had taken leave ($r = -.22, .24$).

Men were more likely to experience fewer specific problems with the leave if they had previous experience with child care ($r = -.27$). This was an interesting finding, given that previous experience with child care had not been found to be a significant correlate of men's taking leave in the first place. Since having other children at home was *not* found to be related to men's experiences with leave, we can assume that the previous experience did not necessarily result from having become a father for a second (or third) time.

Summary

Swedish fathers who took parental leave tended to evaluate the experience in a positive manner. Most liked doing child care, enjoyed being away from their paid jobs for a time, and wanted to take parental leave again if they had another baby. The vast majority reported few problems with loneliness, boredom, or the hard work and stress associated with child care. The most common problems involved circumstances outside the family. Their workplaces experienced disruption, and program rules sometimes led to a cut in their usual salary. These problems were seldom reported to be serious, however.

Might fathers have reported their leaves as positive, even if they were not? What if they were reluctant to admit that they had made a mistake, wasted their time, or failed to live up to the national goal of equal parenthood? While this seems possible, a more likely reason so many men experienced good leaves was because of self-selection. That is, those who thought they would like staying home freely chose to do so, and those predisposed to experiencing a leave negatively did not attempt to take advantage of the leave program in the first place.

Another reason for the high level of satisfaction among the men who took leave may derive from the fact that they did not stay home for long. The amount of time ranged from three to 180 days; only about half of the men who had taken leave (47%) took two or more months of leave. The number of days of leave taken by the father was not related to how well men got along while on leave or their feelings about taking leave again. However, fathers were obligated to establish in advance how long a leave they would take, and they seemed to be able to predict fairly accurately what their tolerance limits would be. Three of the nine fathers interviewed admitted that they were glad to go back to work. A high-level government administrator said:

> I never felt really isolated nor had cabin fever, but I wasn't home very long. . . . It was a nice break.

The gym teacher admitted:

> The first month went fine, but by the second month I became a little bored. . . . If I had been home much longer I would have gone crazy.

The computer consultant said:

> I really wanted to be home for a while, enjoyed getting away from work. I would miss work, however, if I was home too long.

None of the women interviewed made comments such as these.

Not surprisingly, fathers tended to view their leaves more positively when they experienced fewer problems with it. Gender role attitudes and social support were also related to men's willingness to take leave in the future. These results suggest that it may be possible to improve men's chances of having a good leave by providing them with a supportive social environment while on leave. Men's interest in parental leave in the future was also affected by how long their partners stayed home. Perhaps when mothers stay home a longer time, all parties concerned are likely to view mothers as more experienced and interested in child care than fathers. Fathers reported fewer specific problems while on leave if they also reported having had previous practical experience with child care before the child was born. This finding suggests that policymakers may want to provide boys and men with more training and child care experience if they would like to see them experience fewer problems while on leave.

The high numbers of fathers who enjoyed leave and would like to take it again suggest that at least as many Swedish fathers who take parental leave now will continue to do so in the future. Men's access to parental leave might, however, be limited by women's desire to monopolize it. This could occur if women really enjoy their leaves to the point where they would be reluctant to sacrifice portions of future leaves to make room for fathers interested in taking advantage of the program.

MOTHERS' EXPERIENCES WITH PARENTAL LEAVE

Women who agree to share parental leave with their partners are likely to have done so because they had high-status jobs they plan to return to. Even so, mothers have mixed feelings about returning to work, as the following poem suggests:

> I bend down over you
> Breathe in your special scent
> Your temple against my mouth
> Your little hand which lies
> so relaxed on the pillow
> Your mouth a little half-open
> The soft down on your bald head.
> In a little while
> you will waken out of your nice sleep
> I won't be here then
> Another's arms will pick you up
> Arms which you so many
> times safely have slept in
> Your daddy and you
> In the same moment feelings of
> sadness and longing
> but also
> freedom and gladness
> (Hamrin, Nilsson, and Sörman, 1983:132–33, my translation)

Interviews with mothers suggest that the return to work is bitter-sweet because they enjoyed being at home on leave so much. This section of the chapter discusses Swedish mothers' experiences with taking parental leave. Do fathers and mothers experience parental leave similarly, or are there significant differences?

Virtually all Swedish mothers take parental leave; in this study, all mothers had done so. We might expect mothers to evaluate leave more positively and experience fewer problems than fathers. After all, Swedish women have had the opportunity to take postpartum leaves for many decades, while men's opportunity to do so is less than two decades old. Women's taking leave might thus seem more customary, and going along with custom could make for a more pleasant experience. Another reason women might have more satisfactory leaves is related to traditional gender role expectations and socialization processes. Women's identity has long been tied up with motherhood. Since girlhood, females have been led to expect that they will be mothers and will be primarily responsible for child care. Sweden has made major efforts to change these traditional expectations, but it seems likely to take considerable time to undo centuries of social tradition. Yet virtually all Swedish mothers have a permanent attachment to the labor force; the country has the highest rate of maternal employment in the world. Women might thus welcome parental leave as a way to fulfill traditional expectations of full-time motherhood without derailing their careers.

Over-all Evaluation of the Leave

Nearly all mothers (94%) reported that they got along well on parental leave. Almost half (48%) of mothers answered with "very much," in significant contrast to less than one-third of fathers (see table 5.2). Nine out of ten mothers (91%) said they would take parental leave again in the future should the opportunity arise, which was significantly higher than the percentage among fathers (80%). Table 5.3 reports on the statistical tests for differences between mothers' and fathers' experiences with parental leave.

Table 5.2
Mothers' Experiences with Parental Leave
(N=319)

Over-all Evaluation

"How well did you get along in general when you were home caring for the child?"

48%	very well
46%	rather well
3%	neither well nor badly
3%	rather badly
0%	very badly

"If you were to have another baby, would you choose to take parental leave?"

91%	yes
8%	unsure
1%	no

* * *

Specific Problems with Leavetaking

"What were the consequences for your workplace when you went on parental leave?"

39%	no difficulties at the workplace
38%	problem-free for the most part
18%	some difficulties
5%	great problems occurred

"Was your family's income affected adversely by your being at home on parental leave?"

21%	yes, a lot
53%	yes, a little
26%	no

"Indicate whether the following statements applied to your leave."

	Very true	Rather true	No opinion	Not especially true	Not at all true
"I felt lonely."	8%	18%	8%	29%	37%
"I liked caring for the child."	84%	10%	6%	0%	0%
"It was boring."	1%	5%	9%	16%	69%
"It felt good not to be working for awhile."	63%	22%	6%	6%	3%
"It was hard work and stressful."	3%	18%	7%	35%	37%

Table 5.3
Experiences with Parental Leave
Comparisons between Fathers and Mothers

	Group means		
	Leavetaking fathers (N=85)	Leavetaking mothers (N=319)	Leavesharing mothers# N=85)
Getting along well on leave (1=very badly...5=very well)	4.06	4.39*	4.36*
Interest in taking leave again (1=no/2=don't know/3=yes)	2.78	2.90*	2.95*
Problems at the workplace (1=none...4=big)	2.12	1.89*	2.08
Problems with family income (1=none...3=a lot)	1.71	1.95**	1.95**
Loneliness (1=not true...5=very true)	2.38	2.32	2.53
Enjoyment of child care (1=not true...5-very true)	4.35	4.77*	4.78*
Boredom (1=not true...5=very true)	1.84	1.52*	1.59
Enjoyment of absence from work (1=not true...5=very true)	3.46	4.38*	4.30*
Experiencing leave as hard work and stressful (1=not true...5=very true)	2.52	2.14*	2.19

Leavesharing mothers are mothers whose partners took parental leave.

Note: One-tailed t-tests were calculated to see if mothers' scores were significantly different than fathers'. When the coefficient for the mother is marked with one asterisk, it means that mothers experienced significantly fewer problems than fathers. Two asterisks means that the difference was strong in the opposite direction—i.e., mothers experienced significantly more problems than fathers.

Problems Experienced by Women on Parental Leave

In general, mothers (like fathers) experienced few serious problems while on parental leave. The exception to this statement concerned problems of managing on a reduced family income.

Almost three-fourths (74%) of mothers said that their family income suffered while they were on leave. Significantly more mothers than fathers said their leaves caused financial problems, perhaps because the mothers as a group were home much longer and were more likely to take some of the lowly paid "guarantee" days toward the end of the leave.

The second most commonly mentioned problem among mothers (as with fathers) was disruption at the workplace. Three-fifths (61%) of all mothers reported that at least some disruption occurred; only 5%, however, said this was severe. Mothers were significantly less likely to report workplace problems than fathers.

The third most common problem women experienced was loneliness. Over one-fourth (26%) of them mentioned this, about the same proportion as found among the men. A nurse said:

> I got lonely and depressed; it was a cold winter and I couldn't get out much.

A pharmacy worker said:

> I liked being at home... but I missed contact with adults sometimes.

An office manager said:

> I liked being with the child but I disliked the isolation. With two children it was hard to get out; they were stuck in routines.

Mothers were significantly less likely than fathers to find staying home stressful and hard work, although about one-fifth (21%) still did so. An assembly line worker said:

> I disliked the 100% responsibility. It was not *fun.* I couldn't even go to the toilet in peace.

An office manager said:

> Sometimes it was a little hard for me to have control over the day or know what would happen next.

Another mother, an architect, admitted:

> I had to get used to it; it was a very new situation. Messy diapers and throwing up were bad.

Of all the problems considered, the greatest discrepancy between mothers and fathers occurred when it came to missing the job. Most mothers (85%) said that parental leave constituted a welcome respite from their jobs and two-thirds (63%) expressed this sentiment in the strongest terms. (The corresponding figures for the men were 54% and 33% respectively.) Each of the nine mothers who were interviewed in person mentioned that it was fun to get away from work for a time.

Women may have felt more obligated to be at home than men did during this time, and therefore less likely to miss their jobs. Traditional expectations for women to be full-time mothers might lead to this. In the interviews, a nurse revealed how outside opinions and her own feelings about staying home were intertwined:

> At my workplace, people were rather negative to the fact that I wasn't going to be home the whole time. [Her partner took five months of the twelve-month leave.] People said, "How can you think of leaving such a little baby?" . . . The leave *was* very pleasant. It was important for me to be home then—no other relationship is like what mothers have with their newborns.

In response to an open-ended question about how their leaves went, four of the nine women who were interviewed mentioned that one of the benefits of parental leave for them was the opportunity for more independence and autonomy than they had in the workplace. None of the fathers mentioned this. Women seem more likely than men to be low in the power hierarchy at work. This may make them less inclined than men to feel like they miss work while at home on leave. A pharmacy worker said, "I liked the freedom to decide my day." An architect said, "It was nice to have the autonomy, not have specific tasks to do."

A few mothers reported being bored while home on leave. An architect said:

> Doing the same thing like washing got boring—not variable like my job.

A gym teacher who was interviewed said:

> I felt a little isolated, and missed adult contact. Every day became like each other. But the time went fast, and it was very fun to watch her development.

Although few fathers had reported boredom as well, mothers were significantly more likely to strongly disagree that they were bored.

Almost all women (94%) said they enjoyed caregiving activities. While most fathers (81%) said this, too, mothers tended to report their enjoyment in significantly stronger terms.

Mothers who had shared parental leave with their partners tended to experience their leaves in much the same way as other mothers. Comparing the 85 mothers whose partners had taken leave to the 234 leavetaking mothers whose partners had not, the only significant difference was in terms of workplace disturbances. Leavesharing mothers perceived their workplaces to be more disturbed by their absence than mothers who did not share leave with their partners. In fact, leavesharing mothers were no less likely to report workplace disturbances than their male partners (see table 5.3). Couples thus seem to share leave more often when both feel themselves to be indispensable at the workplace. A pharmacy worker said that at her work, "They were glad I could came back so soon—things change fast there and I hadn't missed much."

Correlates of Mothers' Experiences with Parental Leave

The same variables examined as possible correlates of fathers' experiences with parental leave were also looked at for mothers. Over-all evaluation of the leave, desire to take leave again, and the seven-item scale measuring experience with problems were all considered again as well. The average score for mothers on the 5-point problem scale (which had a coefficient of reproducibility of .49) was 2.0, where 1 meant no problems. The range of answers was 1.86 to 5.

Interestingly, workplace disturbances and economic problems caused by their leaves had no effect on women's tendency to rate their leaves as good. These events had caused men to evaluate their leaves negatively. Perhaps men's traditional association with the public sphere makes them more sensitive to problems which originate there, while women's traditional association with the domestic sphere contributes to their ignoring these problems while they are home on leave.

The longer women breastfed part-time, the more highly they evaluated their leaves ($r = .15$). Such women were following guidelines set up by the national health care system for baby nutrition, and would probably feel that their time at home was well spent. Women with more traditional jobs were also more satisfied while on leave, compared to women with nontraditional jobs ($r = .16$). The former may be more traditionally oriented to start with, or their jobs may not provide them with as much self-esteem as full-time child care can.

Almost all the women were interested in taking parental leave again, so it was not worthwhile to look for factors that would explain the little variation. There was a tendency, however, for women with more egalitarian attitudes toward role-sharing and gender-based parenting abilities, as well as those with higher education, to be more likely than other women to be sure they would take the leave again ($r = -.19, -.32, -.15$). Why might this be the case? Perhaps a type of "balancing act" occurs for nontraditional women. Those who embrace egalitarian principles may find themselves departing too far from social tradition and their own upbringing. One way to approach a middle ground would be to embrace wholeheartedly, for a predetermined length of time, the challenges and jobs of full-time motherhood. More traditional-minded women may respond to the leave more realistically; they seem likely to have had primary responsibility for any children born earlier and would continue to have more responsibility for the child even once both partners have returned to work. For them, parental leave would not represent such a welcome break from their usual routine.

Mothers, like fathers, reported fewer specific problems while on leave if they had had previous experience with child care before the child was born. Again, having had a child before was not related to enjoyment of parental leave, so we can assume that this experience was obtained well before parenting began. Several other variables were significantly correlated with the scale of items measuring mothers' problems while on leave. Three of these concerned the woman herself. Women experienced fewer problems while on leave when they held more traditional attitudes toward gender-based parenting abilities, when they had paid less attention to the debate about fathers taking parental leave, and when they had breastfed babies a greater number of months ($r = -.17$, $-.14$, and $-.13$ respectively). Two variables concerned the woman's partner. Women were more likely to have trouble-free leaves if their partners had taken fewer or no days of parental leave and if their partners earned higher incomes ($r = .12$ and $-.12$ respectively).

Multivariate analysis showed that three of the six variables significantly correlated with women's experience of problems were the strongest independent predictors—months of breastfeeding, attitudes toward gender-based parenting abilities, and attention to the mass media debate (beta coefficients were $-.12$, $-.16$ and $-.14$ respectively). These results suggest that adherence to traditional gender roles helps to lead to a more problem-free leave for women.

Summary

While parental leave was perceived positively by most of the men and women who took it, women still reported higher levels of satisfaction and fewer problems than men did. A potential conflict seems evident: Will women *let* men take parental leave when they like it so much? The unexpected finding that women who held nontraditional gender role attitudes were even more likely than traditionally minded women to want to take parental leave again becomes interesting in this regard. If women we might otherwise expect to be supportive of their partners' sharing parental leave look forward so much to parental leave, it may indeed be difficult for men to get opportunities to take (and enjoy) parental leave. The amount of time women spent in breastfeeding was also positively associated with women's viewing their leaves positively and experiencing less problems. Women's unique ability to breastfeed may constitute an advantage over men that will be difficult to overcome in the first year of child care.

On the other hand, the study suggests that expanding economic opportunities for women outside the home may make parental leave less appealing to women and thereby more available to men. Women had more problem-free leaves when the jobs they held before childbirth were traditional women's jobs. Interviews also suggested that even professional women found being at home gave them more opportunities for independence and autonomy than their regular jobs. When women have more opportunities for self-fulfillment outside the home, we might expect them to make way for their partners to take and enjoy parental leave.

IMPLICATIONS

Although a relatively small proportion of Swedish fathers elect to take parental leave, when they do so they tend to manage well, experience few problems, and wish to repeat the experience in the future. An examination of the factors associated with a more positive leavetaking experience suggests that policymakers who want to make parental leave attractive and enjoyable to men might want to pay attention to three things.

First, the current income ceiling and tendency to reimburse only 90% of salary under that ceiling appears to lead not only to family budget problems but also to a less enjoyable leave. The most common problem noted for fathers in this study concerned worries about income loss. Policymakers might consider raising the ceiling and also providing 100% reimbursement of salary.

Second, policymakers might take note that what happens at the workplace when fathers take leave has an important impact on their over-all experience with taking leave. When leaves cause disruption at the workplace, men are likely to say their leaves have not gone well. It may be important to work with employers and unions to reduce disruptions at the workplace.

Third, findings show that women enjoy parental leave even more than men. Efforts to dissuade women from monopolizing parental leave may be in order. This may need to take the form of an incentive system that grants couples more leave when fathers take a higher portion of it. But perhaps the best way to ensure that women do not find parental leave exceedingly attractive is to encourage their permanent attachment to the labor force and provide them opportunities for meaningful employment. When women are oriented to the public sphere as well as the domestic, they are anxious to return to work and make way for their partners to take over. The group of nine women who had shared parental leave fairly equitably with their partners were all very interested in their jobs. Quotes from their interviews reveal how relieved they were to return to work and leave their babies in such good hands. A nurse confided:

> The best part about Peter being home on parental leave was that I could go back to work, which is very important to me. . . . I enjoy it very much.

A preschool teacher said:

> When it came time for me to go back to work, I felt a little emotional about it. But after a week, things were *great*. It was really fun to go back to work.

This chapter has focused on the experiences fathers and mothers reported having while on parental leave. The next chapter considers whether or not parental leave has a longer lasting effect on parents' involvement in the labor force and in child care.

6

CONSEQUENCES OF FATHERS TAKING PARENTAL LEAVE FOR GENDER EQUALITY IN THE FAMILY

Feminist theorists (e.g., Chafetz, 1988; Eisenstein, 1984) maintain that gender stratification in industrial societies is reinforced by the division of labor in the family, particularly by women's having primary responsibility for child care. When women are more responsible for taking care of children, then by necessity their interest and involvement in the labor force are limited. Men thus have easier access to the more rewarding work roles. This in turn gives men considerable power, both within the family and outside. Within the family, men can use this power to avoid domestic tasks that they deem uninteresting. Outside the family, the power can be used to control institutions (e.g., education, mass media, religion) which generate ideological justifications for the traditional division of labor by gender. Socialized to accept such ideology, most women accept primary responsibility for child care and come to see motherhood as their chief vocation in life. They typically do not view this as inequitable.

As mention in Chapter 2, Swedish policymakers promote a new model for relations between men and women. Policies like parental leave for men were designed to undermine existing gender stratification. The government's rationale for extending maternity leave provisions to men back in 1974 read as follows:

> The change from maternity leave to parental leave is an important sign that the father and mother share the responsibility for the care of the child. . . . It is an important step in a policy which aims through different measures in different areas to further increased equality not only formally but in reality, between men and women in the home, work life, and society. (quoted in Sellström and Swedin, 1987, my translation)

The purpose of this chapter is to report whether fathers' participation in parental leave eliminates gender differences in parenting and employment after the leave is over. The prospects of eliminating gender stratification in Sweden are also discussed.

EFFECTS OF SHARED LEAVE ON LATER CHILD CARE SHARING

Fathers who participate in parental leave would seem likely to gain an early start on becoming knowledgeable about child care as well as an enhanced interest in the child's well-being. In a study of Scottish families with preschool-aged children, Backett (1982) found that mothers' early monopolization of child care led to couples' defining mothers as more knowledgeable about children's needs and personalities, and this in turn led to mothers' assuming over-all responsibility for child care. When mothers seemed to respond to their needs more effectively, children themselves relied more heavily on mothers to meet their needs, shutting out fathers even more.

The interviews with nine Gothenburg couples who shared parental leave fairly equitably suggested that fathers' early involvement in child care set the stage for continued sharing of this responsibility. A year after he had finished taking leave, a gym teacher commented on his relationship with his daughter:

> I know her, what she wants, I am not a foreigner to her. She knows us both equally well. I'm not just a babysitter filling in for Mom.

His wife agreed:

> She is secure with both of us. . . . I am not raising a child alone. He can do things as well, knows her as well.

A nurse said about her husband:

> It is taken for granted that he can take care of her now, that he knows how. Some fathers don't know where the clothes are, what the child should eat. He does because he was home.

A father who was an auto assembly line worker said:

> The child has learned that not only Mommy can take care of all his practical needs.... If one isn't obligated to do child care, it is very easy to fall into the traditional pattern.

Other researchers have addressed the issue of whether fathers' early involvement in child care affects their later involvement. One study of fifty Swedish fathers compared those who had taken parental leave for at least one month to fathers who had taken little or no leave, in terms of their involvement with their babies at eight months and at sixteen months. Parents were observed in their homes for about two hours on each occasion. Fathers who had taken parental leave were no more likely than fathers who had taken little or no leave to vocalize, show affection, tend, touch, play, or hold their children (Lamb Frodi, Frodi, and Hwang, 1982a; Lamb, Frodi, Hwang, Frodi, and Steinberg, 1982b; Lamb, Frodi, Hwang, and Frodi, 1983). Sex differences in parenting were also found for both groups. The researchers suggested that gender differences in parenting behaviors might be either biologically based or heavily influenced by traditional socialization practices. However, one month home on parental leave might not be long enough for fathers to become as interested in parenting as mothers who might be home ten times as long.

In a more recent study the same researchers used a larger, more random sample of couples (N = 130) and a longer timeframe. Using self-reports to assess the situation when the children were twenty-eight months of age, the investigators came to a different conclusion. They found that fathers who took parental leave were more likely to participate in child care than fathers with little early involvement (Lamb et al., 1988).

Another study was done by the Swedish Census Bureau in 1975–1976 (Statens Offentliga Utredningar, 1978). Researchers found that fathers' participation in parental leave was associated with greater participation of the father in child care after the leave was over. While one-third of all fathers were said to assume equal responsibility for parenting, the rate was considerably higher (half) among fathers who had taken parental leave.

Some qualitative studies have examined fathers' relationships with children following an opportunity for the father to be at home for various reasons; these include job-sharing (Grønseth, 1978), unemployment (Russell, 1982), and shift-work (Hood and Golden, 1979). These studies have all found that fathers report themselves to feel closer to their children after such experiences made it possible for them to participate in child care.

Measures

The Gothenburg survey allowed an investigation of the impact of fathers' taking parental leave on the subsequent division of labor for child care. Parents were asked several questions about their child care arrangements at the time of the survey, which occurred when their children were toddlers between fifteen and twenty-seven months of age. Instead of relying upon such self assessments, some social scientists advocate time budgets as a more precise way to measure fathers' participation in child care. However, such budgets are difficult to obtain, since they require respondents to monitor very carefully how they spend their time. Pleck's (1983) review of the literature suggests that ordinary self-reports yield similar results to those found when time budgets are employed.

To see if fathers' participation in parental leave would result in greater sharing of child care, several dimensions of the latter were measured. For all the indicators used, mothers' and fathers' responses were averaged to arrive at a composite picture of the division of labor in the family. Other researchers have noted that such averaging has the advantage of balancing out any distorted views fathers and mothers might have of their division of labor (e.g., Warner, 1986).

A general item in the Gothenburg survey asked, "Who has main responsibility for the care and upbringing of your child born in 1984–the woman mostly, the woman a little more, the woman and man equally, the man a little more, or the man mostly?" Using the same categories, respondents were asked which parent performed various specific tasks for the child: bought food, prepared food, fed, changed diapers, bathed, bought clothes, washed clothes, arranged babysitting, played, read books, taught something new, comforted when sick or tired, took to the doctor for checkups, and got up at night when the child cried. These fourteen items were analyzed separately and also summed to form a scale with high reliability (Cronbach's *alpha* = .81).

A set of measures was developed to examine the amount of time fathers spent doing things for or with their children. Individuals were asked, "How many hours approximately do you take care of or are you together with your child during a day when you work? . . . when you don't work?" They were also asked to estimate their mates' child care time. Averaging the man's and woman's responses to these questions, the following measures were developed:

—the actual amount of time fathers spent with children on a workday;
—the *relative* amount of time fathers spent with children on a workday, compared to their partners (the percentage of time fathers spent with child on a workday of all the time the couple spent);
—the actual amount of time fathers spent doing things for or with children on a nonworkday;
—the *relative* amount of time fathers spent with children on a nonworkday, compared to their partners (the percentage of time fathers spent with children on a nonworkday of all the time the couple spent);
—the actual amount of time fathers spent on child care in a week (calculated by multiplying the workday time by five, the nonworkday time by two, and summing the two figures);
—the *relative* amount of time fathers spent with children in a week's time.

There were three measures of fathers' parenting abilities. One involved asking parents, "Which of you can best comfort the child—the mother, both equally, or the father?" The second involved averaging fathers' responses to "How good do you think you are at caring for a child now?" with their partners' answers to "How good do you think that your partner is at caring for a child—very good, rather good, or not so good?" The third measure involved using responses to the above question to compare what the fathers' and mothers' abilities were in regard to child care. When they thought the father was at least as capable as the mother, the case was put in one category; if the father was judged to have less ability, the case was put in another.

High correlations were found between mothers' and fathers' replies, yet significant differences were detected (with two-tailed t-tests on means) for half of the twenty items presented above. In general, mothers tended to report less child care sharing than fathers reported. For example, mothers reported spending more time on child care than fathers reported for their partners. For six of the fourteen specific child care tasks examined, mothers claimed there was a less egalitarian division of labor than fathers claimed. On the other hand, mothers rated fathers higher in parenting abilities than fathers rated themselves.

As in earlier chapters, fathers' participation in parental leave was measured in two ways. For the first indicator, fathers who had taken leave and those who had not were compared in terms of their means on various aspects of subsequent child care, with t-tests applied to the group differences. To assess the impact of the other variable (percentage of couple's total leave taken by father) on later child care, correlation coefficients (Pearson's r) were calculated.

Findings

Fathers who had taken parental leave were found to be significantly more likely to share in the general responsibility for child care. (See Table 6.1.) Over two-fifths (41%) were reported to share equally in the responsibility for child care, compared to only one-fifth of fathers who had not taken leave.

Fathers who had taken parental leave were also significantly more likely to perform most child care tasks, including food buying, feeding, cooking, diapering, bathing, laundry, reading, comforting, going to the doctor, and getting up at night. There were no differences between the two groups in terms of how much playing or teaching they did, which were the tasks performed most often by fathers in general. There were also no group differences in arranging for babysitting or in shopping for clothes. The latter chore was the task least likely to be performed by the fathers in general.

Fathers who took leave were reported to have higher levels of ability. Two-fifths of them were reported to be 'very good" at doing child care, compared to less than one-fifth (19%) of fathers who had not taken leave. The fathers' child care ability *relative* to the mothers' also improved if the former took parental leave. Two-thirds (66%) of leavesharing fathers were said to be as capable as mothers at child care, or even more so, compared to only half (51%) of fathers who did not take leave. However, the amount of time fathers spent with children was not affected by taking parental leave. Fathers on the average spent a great deal of time with their toddlers: about 3 hours on workdays and 10½ hours a day on nonworkdays. On the latter days, fathers were reported as sharing equally the time spent with children—an average of 45% of all the time spent by the couple. On workdays, the division of time was less equitable, with fathers' share dropping to 37%.

There were also no effects of leavetaking on fathers' ability to comfort the child. Half of all couples felt that both parents were equally good at this, with 39% saying the mother was better and 12% the father.

The effects of fathers' taking a higher proportion of leave were also investigated. Table 6.1 shows the results (far right column). Fathers who took a greater proportion of parental leave were found to participate more equally in child care by most measures used in the study. They were significantly more likely to share in the general responsibility for child care, perform more specific child care tasks, spend time with children more equally when compared to mothers over a week's time, and to rate highly in terms of parenting ability, in both absolute terms and relative to mothers.

Taking 20% or more of all the leave days taken by the couple had the effect of increasing even further men's share of responsibility for child care, participation in specific child care tasks, time spent on child care on a workday, and general parenting ability (see table 6.2). Indeed, fathers who took less than 20% of the couple's leave resembled more the groups of fathers who

Table 6.1
Effects of Fathers' Participation in Parental Leave on Child Care Sharing

	Means			*Correlations*
	Father did not take leave (N=234)		Father did take leave (N=85)	Father's %age of couple's (total) leave (N=85)
Father's responsibility for child care (1=mother most...3=shared... 5=father most)	2.05	*	2.31	.36*
Father's participation in specific child care tasks (1=mother most...3=shared... 5=father most)				
Buying food	1.83	*	2.16	.20*
Feeding	1.93	*	2.31	.26*
Cooking	1.57	*	1.98	.34*
Diapering	2.05	*	2.42	.41*
Bathing	2.32	*	2.75	.23*
Shopping for clothes	1.33		1.40	-.05
Washing clothes	1.48	*	1.81	.22*
Arranging sitting	2.16		2.30	.29*
Playing	2.74		2.80	.08
Reading	2.53	*	2.75	.05
Teaching	2.61		2.69	.25*
Comforting	2.26	*	2.49	.25*
Taking to doctor	1.53	*	1.96	.31*
Getting up at night	2.38	*	2.64	.15
Total	2.05	*	2.32	.39*

did not take leave than they did those who took 20% or more of the leave, when it came to sharing various aspects of child care (see table 6.3).

Radin (1988) has suggested that fathers' continued involvement in child care, once a pattern of sharing has been established, depends heavily on the labor force participation of mothers. In support of this, Lamb and others (1988) found that Swedish fathers who had taken parental leave tended to do more child care later if their partners remained in the labor force. It was possible to investigate in the present study whether

Table 6.1 (Cont.)

	Means			*Correlations*
	Father did not take leave (N=234)		Father did take leave (N=85)	Father's %age of couple's (total) leave (N=85)
Father's child care time				
Hours per workday**	3.17		3.09	.15
As percent of couple's time**	.39		.39	.22
Hours per non-workday**	10.48		10.58	-.08
As percent of couple's time**	.45		.46	.13
Hours per week**	36.80		36.89	.05
As percent of couple's time**	.43		.43	.25*
Father's parenting abilities				
Father comforting ability (1=mom comforts best/ 2=both/3=dad best)	1.78		1.71	.19*
Father's child care ability (1=not good...3=very good)	1.38	*	1.56	.24*
Father's relative ability (1=not as capable as mother/ 2=at least as capable)	1.51	*	1.66	.22*

* Between the two columns of means, this signifies that the means were significantly different at the .05 level, in a one-tailed t-test. For correlations, this signifies that the linear relationship was a significant, at the .05 level in a one-tailed test.

** Calculations concerning this variable were performed only for individuals who were in the labor force at the time of the survey. For nonleavesharing couples, N=181; for leavesharing couples, N=61.

mothers' continued labor force participation improved the chances that leavetaking fathers would do child care later. Over three-fourths (78%) of the mothers had returned to work at the time of the survey, but only one-fourth of these (27%) worked full-time (thirty-five hours or more per week). Mothers' employment status turned out not to be related to leavetaking fathers' tendency to participate in child care, however. Fathers who took leave were just as likely to share child care if their partners were still employed as in situations when they were not. If the mother worked full-time, however, fathers who took leave tended to be more involved in child care than in families where the mother worked part-time. They were more likely to

Table 6.2
Fathers' Participation in Child Care by Proportion of Parental Leave Taken

	Means		
	Father took 19% or less of all leave days taken by couple (N=54)		Father took 20% or more of all leave days taken by couple (N=31)
Father's responsibility for child care	2.22	*	2.53
Father's participation in specific child care tasks			
Buying food	1.99	*	2.46
Feeding	2.20	*	2.48
Cooking	1.79	*	2.31
Diapering	2.25	*	2.73
Bathing	2.64		2.95
Shopping for clothes	1.38		1.44
Washing clothes	1.69		2.03
Arranging sitting	2.11	*	2.63
Playing	2.77		2.85
Reading	2.72		2.80
Teaching	2.61	*	2.84
Comforting	2.39	*	2.66
Taking to doctor	1.72	*	2.37
Getting up at night	2.55		2.79
Total	2.28	*	2.52
Father's child care time			
Hours per workday**	2.93	*	3.45
As percent of couple's time**	.37	*	.43
Hours per non-workday**	10.69		10.42
As percent of couple's time**	.46		.48
Hours per week**	36.68		37.58
As percent of couple's time**	.42	*	.46
Father's parenting abilities			
Father's comforting ability	1.66		1.80
Father's child care ability	2.49	*	2.65
Father's relative ability	1.59	*	1.77

* Between the two columns of means, this signifies that the means were significantly different at the .05 level, according to one-tailed t-tests.

** Calculations concerning this variable were performed only for individuals who were in the labor force at the time of the survey. For the subsample of couples where the father took 1–19% of the leave, N=52; for the subsample of couples where the father took 20% or more of the leave, N=30.

Table 6.3
Equal Sharing of Child Care

	Percent of fathers sharing child care equally with mothers				
	Fathers took 20% or more of leave (N=31)		Fathers took 1–19% of leave (N=54)		Fathers did not take leave (N=234)
General responsibility for child care	65	*	28		20
Specific child care tasks					
Buying food	52	*	28		20
Feeding	52	*	32	*	20
Cooking	39	*	19		11
Diapering	71	*	33	*	20
Bathing	66	*	46	*	33
Shopping for clothes	10		8		6
Washing clothes	29		17		8
Arranging sitting	52	*	28		32
Playing	74	*	54		57
Reading	74	*	56		45
Teaching	74	*	44		53
Comforting	64	*	44		31
Taking to doctor	42	*	17		7
Getting up at night	64	*	37		37
Child care time (father accounted for at least 40% of couple's time)**	90	*	67		74
Parenting abilities					
Comforting ability (father at least as good as mother)	71		57		51
Child care ability (father at least as good as mother)	77	*	59		51

* Indicates that the percentages on either side are significantly different, according to one-tailed z-tests.

** Calculated only for those couples where both partners were employed. N=19 for couples where the father took 20% or more of the leave; N=46 for couples where the father took 1–19% of the leave.

Table 6.4
Effects of Mothers' Employment Status on Fathers' Participation in Child Care
(Leavetaking fathers only, N=85)

	Means				
	Mother employed		Mother employed		
	Yes (N=62)	No (N=23)	Full-time (N=21)		Part-time (N=41)
Father's responsibility for child care	2.31	2.28	2.62	*	2.16
Father's (total) participation in specific child care tasks	2.31	2.34	2.49	*	2.22
Father's child care time					
Hours per workday**	3.10	3.36	3.43		2.93
As percent of couple's time**	.36	***	.37		.35
Hours per non-workday**	10.85	9.85	11.45		10.55
As percent of couple's time**	.47	.47	.49	*	.46
Hours per week**	37.19	36.50	40.05		35.73
As percent of couple's time**	.41	***	.43		.42
Father's parenting abilities					
Father's comforting ability	1.72	1.70	1.83	*	1.66
Father's child care ability	2.56	2.52	2.62		2.52
Father's relative ability	1.65	1.70	1.71		1.61

* Between the two columns of means, this signifies that the means were significantly different at the .05 level, according to one-tailed t-tests.

** Calculations concerning this variable were performed where fathers were in the labor force at the time of the survey. The subsample sizes were 61, 21, 20, and 41 for columns left to right.

*** Since the mother was not in the workforce and did not have a measure for amount of time spent in child care on a workday, this percentage was not calculated.

share in the responsibility for child care, perform more specific child care tasks, spend more time with children on a nonworkday, and rate as equally good as the mother at comforting the child (see table 6.4).

Fathers' own work hours had little effect on their tendency to continue sharing child care after taking parental leave. Since so few fathers worked part-time, it was not feasible to compare full-time working fathers to part-time working fathers in terms of child care sharing. Because of variations in overtime hours, however, it was possible to consider the impact of the number of hours fathers were employed at the time of the survey. Fathers who worked a greater number of hours were no less likely to participate in child care than men who worked fewer hours. This is in accord with other studies that have found fathers' work hours to be unrelated to their participation in child care (Ellingsaeter, 1990; Hochschild, 1989; Kalleberg and Rosenfeld, 1990). Parenting ability, however, was rated lower in those cases where the father worked more hours ($r = -.19$).

Discussion

Results from this study of 319 sets of new parents in Gothenburg revealed that fathers' participation in parental leave did lead to fathers' greater involvement in child care after the leave was over. Fathers took more responsibility for child care, did various specific child care tasks more often, and were rated as better parents if they had taken leave. While fathers did not spend more time with children if they had taken leave, they seem to do more parenting in the time they have.

Since most fathers took relatively short leaves, this finding supports Pleck's (1985) belief that even short leaves can facilitate fathers' later involvement in child care. However, gains were magnified when fathers had taken a high proportion of the leave (at least 20%) and when mothers remained employed on a full-time basis after leaves were over.

On the other hand, the results show that Swedish couples are far from the goal of equal parenthood. Even among families where the father took leave, the majority of mothers (60%) were still more responsible for child care. Why might this be the case? Fathers may be reluctant to take on this difficult as well as low-status role, given their heavy involvement in the labor market. It is also possible that mothers' own wishes to care for children led them to block men's opportunities to do the same.

Several specific child care tasks remained the province of mothers, particularly tasks involving noninteractive domestic work, such as laundry, shopping, and cooking. The most progress toward the goal of equal parenthood was found for emotional caregiving tasks (e.g., playing, teaching, reading) and for the amount of time fathers spent with children. Fathers who took leave were also rated as highly capable parents. It is possible that becoming comfortable with emotional caregiving, spending a lot of time around children, and feeling confident about parenting abilities are first steps in a long road toward men's equal involvement in all dimensions of parenting.

EFFECTS OF SHARED PARENTAL LEAVE ON MOTHERS' EMPLOYMENT

Sociologist Lois Hoffman (1983) predicts that greater male involvement in child care would have several positive consequences for women's employment. She believes that women's occupational commitment would increase as sharing of child care would allow them to appreciate the benefits of employment. She believes women would be freer to choose occupations without being constrained by child care obligations. Finally, she expects employers would be more likely to hire women in a wider range of higher-status occupations if women were not uniquely saddled with child care responsibilities.

When Swedish policymakers introduced parental leave for both sexes, they assumed that this would improve women's economic opportunities. On one hand, mothers who took leave would be assured of the same jobs when they returned to work; their seniority rights were protected as well. On the other hand, by making leave available to fathers and encouraging them to take advantage of the program, policymakers hoped that this would free women from feeling as if they were the primary caretakers of children and encourage them to look to other sources of self-fulfillment, such as a career. The present study investigated whether the expectations that Swedish policymakers had for parental leave are borne out. Is fathers' participation in parental leave associated with mothers' greater commitment to work, participation in the labor force, and labor market status?

Measures

Work commitment was measured in two ways. First, respondents were asked, "What would you rather do now—work full-time, work part-time, or be at home?" The second question was "How important is employment to you just now in comparison with your other interests and activities—the main interest in your life, a main interest but not the only interest, one of several important interests, a less important interest, or not at all important compared with your other interests?"

To measure labor force participation, individuals were asked if they were presently employed for pay and how many days per week they worked on the average. They were also asked how many hours per week they worked before the baby was born and at the time of the survey. A measure of change was obtained by subtracting the number of hours worked before the baby was born from present work hours.

Labor market status was examined in terms of promotion opportunities, job satisfaction, and income. Respondents were asked, "Compared to the time before the child's birth, have your chances for advancement on the job improved, worsened, or stayed the same?" Job satisfaction was assessed by this item: "In general, how good is the job which you now have, compared to the job which you really would rather have—precisely like the job you really want to have, very much like it, something like it, not especially like it, or not at all like it?" Since respondents were also asked this question about the job they had before the baby was born, a change score could be obtained by subtracting the job satisfaction level before childbirth from the level reported after parental leave was over. Income was measured by having respondents mark which of six categories their monthly pay fell into after taxes, both before and after the baby was born. The pre-childbirth level was subtracted from the post-childbirth one to get a measure of change.

Findings

As shown in table 6.5, fathers' taking parental leave had no significant influence on mothers' work commitment. Women whose partners had taken parental leave and those whose mates had not were quite similar in terms of their preference for part-time work, with only 8% of leavesharing mothers and 5% of other

Table 6.5
Effects of Fathers' Participation in Parental Leave on Mothers' Employment

	Means			*Correlations*
	Father did not take leave (N=234)		Father did take leave (N=85)	Father's percentage of couple's (total) leave (N=85)
Work commitment				
Preference for full-time employment (1=prefer staying home... 3=prefer working full-time)	1.76		1.86	-.07
Importance of work (1=least...5=most important)	2.83		2.96	-.11
Labor force participation				
Current employment (0=no/1=yes)	.79		.73	.15
Days employed per week**	4.08		4.16	.21
Hours employed per week**	29.56		30.10	.19
Change in hours employed/week**	-5.54		-3.47	.17
Labor market status				
Improvement in promotion opportunities** (1=worse...3=better)	1.85		1.94	-.09
Job satisfaction** (1=low...5=high)	3.59	*	3.94	-.07
Change in job satisfaction**	.15		.02	.02
Present income level** (1=5000 or less... 5=9000 + crowns/month)	1.66	*	1.98	.20
Change in income**	.02		.08	.29*

* Between the two columns of means, this signifies that the means were significantly different at the .05 level, according to one-tailed t-tests. For the correlation coefficients, this signifies that the linear relationship was significant, at the .05 level in a one-tailed test.

** Calculations concerning this variable were performed only for individuals who were in the labor force at the time of the survey. For the sample of couples which did not share parental leave, N=186; for the sample of couples who did, N=62.

mothers wanting to work full-time. (22% of leavesharing mothers would rather stay home, compared to 29% of other mothers.) Both groups of women tended to report work as being of medium importance (scoring at three on a scale of one to five).

Fathers' taking leave also had no significant effect on mothers' labor force participation. Regardless of whether the man took leave or not, about three-quarters of these women had returned to the labor force at the time of the survey, generally working a four-day week for about thirty hours.

Some effects of fathers' leavetaking were found on mothers' labor market status. Women whose partners had taken leave reported higher job satisfaction and more income. It seemed possible that these relationships might be spurious ones. A woman who was more satisfied with her job before childbirth, as well as a woman who earned more income, might be more prone to encourage her partner to take parental leave. Afterwards she would be likely to enjoy a high level of job satisfaction and income because she already did so before the child was born. To test whether or not parental leave by itself led to an improvement in mothers' postbirth job satisfaction and income, partial correlation coefficients were calculated between leavetaking and women's job satisfaction or income. When controlling for prebirth levels of the latter, a significant relationship remained for satisfaction ($r = .12$), indicating that a man's participation in parental leave had positive effects on the woman's job satisfaction independent of the satisfaction level she enjoyed before the baby was born. No significant correlation remained, however, between fathers' leavetaking and mothers' postbirth income when mothers' prebirth income was taken into account. This suggests that women's income level should probably be considered more of a determinant of fathers' leavetaking, rather than a consequence.

The proportion of parental leave days the father took had significant effects on only one aspect of mothers' employment. When the father took a greater percentage of a couple's total parental leave, the mother tended to experience less of a drop in postbirth income from the prebirth level.

More effects of fathers' leavetaking on mothers' employment were discovered for the subsample of couples where the father

Table 6.6
Mothers' Employment
by Proportion of Parental Leave Taken by Fathers

	Means		
	Father took 1–19% of all leave days taken by couple (N=54)		Father took 20% or more of all leave days taken by couple (N=31)
Work commitment			
Preference for full-time employment	1.91		1.77
Importance of work	2.98		2.94
Labor force participation			
Current employment	.78		.65
Days employed per week**	4.02		4.45
Hours employed per week**	28.57	*	33.30
Change in hours employed/week**	-4.88		-.50
Labor market status			
Improvement in promotion opportunities**	1.93		1.95
Job satisfaction**	3.95		3.90
Change in job satisfaction**	-.00		.05
Present income level**	1.81	*	2.35
Change in income**	-.10	*	.45

* Between the two columns of means, this signifies that the means were significantly different at the .05 level, according to one-tailed t-tests.

** Calculations concerning this variable were performed only for individuals who were in the labor force at the time of the survey. For the subsample of couples where the father took 1-19% of the leave, N=42; for the subsample of couples where the father took 20% or more of the leave, N=20.

took at least 20% or more of the leave. If their partners had taken a more equitable proportion of leave, mothers tended to work more hours per week, earn higher incomes, and experience less of a drop in income from pre-childbirth levels (see table 6.6). The relationship between fathers' taking a high portion of the leave and mothers' income could have been spurious, due to mothers' having high income potentials to start with in these situations. To check this possibility, a partial correlation coefficient was calculated while controlling for prebirth income. The relationship between fathers' percentage of leave taken and mothers' postbirth income remained significant, however (r = .29).

The subsample of women in professional, technical, and managerial occupations living with men with similar occupations was examined separately to seek if men's leavetaking had a special impact on this subgroup. (This group consisted of 96 women, or 30% of the total sample.) No special advantages of having a partner who took parental leave, however, was found for this group of women living in dual-career households.

Comparisons between Mothers and Fathers

Will fathers' participation in parental leave result in the elimination of gender differences in employment patterns? Table 6.7 lists the results of t-tests which gauged whether mothers and fathers had significantly different employment profiles. Couples where the father had taken leave were compared with cases where the father had not done so.

Fathers' participation in parental leave did not reduce all the inequities between women's and men's employment situations. Regardless of whether or not the father had taken leave, significant sex differences existed in terms of preference for part-time work, labor force participation, and income. For example, over two-thirds (67%) of all mothers preferred part-time work, compared to less than one-fourth (24%) of all fathers. Only 3% of all fathers were not employed, compared to 22% of mothers. Mothers worked an average of 30 hours a week over four days a week when they were employed, compared to fathers working an average of 43 hours over five days. Only 2% of working mothers placed in the top two income levels, compared to 31% of fathers. (This wide income discrepancy could not be blamed entirely on differences in work hours; only 12% of full-time working women earned in the top two income categories, compared to 33% of full-time working men.) After parental leave, greater drops in hours and income were observed for mothers in comparison to fathers, regardless of whether or not the father had taken leave.

There were, nevertheless, some important respects in which women's employment situations in comparison to men's was

Table 6.7
Sex Differences in Employment by Fathers' Leavetaking Status

	Means						
	Fathers took leave (N=85)				Fathers did not take leave (N=234)		
	Mothers		Fathers		Mothers		Fathers
Work commitment							
Preference for full-time employment	1.86	*	2.61	***	1.76	*	2.79
Importance of work	2.96		3.16	***	2.83	*	3.34
Labor force participation							
Current employment	.73	*	.96		.79	*	.97
Days employed per week**	4.15	*	4.98		4.07	*	5.10
Hours employed per week**	29.93	*	42.31		29.59	*	43.71
Change in hours employed/week**	-3.52		-1.03		-5.46	*	-.04
Labor market status							
Improvement in promotion opportunities**	1.93		2.05		1.86	*	2.10
Job satisfaction**	3.93		3.72		3.58		3.75
Change in job satisfaction**	.02		.20		.14	*	-.12
Present income level**	1.98	*	3.64	***	1.67	*	3.82
Change in income**	.07	*	.52		.02	*	.66

* Between the two columns of means for mothers and fathers, this signifies that the means were significantly different at the .05 level, according to one-tailed tests.

** Calculations concerning this variable were performed only for individuals who were in the labor force at the time of the survey. For the subsample of leavesharing couples, N=61; for the subsample of nonsharing couples, N=181.

*** This indicates that the absolute difference between male and female partners' answers is significantly less (at the .05 level) among leavesharing couples than among those couples where the father did not take leave.

more equal when men took parental leave. In significant contrast to couples where the father did not take leave, leavesharing couples tended to rate work similarly in terms of personal importance, and their subsequent experiences with promotion opportunities and job satisfaction were similar. Furthermore, in some cases where a substantial sex difference in employment remained, the gap between the partners turned out to be significantly smaller among leavesharing couples. Such instances of substantially smaller (though still significant) discrepancies between partners were found with regard to the preference of full-time work and post-childbirth income.

When the subsample of couples where the father had taken leave was examined separately, it was found that women's work hours and income were greater when the father had taken 20% or more of the couple's leave than when he had taken 19% or less (see table 6.8). When leave was shared more equitably, mothers were also likely to experience less of a change in work hours and in income, compared to the time before childbirth. Although gender differences in labor force participation and income remained for the small group of couples where the father took 20% or more of the couple's leave, most of these differences turned out to be significantly smaller than those in the subgroup of couples where the father had taken 19% or less of the leave.

Discussion

In summary, then, study findings indicate that fathers' participation in parental leave did bring about improvements in mothers' employment situation in several respects, particularly when fathers took 20% or more of the couple's leave. However, mothers' employment attitudes and profiles remained quite different from fathers', particularly with regard to part-time work and income. A major goal of Swedish parental leave policy—to enhance women's employment participation and opportunities—is not being fully realized.

Why doesn't men's sharing parental leave improve women's employment situation more dramatically? One possible reason is that women generally take most of the parental leave offered, even in families where the father takes leave. Taking leave themselves might reinforce women's unequal position in the labor market. Sharing a small part of the leave is not enough to remedy this.

There is some evidence for this position from three separate sources. Social scientists in Sweden maintain that employment

Table 6.8
Sex Differences in Employment by Fathers' Leavetaking Category

	Means						
	Fathers took 1–19% of leave (N=54)				Fathers took 20% or more of leave (N=31)		
	Mothers		Fathers		Mothers		Fathers
Work commitment							
Preference for full-time employment	1.91	*	2.76		1.77	*	2.35
Importance of work	2.98	*	3.31		2.94		2.90
Labor force participation							
Current employment	.78	*	.96		.65	*	.97
Days employed per week**	4.02	*	5.00		4.42		4.95
Hours employed per week**	28.57	*	42.81	***	32.95	*	41.21
Change in hours employed/week**	-4.88	*	-.57		-.53		-2.05
Labor market status							
Improvement in promotion opportunities**	1.93		2.10		1.95		1.95
Job satisfaction**	3.95		3.83		3.89		3.47
Change in job satisfaction**	.00		.10		.05		.42
Present income level**	1.81	*	3.79	***	2.37	*	3.32
Change in income**	-.10	*	.64	***	.42	*	.26

* Between the two columns of means for mothers and fathers, this signifies that the means were significantly different at the .05 level, according to one-tailed tests.

** Calculations concerning this variable were performed only for individuals who were in the labor force at the time of the survey. For the subsample of couples where the father took 1–19% of the leave, N=42; for the subsample of couples where the father took 20% or more of the leave, N=19.

*** This indicates that the absolute difference between male and female partners' answers is significantly less (at the .05 level) among couples where the father took 20% or more of the leave, than among couples where the father took 1–19% of the leave.

discrimination against women has in fact worsened as a result of work-family policies. According to Dowd (1989:327):

> Employers apparently quite readily admit that they avoid hiring women of childbearing age, or give preference to hiring men over women, because women are more likely to take extended parental leaves and request part-time work.

A study of working class women in hospital, office, factory, and department store workplaces (Calleman et al., 1984; Widerberg, 1985) found that women who took leave returned to a "pool" where they were assigned to temporary jobs on a day-to-day basis, substituting for workers who were out or assisting in a rush period. Such work tended to be reported as yielding little intrinsic satisfaction and few chances for advancement. Some women found that the jobs they had before their leaves had been "rationalized" out of existence because of technological innovations, which forced them into other jobs. Calleman and Widerberg maintain that sharing parental leave with men does not alleviate women's employment difficulties; indeed, it may exacerbate them. Men usually take leave for only a short amount of time (under two months), and this often falls in the middle of the year parents are allowed to take. A woman worker is thus likely to return to work once when the baby is five or six months old so her partner can stay home for a month or two, and then leave work once again to return home and finish out the rest of the parental leave. This tendency makes it difficult for supervisors and employers to make plans, and results in women's relegation to different, less satisfying tasks than they had before parental leave.

The Gothenburg survey also reveals that parental leave tends to reduce women's level of job satisfaction and promotion chances. About one-fourth (23%) of mothers who returned to work reported a drop in their levels of job satisfaction, compared to 16% of fathers who had taken leave. This drop appeared to be related to women's being assigned different tasks upon their return to work. Forty-three percent of women were assigned different tasks after taking parental leave, compared to 32% of men who took parental leave. A more recent study found that between one-fourth and one-third of mothers had been assigned different tasks upon their return to work; another one-third who got their old jobs back said the pace was quicker and their pay had been lowered (Török, 1990). When women in the Gothenburg survey were assigned different tasks, they tended to report lower job satisfaction ($r = -.18$). Leavesharing fathers' assignment to new tasks was not associated with a decline in their job satisfaction; indeed, it was associated with an increase in satisfaction. It appears that leavesharing men, like other men, were being promoted to more interesting work. Almost the same percentage of men who did *not* take parental leave reported having different job tasks at the time of the survey compared to the time before their babies were born, and for these men as well, new tasks were significantly associated with greater job satisfaction. A sizeable proportion of women who had taken parental leave—one-fifth—said their promotion opportunities had worsened since taking leave, compared to only 8% of men who had taken parental leave. Sharing parental leave with their partners did not change this.

While Calleman and Widerberg suggest that parental leave can be especially detrimental to the employment situation of working class women, the Gothenburg survey actually found little difference between women in professional or managerial jobs and women in other types of jobs in terms of drops in job satisfaction or assignment to new tasks. One difference by job type that was found was this: a significantly higher proportion of professional or managerial women reported worsened promotion opportunities after taking parental leave than did women in other occupations.

A second reason parental leave may not markedly enhance women's employment opportunities might be the nature of government policy regarding daycare. Elisabet Näsman, who has recently researched the effects of parental leave on women's employment, has said:

> Mothers actively try to adjust their working conditions to parenthood and the child. If the work hours won't work any longer, they try to change them and if they cannot get a daycare place they can perhaps be obligated to quit. (quoted in Török, 1990:16; my translation).

This last remark about daycare needs further elaboration. Calleman and Widerberg noted that women who took parental leave found it difficult to return the job, if they worked in a setting with shift work (common in factories and hospitals), since shifts start earlier than day care centers open their doors. The general supply of daycare has also changed in recent years. In an effort to involve as many children as possible in government-subsidized child care, the Swedish government has elected to provide less space for the youngest children, whose care costs substantially more than that of older children. At first, this involved children under the age of one, and now involves children under eighteen months or even two years old in some areas. This means it is increasingly difficult for families to find child care for children after parental leave is over, necessitating changes in parental employment (usually the mother's). Because this problem is increasing, we might expect women's employment to be even more adversely affected by childbearing and parental leave in the future.

Calleman and Widerberg's work suggests a last possible explanation for the lack of important effects of fathers' sharing parental leave on mothers' employment. The women they interviewed prioritized parenthood over employment. As long as this happens, we might expect that increased early involvement of fathers in child care, as on parental leave, will not suffice for equalizing women's and men's employment situations.

Interviews with some of the women who had shared parental leave in the Gothenburg study also revealed this desire women had to participate in both worlds while still prioritizing motherhood. A nurse said, "I wouldn't have minded staying home longer on parental leave, but I was glad to get back to work, too." When asked about difficulties in combining employment and parenthood, she said, "It is hard to do both. Parenting is the most important thing, but sometimes work must come first." An office manager said, "Children are more important, but work is still very important."

The women in the Gothenburg survey also reported work to be of only medium importance in their lives. This feeling did not change just because their partners took parental leave. When women deemed work to be of lesser importance, they tended to work fewer hours, earn less money, and hold less satisfying jobs ($r = .16, .33$, and $.35$ respectively). Women's devaluation of employment might very well be due to traditional socialization practices and to inadequate daycare. Women with fewer opportunities for rewarding jobs might also reasonably choose to prioritize motherhood over employment as a way to enjoy some self-esteem.

EFFECTS OF SHARED PARENTAL LEAVE ON FATHERS' EMPLOYMENT

Traditionally, success for men has been defined in terms of occupational and economic achievement (Pleck, 1983). The childbearing years tend to come right at the time when men have typically been busy building their careers and gaining important experience in their jobs. Previous studies have found that fathers perceive an active caregiving role on their part as a drain on their energy for work and consequently a potential hindrance to their success on the job (Radin, 1982). Men who are househusbands because of unemployment report problems with adjustment to the primary caregiving role because they see occupational success as the major criterion for happiness (Russell, 1982). A study of fifty dual-career American couples found that nearly all fathers reported that their lifestyle of combining a career and major parenting responsibilities was a very demanding one, and only one of fifty felt he was coping well (Jump and Haas, 1987).

While men find it difficult to combine parenting and employment, there is little evidence that they reduce their labor force commitment and involvement during the years their children are small in order to reduce potential conflicts. Previous studies in Sweden have found that parenthood did not affect men's involvement in the labor force as it did women's. In one study, only 5% of men were found to shorten their work hours after childbirth, in contrast to 62% of women (Statens Offentliga Utredningar, 1982b.) A more recent study found 8% of men, compared to 60% of women, worked fewer hours after childbirth for child care purposes (Török, 1990). In another study, even fathers who had taken parental leave rarely changed their work patterns, for only 10% lessened or changed their hours (Statens Offentliga Utredningar, 1978). Swedish fathers who have taken parental leave have also been reported as saying that the experience did not affect their careers in any negative way (Statens Offentliga Utredningar, 1982a). In the Gothenburg study, a physician who was interviewed as part of the group of nine couples that shared parental leave fairly equitably discussed differences in her and her husband's response to parental leave:

> I found myself completely changed after the first child. Before, I was very interested in equality, but now I feel that there is a special tie between mother and child. I find myself giving priority to family over work. There might not be any noticeable objective effects of staying home on my career, but I am subjectively different. I am not as psychologically involved; I now prefer a specialty more combinable with family life. I will have to act like I am more interested than I am so I won't get into any trouble. For my husband, career and family are equally important. He doesn't think you have to choose, or that there are inherent conflicts.

In this study, it was possible to test if fathers became less absorbed in occupational pursuits when they took parental leave. The same measures for work commitment, labor force participation, and labor market status used for mothers above were also used for fathers.

Findings

Three employment variables were significantly associated with fathers' participation in parental leave. First, men who had taken leave were more likely to prefer part-time over full-time work. Second, they worked significantly fewer days at the time of the survey although they still worked the same number of hours as the men who had not taken leave. Third, fathers who had taken leave reported job satisfaction levels that were significantly lower than those reported before the child was born. As noted earlier, lower job satisfaction for fathers was not a consequence of their being assigned different tasks when they returned to work (see table 6.9).

Perhaps leavetaking fathers became more dissatisfied with their jobs because they began to prefer jobs more compatible with active parenting. Interviews with fathers who took a considerable amount of leave suggest this might be the case. Men seemed to express more satisfaction with their jobs when their work was perceived as being easy to combine with their new interest in child care. A high-level government administrator who reported continued enjoyment of his "stimulating and engaging" job after his leave was over noted: "I have a flexible job;

Table 6.9
Effects of Fathers' Participation in Parental Leave on Fathers' Employment

	Means			*Correlations*
	Father did not take leave (N=234)		Father did take leave (N=85)	Father's percentage of couple's (total) leave (N=85)
Work commitment				
Preference for full-time employment	2.79	*	2.61	-.40*
Importance of work	3.34		3.16	-.24*
Labor force participation				
Current employment	.97		.96	.00
Days employed per week**	5.11	*	4.96	-.10
Hours employed per week**	43.66		42.26	-.17
Change in hours employed/week**	.10		-.80	-.29*
Labor market status				
Improvement in promotion opportunities**	2.13		2.05	-.23*
Job satisfaction**	3.72		3.73	-.18
Change in job satisfaction**	-.09	*	.11	.06
Present income level**	3.85		3.52	-.31*
Change in income**	.61		.52	-.12

* Between the two columns of means, this signifies that the means were significantly different at the .05 level, according to one-tailed t-tests. For the correlation coefficients, this signifies that the linear relationship was significant, at the .05 level in a one-tailed test.

** Calculations concerning this variable were performed only for individuals who were in the labor force at the time of the survey. For fathers who did not take parental leave, N=228; for fathers who did take leave, N=82.

I can leave work to go home when I want." Similarly, a teacher who reported continued satisfaction with his job said:

> I have a very short actual work week and flexible hours, even though it is officially full-time. Some days I can go in around noon and be home at 4. I often have Fridays off. Instead, I can bring work home.

An architect reported on his job after taking parental leave:

> The work I went back to was fun. There was enough work to keep me busy but not so much to keep me from going home when I wanted.

Fathers who took a greater portion of the leave showed more of a preference for part-time work, felt work was less important in life, had fewer work hours, had fewer promotion opportunities, and earned less income (even when prebirth income was controlled). When the men who had taken at least 20% of the couple's leave was examined separately, even greater decreases in fathers' work commitment, preference for full-time work, and income-earning were found (see table 6.10). Of the nine couples interviewed who had shared parental leave fairly equitably, it was found that in every case but one, the father had changed his orientation to employment significantly. (In that one case, both the mother and father continued to work full-time as physicians.) In four of the nine couples, the father worked part-time at the time of the survey; in two of these cases their partners also worked part-time. In three of the nine couples, the father took advantage of considerable flexibility in his job as teacher, administrator, or professor to leave work earlier and bring more work home to do. In the remaining case, the father worked a compressed work week of four days so that he could be home for child care on Fridays.

Discussion

In summary, then, fathers' participation in parental leave has important effects on men's employment attitudes and behavior. Results suggest that fathers' early involvement in child care, especially when this involvement approximates mothers', does have the effect of substantially reducing men's absorption in occupational achievement outside the home. As we have seen, however, such reductions are not so dramatic as to result in the elimination of differences between mothers and fathers in employment patterns. The results suggest that equalization of parents' employment opportunities might be just likely to come about through a lowering of men's involvement in the labor market as through the raising of women's.

Table 6.10
Father's Employment
by Proportion of Parental Leave Taken by Fathers

	Means		
	Father took 1–19% of all leave days taken by couple (N=54)		Father took 20% or more of all leave days taken by couple (N=31)
Work commitment			
Preference for full-time employment	2.76	*	2.35
Importance of work	3.31	*	2.90
Labor force participation			
Current employment	.96		.97
Days employed per week**	5.00		4.90
Hours employed per week**	43.38	*	40.30
Change in hours employed/week**	-.27		-1.73
Labor market status			
Improvement in promotion opportunities**	2.10		1.97
Job satisfaction**	3.87		3.50
Change in job satisfaction**	.08		.17
Present income level**	3.77	*	3.10
Change in income**	.58		.43

* Between the two columns of means, this signifies that the means were significantly different at the .05 level, according to one-tailed t-tests.

** Calculations concerning this variable were performed only for individuals who were in the labor force at the time of the survey. For the subsample of couples where the father took 1–19% of the leave, N=52; for the subsample of couples where the father took 20% or more of the leave, N=30.

One promising way to equalize parents' employment might be the establishment of a six-hour work day for all Swedish workers. Since 1978, parents of preschool-aged children have been allowed to reduce their workday to six hours, with a corresponding cut in pay. Since the 1970's, however, feminists in the Social Democratic Party have argued that a six-hour workday for all is the solution to gender stratification in the labor market as well as women's double role in the home. In a circular pattern which is difficult to break, Swedish women work fewer hours in a narrow range of occupations for lower pay in order to be able to combine work and family responsibilities; their primary responsibility for child care and housework in turn becomes justified because they are home more. This process was illustrated in an interview with a couple who had shared parental leave fairly evenly but were nevertheless unequally responsible for child care after the leave was over. When asked how they managed combining parenthood and working, the mother said: "It is hard sometimes.... I have worked part-time—twenty-five hours a week—for the past thirteen years [in order to raise their three children]." When asked who had more responsibility for child care at the present time, the father said, "She does, because she has more time. I work sixty hours a week and travel—they are often asleep when I get home." She said, "I do, because I have more time. I work part-time, I have more time for the practical details." If full-time workers' hours were reduced to thirty hours a week across the board, there might be less rationale for women restricting their employment and for their being primarily responsible for child care.

The general Swedish population supports such a reduction in work hours. In a recent study, 71% of women and 62% of men said they would prefer shorter working hours to higher pay (Ericsson and Jacobsson, 1985). In the late 1980s, two small political parties, the Communists and the Greens (environmentalists), also demanded a six-hour day (Pettersson, 1989). Despite this popular interest and political pressure, the Social Democratic Party, along with the major trade union and employers federations, has regarded this reform as much too utopian. They worry about a decline in workers' purchasing power and lack of growth in the gross national product (Scott, 1982). Among Social Democrats and trade unionists, much more interest has been shown in legislating a sixth week of vacation for all workers (40% now have this through labor contract, while the remaining 60% have a five-week vacation). Employers, as might be expected, oppose both a longer vacation and a shorter work week (Pettersson, 1989).

IMPLICATIONS

Sweden boasts the world's most generous and lengthy parental leave available to working parents. The program was explicitly designed as a tool for undoing the traditional gender-based stratification system in society. In particular, it was intended to increase men's involvement in child care and to equalize women's involvement in the labor force with men's. Results from a study of the Swedish case can give us some ideas how effective parental leave might be as a policy to promote equality between the sexes.

Findings from this study of 319 sets of new parents in Gothenburg revealed that fathers' participation in parental leave did lead them to greater involvement in child care after the leave was over. There is considerable pressure placed on all Swedish fathers to be heavily involved in child care. It is therefore possible that parental leave would not have such positive effects on child care sharing in societies where popular support for equal parenthood is less.

Swedish fathers' taking parental leave tended only to reduce, rather than eliminate, inequality in child care, unless they took a high proportion of leave and mothers continued to work full-time. Neither of these circumstances was common, however. Efforts to increase men's proportion of leave, as well as efforts to equalize men's and women's work hours (perhaps through a thirty-hour work week for all), may prove necessary to bring about equal parenthood. Such efforts are under way in Sweden to a small extent.

Past research on fathering has suggested that men perceive conflicts between breadwinning and childrearing but actually do little to alleviate these conflicts (e.g., by reducing their work involvement). This study suggests that if men are involved with children early enough, they will seek to enhance their involvement in their children's lives by becoming less absorbed in occupational achievement. Participation of fathers in parental leave may thus be important as a way to convince men that they will need to lessen their occupational involvement in order to manage work and family roles. Only when men become actively interested in parenting will there likely be pressure on social institutions to change in major ways so that individuals can combine employment and parenting. Men are more often in positions of power and perceived as an indispensable part of the labor force, so if they push for more family-friendly policies in the workplace, major changes seem inevitable.

Fathers' participation in parental leave also had noteworthy effects on mothers' employment situations, particularly when the proportion of leave fathers took was substantial. Gender differences in preference for part-time work, labor force participation, and income persisted, however. Deeply rooted traditional socialization practices which lead women to prioritize motherhood over employment, as well as institutional discrimination against women (particularly pay policies) and day care priorities, seem responsible for women's lower interest and involvement in the labor force.

For parental leave to be more successful in eliminating gender-based role responsibilities in the family, more fathers must take it for greater periods of time. In addition, efforts that would lead to both males' and females' valuing employment and parenthood equally are required. Swedes are currently involved in significant efforts to bring both of these about, through education and information campaigns organized by political parties and trade unions and publicized in the mass media. However, major changes in the structure of the labor market, particularly the length of the work week and compensation levels for women's jobs, also appear to be necessary. These are likely to be more difficult to realize.

7

IMPLICATIONS FOR THE UNITED STATES

Previous chapters have described the development of the parental leave program in Sweden, fathers' usage of the benefits and their experiences while on leave, and the determinants and consequences of fathers' participation in parental leave. The import of these findings for the Swedish situation have already been addressed. This chapter focuses on potential implications of the findings for the United States. Specifically, it analyzes the likelihood that the United States will develop a policy like the Swedish paid parental leave program in the near future. Then, based on knowledge of the actual operation and success of the Swedish program, the chapter examines possible consequences of an American parental leave policy. The discussion here might also apply to other societies in the process of developing parental leave programs designed to involve fathers in early child care.

It is not only difficult but perhaps even foolhardy to assess one country's family policy based on results from a study of another's. Each society is a unique configuration of social and economic forces, and programs existing in one cannot be readily extrapolated to another. Appreciation of the differences in cultural settings is integrated into the discussion which follows, but caution should still be exercised in assuming that the Swedish findings are readily applicable to the U.S. case.

THE DEVELOPMENT OF PARENTAL LEAVE POLICY IN THE U.S.

Historical Perspectives

Policies to help individuals combine work and family roles, including parental leave, have been very slow to develop in the United States. Unlike Sweden, the U.S. has a long history of denying employment rights to women on the basis of their childbearing capacities. In the late 1800s, many states passed laws which limited women's work hours; long hours were seen as weakening women's childbearing potential. The Supreme Court upheld this sort of "protective legislation" in 1908. By 1912, thirty-four states had such laws (Kamerman, Kahn, and Kingston, 1983). Until World War II it was quite common for American employers to refuse to hire or to retain married women and pregnant workers (Gladstone, Williams, and Belous, 1985). Employed married women were seen "as a menace to the race . . . accountable for the falling birth rate, declining parental responsibility, and decadence in home and family life" (Kamerman, Kahn, and Kingston, 1983).

During World War II, women, including wives and mothers, were actively recruited into the labor force to replace men taken into the armed forces. To encourage women to retain an attachment to the labor force, the U.S. Department of Labor's Women's Bureau recommended six weeks' prenatal and eight weeks' postnatal leaves for women workers bearing children. In practice, however, the unpaid leaves were forced on women whether or not they wanted or needed them. In 1942–1943, the U.S. Children's Bureau issued a report which examined workplace practices in regard to maternity leave. According to this report, employers admitted mandating maternity leave for women, not so much for health reasons, but because "it was 'not nice' for pregnant women to work in factories and that the sight of them had 'a bad effect' on male employees" (Gladstone, Williams, and Belous, 1985:10). Upon their return to the workplace, women seldom got their old jobs back (Frank and Lipner, 1988). During the 1950s and 1960s, some states passed legislation which prohibited women's employment for up to two months after childbirth; in other states pregnant women were fired (Caplan-Cotenoff, 1987).

Women's access to paid maternity leaves with job guarantees remained extremely limited until the 1978 Pregnancy Discrimination Act. This legislation was written by a coalition of feminist unionists, lawyers, and government officials, because they felt employers used women's childbearing capacity as their main justification for employment discrimination against women (Frank and Lipner, 1988). This law amended the 1964 Civil Rights Act to prohibit employment discrimination against pregnant women, and it required employers who provided health insurance and temporary disability plans to allow pregnant women to use these at childbirth (Gladstone, Williams, and Belous, 1985). Before the 1978 act, the majority of states had laws which *prevented* pregnant women from using companies' temporary disability plans for maternity leave, so this was a dramatic change in policy (Frank and Lipner, 1988). Social scientists have estimated that the Pregnancy Discrimination Act led to about 40% of American women workers gaining access to job-protected leaves at childbirth, through their companies' temporary disability plans. The remaining women are forced to leave their jobs and find a new one later. Women are more likely to have access to this type of paid maternity leave in large firms and in banking, finance, and insurance companies. Five states (California, Hawaii, New Jersey, New York, and Rhode Island) now have temporary disability insurance (TDI) plans that apply to all workers in the state, whereby all women workers in these states can receive partial wage replacement when they take a childbirth leave (Kamerman and Kahn, 1987; Piccirillo, 1988).

The reliance on temporary disability plans for access to job-protected maternity leave in the United States means that the leaves available have been designed for mothers' physical recuperation from childbirth, not for infant care (Caplan-Cotenoff, 1987). Some companies have developed their own programs to allow time off for infant care; in other cases, unions have negotiated rights to take parental leave (Bernstein, 1986; Bureau of National Affairs, 1986; Kantrowitz, 1989; Pleck, 1986; Pleck, 1990). A recent government study of full-time employees at establishments employing one hundred or more workers found that 36% of women and 17% of men have access to unpaid child care leaves (defined as separate from disability leaves for women at childbirth). The common maximum allowable duration is between six and twenty-six weeks. Only 2% of women and 1% of men have access to paid parental leave, which is typically limited to one to three days (Meisenheimer, 1989). Opportunities for such leaves seem to be greater in firms with more than five hundred employees and for salaried employees (who would be hard to replace). In small establishments, the leaves are often discretionary on the part of supervisors, and come under the rubric of "personal leave" (Friedman, 1985).

While an increasing number of companies have introduced parental leave benefits, most still have no formal mechanism in place. Businesses continue to rely mostly on informal means of handling the needs of their employees for parental leave—for example, allowing employees to take personal, vacation, or sick leave. Zacur, Greenfield, and Drost (1989) maintain that companies are not interested in developing parental leave because of the costs involved in replacement or in lost productivity from less experienced replacements. These costs are greater for occupations where substitutes are difficult to recruit—in nursing and engineering, for example. Policy analyst Paul Kingston is not surprised that the enthusiasm of employers for parental leave has been less than overwhelming. According to Kingston (1990:439–440):

> [I]t is illusory to expect that market solutions will deliver good and equitable family policy in the foreseeable future. Within the calculus of profitability and managerial desires to retain control, the forces for family responsiveness fall short.

To overcome the hesitancy of the private sector to get involved in parental leave, national legislation was proposed in 1985 which would grant both fathers and mothers time off to care for a newborn or adopted child. National opinion surveys indicate that the vast majority of American voters approve of such legislation (McEntee, 1989; Shapiro et al., 1987). The first such proposal in the House of Representatives was developed by a group of feminist lobbyists, whose ideas formed the basis of a bill presented by Rep. Patricia Schroeder. This bill would have granted workers eighteen weeks of unpaid leave for child care purposes (Radigan, 1988). A Senate version, sponsored by Senator Christopher Dodd, was first proposed in 1986. It limited leaves to those workers in firms with more than fifteen employees. Neither bill made it to a floor vote during 1985–1988. Over time, both bills' coverage has become more limited to increase the chances for passage. In the latest version only twelve weeks of family leave would be granted. (In addition to parental leave benefits, the bill also involves medical leave for the worker or time off to care for a close family member.) The legislation would guarantee continued employment, health insurance, and job seniority if workers choose to stay home to recuperate from childbirth of take care of a baby. Several groups of workers would be denied a right to take leave, including those working in establishments with less than fifty employees, those with less than one year of service, those working less than twenty hours a week, and those in the highest paid key positions. The U.S. Government Accounting Office estimated that only 39% of American employees and 5% of U.S. firms would be covered by this legislation (Gainer, 1989).

Most family legislation in the United States (such as Aid to Families with Dependent Children as well as child abuse legislation) has occurred at the state level, so it is probably not surprising that national parental leave legislation has been difficult to enact. Progress toward parental leave has in fact been more noticeable at the state level. Thirty states have considered some form of unpaid parental leave legislation (Kantrowitz, 1989). At least fourteen others have guidelines which recommend but do not require leave to state employees (Makuen, 1988).

The first statutory provision for parental leave in the U.S. came in 1987, when four states enacted such legislation (Wisensale and Allison, 1989). As of 1989, six states mandate unpaid parental leave for men and women: Maine, Minnesota, Oregon, Rhode Island, Wisconsin, and Vermont. The length of the leaves ranges from six to thirteen weeks (Meisenheimer, 1989). It seems likely that more states will pass parental leave legislation before any federal law is enacted. This would be consonant with the historical tradition of American family law being made at the state level and also with the push to shift power from the federal government to the states, which started during the Reagan years (Nelson, 1988).

The recent interest in unpaid parental leave manifested in proposals for federal and state legislation and among some employers seems to be mainly a response to a growing recognition that American mothers are in the labor force to stay. In 1960 less than one-fifth (19%) of mothers with preschool-aged children were in the labor force; in 1988 over half (53%) were (Shehan and Scanzoni, 1988; Sorrentino, 1990).

The three concerns that led Sweden to adopt a much lengthier paid parental leave in 1974—worry about a low birth rate, recognition of a need for women's labor power (not just resigned fatalism regarding women's growing labor force participation), and an interest in men's liberation—have up to now been virtually absent in the United States. This appears, however, to be changing. We might therefore expect to find these concerns motivating American policymakers to consider paid parental leave in the future.

Birth Rate

By 1985 the U.S. birth rate had dropped to 1.8 children per woman, which is below the rate needed to replace the population and even lower than Sweden's current level (Norgren, 1988). Over one-fourth (26%) of women ages 30–34 were still childless, a substantial increase from ten years previously when the figure was 16% (Shehan and Scanzoni, 1988). The low birth rate followed a "baby boom" of tremendous proportions which began in the United States after World War II and lasted through the 1950s.

The declining birth rate has been attributed to women's rising educational levels, more reliable birth control technology, and women's greater participation in the labor market. Social science research has consistently shown that employment has a negative impact on childbearing, perhaps because women find it difficult to combine motherhood and employment roles without social supports (Kagan, Klugman, and Zigler, 1983).

The effects of the declining birth rate have been somewhat masked by the current births to the numerous members of the "baby boom" cohort. When the "baby boomers" move out of the childbearing years, a noticeable drop in the number of births is expected. Economists are beginning to issue warnings about the dire economic consequences of a demographic profile which makes a decreasing number of workers economically responsible for an increasing number of retired persons. It seems likely, as the message catches on, that there might be greater interest in policies to help working women combine childbearing and employment.

Need for Women's Labor Power

As discussed previously, American business and government have not been supportive of wives' and mothers' being in the labor market. Not surprisingly, there has up to now been little acknowledgement of the crucial economic role women play. For example, in 1986, a government official in the Reagan administration praised mothers of small children who were not employed: "... unlike Sweden ... [these] mothers have managed to avoid becoming just so many cogs in the wheels of commerce" (Shehan and Scanzoni, 1988:44). Policymakers have been slow to notice that most mothers have already entered the labor force out of economic necessity. There is no longer such a thing as a "family wage"—an income earned traditionally by the husband which would financially support a family. By 1985 it took two incomes to maintain the same standard of living that was possible on one income in the 1950s (Schroeder, 1988). In 1989 families with one male breadwinner earned an average of almost $26,000 a year, while families where both the wife and husband were employed earned almost $44,000 (U.S. Department of Labor, 1989).

Policymakers have also tended to ignore the reliance of the economy itself on women workers. Women fill positions in the service sector and information industries not filled by men, and serve as low paid workers in textile and small appliance industries. In 1960 women made up less than one-third (31%) of the members of the American labor force; by the year 2000, economists estimate, they will comprise 47% (Kamerman and Kahn, 1987; Wall Street Journal, 1988).

Recognition of the importance of women as workers may be on the horizon. Economists are warning employers and government officials that because of the declining birth rate, fewer men will be available for the work force, and the activation of women who are not yet in the labor force with become increasingly important. By the year 2000, two-thirds of the new entrants into the labor force are expected to be women (Wall Street Journal, 1988). Eighty percent of women workers will be in their childbearing years (ages twenty-one to forty). At least 75% of these women will get pregnant sometime during their employment, and at least one-half will return to their jobs within the first year after childbirth (Friedman, 1987; *Wall Street Journal,* 1988). Companies will find themselves in intensifying competition to recruit women into the labor force; one recruitment tool might be policies, like parental leave, which are appealing to individuals who wish to combine employment and parenthood.

Retention is also an issue. At Aetna Life and Casualty Insurance Company, the philosophy is that it is cheaper "to manage absences than replace" workers (Zacur, Greenfield, and Drost, 1989:8). It can be good for business to adjust to present employees' needs rather than pay the extra recruitment and training costs generated by high employee turnover in a tight labor market (Zacur, Greenfield, and Drost, 1989).

The declining rate of productivity in the United States and growing foreign competition for business may also prompt employers to make changes in employee benefit packages. They will need to motivate all employees to produce at high levels, through the development of policies which improve morale, lower absenteeism, and are responsive to a new cohort where both men and women value a strong family life (Kamerman and Kahn, 1987; Friedman, 1987). Elimination of workplace discrimination in terms of hiring, promoting, and paying women promises to be insufficient to recruit and retain women workers. Affirmative action policies which help women obtain jobs in nontraditional fields which might better suit their talents and interests (as well as simultaneously meeting national needs for scientific and technical workers) appear to be necessary. "Family-enhancing employment policies" (Schroeder, 1988:327) are also called for, including programs such as subsidized child care and elder care, flextime, and paid parental leave (Ratner, 1980).

Gustafsson (1979) outlines three types of possible attitudes toward women's employment: attitudes that show support for "patriarchy," "conditional equality," and "full equality." In the

United States, attitudes toward women's employment seem to be moving slowly but inexorably away from the patriarchal approach, where women are discouraged from being employed. There is increasing support for conditional equality, whereby women can work as long as it does not interfere with their family responsibilities. An ideology of "full equality," which regards both sexes as having equal rights and responsibilities for breadwinning and parenthood (as advocated in Sweden), is still mostly absent in the United States.

Concern for Men's Liberation

Of all those concerns which precipitated parental leave in Sweden, probably least developed in the U.S. is a concern for men's liberation and acceptance of the "full equality" model. There is an increased interest in changing men's roles, at least in women's magazines and on talk shows (LaRossa, 1988). There are men's liberation organizations (e.g., the National Organization for Changing Men) and a growing list of popular books on men's roles (including the "new father"). Opinion polls show that the public is more favorably disposed to the concept of gender equality than ever before (Fleming, 1988).

Much of the interest in changing men's roles in America centers around issues of fatherhood. According to Morgan (1990), these issues have been put on the agenda because of three factors. One of these involves changes in employment patterns and the economy. The increase in mothers' rates of labor force participation and the rise in male unemployment rates have led to the realization that males can no longer view their parenting role merely in terms of breadwinning. Some men are also growing increasingly dissatisfied with the demands of their occupational role and have turned to the father role for self-fulfillment. The second factor responsible for a reconsideration of men's role as fathers is the high divorce rate. Men often report that they want more contact with their children after divorce than they wanted before. Yet their opportunities for contact are limited by traditional practices that typically grant child custody to women and serve to perpetuate men's marginal role in raising children. Lastly, feminism has led to a more critical examination of men's role in families. As women come to protest the undue burdens of their double role as workers and mothers, men are pressured to participate more in domestic and child care activities.

Reexamination of men's roles in families in the U.S. has not progressed to the point where men are as strongly encouraged to participate in early child care as they are in Sweden. Nevertheless, there is a tendency to move in the same direction. American men are becoming more interested in their children and more involved with them. While the precipitating conditions for parental leave noted for Sweden may now be emerging in the United States, unique features of American political and economic institutions as well as basic cultural values still promise to make it very difficult for a policy like Sweden's parental leave program to be adopted in the near future.

Political Obstacles

Sociologist Alvin Schorr (1979) has outlined three major American political traditions that could explain why the United States will have difficulty developing a parental leave program such as Sweden's. The first such tradition is individualism. In a study of thirty-nine countries, Americans scored higher than all others in terms of this value (Hofstede, 1984). Individualism denotes a lack of concern for the common good; the concept that children are society's resource to be supported by all is absent (Brazelton, 1989; Bronfenbrenner, 1986). This tradition makes unpalatable to many Americans the idea that society will pay for parental leave through employers' payroll taxes or government revenues. Americans resent being taxed to pay for services they as individuals may not receive. Public opinion surveys indicate that only 38% of Americans support the concept of paid parental leave (Shapiro et al., 1987). People may also be unwilling to accept the possibility of an increased workload when a colleague is off work to care for children. In Sweden, temporary workers are hard to find; the most common approach to coping with an employee on parental leave is for co-workers to take up the slack. The emphasis on individualism takes another form when mandated parental leave is considered. Employers point out that a relatively small percentage of employees would want or use parental leave. By requiring parental leave be made available to all, this is said to reduce workers' freedom to choose other benefits (such as dental care). In this vein, objections are raised to having Congress define and regulate the individual needs of employees (Motley, 1989).

The second political tradition mentioned by Schorr that may operate against the development of parental leave in the United States is suspicion of government, particularly in "private, sentimental, or sexual" matters (Schorr, 1979:465). This applies, first and foremost, to the family. This value seems to descend from the influence that European liberals, notably Locke, had on the development of culture and legal traditions in the United States. Early in American history, families were regarded as sacrosanct, in need of protection from government interference (Adams and Winston, 1980). This tradition has retarded the development of national social welfare policies, child abuse legislation, support for battered women's shelters, and a national child care policy (Adams and Winston, 1980). Not surprisingly, a program like parental leave is seen by some as a meddlesome program preventing individual families from solving their own needs for infant care. Even the most ardent proponent of American family policy, Walter Mondale—who chaired a Senate committee on children and families, sponsored bills on day care and family services, and ran on a profamily platform against Reagan in 1984—said:

> Above all, we are proceeding with caution. Families involve the most personal and intimate relationships between human beings, and government must be sensitive to that fact. We can't afford any national crusades to 'save the family'. We don't need or want any new bureaucracies intruding on the privacy of family life. (Adams and Winston, 1980:204)

Third, the nature of our political process works against the development of parental leave policy. That process, Schorr maintains, "does not lend itself to broad agreement on principles to which subsequent policies are subordinated" (1979:465).

Swedes agree on principles such as children's welfare and equality between the sexes; Americans do not. Such agreement is possible in a society that is fairly homogeneous in terms of religion and ethnicity (although one out of eight Swedes is foreign-born); it is more difficult in a society like the U.S., which has a population twenty-six times larger with more dramatic social divisions.

The American political system also encourages disconnected reforms. Historically, the United States has not had a family policy, such as exists in approximately one hundred Western European and developing nations (Dowd, 1989). A variety of programs have been developed in the U.S., usually at the state level, with widely variable coverage and levels of benefits. These programs have not been instituted with any particular ideology or set of goals in mind, except perhaps the maintenance of the traditional nuclear family with its gender-based division of labor (Scanzoni, 1983). Moreover, the programs which exist tend not to treat the underlying cause of problems, but rather to alleviate some of their symptoms (Adams and Winston, 1980; Dumon and Aldous, 1979; Grubb and Lazerson, 1984; Spakes, 1983). The Swedish legislative style, in contrast, is not only social problem-oriented, but more "organized" in pursuit of specific goals (Qvarfort, McCrae, and Kolunda, 1988).

There are additional political obstacles to the development of paid parental leave legislation in the U.S. In comparison to Sweden, American feminists have been a less important political force. A "winner-take-all" electoral system and personality-focused candidate (vs. party) elections have limited women's opportunities for political office in the United States. After the 1988 election, they still made up only 5% of the members of the U.S. Congress, compared to 33% in Sweden.

Feminists in the United States have relied upon autonomous organizations to press for political change, perhaps because of their limited access to formal positions of power. These organizations have worked for legislation that would help all women, rather than legislation that would help only some (e.g., working mothers) (Adams and Winston, 1980). They have pushed for enforcement of the provisions for employment rights extended to women in the Civil Rights Act, and worked to have the 1964 act extended to deal with education and to apply to pregnant women. (The Pregnancy Discrimination Act was not a departure from the practice of supporting legislation aimed at all workers, since women's childbearing capacity was seen as a grounds for discrimination against all women.) They have fought for women's reproductive rights and for a constitutional amendment guaranteeing women legal equality with men. Reproductive and employment rights are necessary prerequisites for women's opportunities for independence and equality with men. Swedish feminists did not need to press so much for these concerns, since they were already agreed upon by the Social Democratic Party as early as the 1930s (even if not fully acted upon until the 1960s and 1970s).

In contrast to Swedish feminists, American feminists seem to be more comfortable promoting the "conditional equality" model for women over the model of "full equality" advocated in Sweden. Most American feminists argue that women should have the "choice" whether or not to be employed, which implies that women are not as obligated as men to earn family income. While American feminists seem interested in domestic arrangements that would make men more responsible for domestic work and housework, more attention seems to be paid to the need for changes in social institutions—for example, government subsidy for organized child care. This may be due to interest in improving employment opportunities for single mothers, who cannot count on the generous welfare benefits which exist in Sweden (Sandqvist, 1989).

For these reasons, American feminists and their organizations have not become driving forces behind work-family legislation in the U.S., such as parental leave. This is not to say that American women's organizations oppose such legislation. Indeed, the National Organization for Women, the Women's Equality Action League, the League of Women Voters, the Women's Legal Defense Fund, 9 to 5, and the National Federation of Business and Professional Women have all been supporters of the national legislation for unpaid parental leave. But these groups are in league with a far greater number of organizations, including labor unions (e.g., the AFL-CIO, AFT, United Mine Workers), social scientists (e.g., the Bush Center in Child Development and Social Policy), childbearing experts (e.g., Dr. T. Berry Brazelton, 1988), the Children's Defense Fund, the National Association of Junior Leagues, religious groups (e.g., the U.S. Catholic Conference), the American Civil Liberties Union, and some liberal-minded employers who conduct business across interstate lines and would like to see national legislation on this issue (e.g., International Paper Company, Warner Communications, Hewlett) (Bernstein, 1986; Congressional Digest, 1988; Kantrowitz, 1988; Kovach, 1987; Sciabarrasi and Johnson, 1988; *U.S. News and World Report*, 1986).

A final political obstacle to paid parental leave in the U.S. has to do with funding priorities. Revenues for social programs are more difficult to come by in the U.S. than in Sweden because of a strong American emphasis on a pugnacious and highly technological (and therefore expensive) military establishment. While Sweden has not been involved in a war for two hundred years, the U.S. has fought five major ones in this century alone. The U.S. spends proportionately twice the amount for defense than Sweden does. In 1988 American military expenditures constituted 5.8% of the gross national product (GNP), while in Sweden defense made up 3.0%. This amount averaged $1245 per person in the U.S., compared to $600 per person in Sweden (Sandqvist, 1989; Swedish Institute, 1988; World Almanac, 1989).

Economic Hindrances

American individualism takes another form not discussed above: the extremely high regard in which small business is held in the United States. Almost one-third of the American workforce is employed in companies with fewer than twenty-five workers. Small businesses have generated 70% of new jobs since 1980 (Motley, 1989). The majority of Americans aspire to own their own business someday, and this, combined with the image of America as the land of opportunity, gives small businesses and their lobbying organizations (e.g., state and national chambers of commerce, the National Federation of Independent Businesses) considerable political influence in American society (Butler and Wasserman, 1988). Owners of small businesses, including even female entrepreneurs, tend to be adamantly opposed to even unpaid parental leave (Doherty, 1990). The U.S. Chamber of Commerce combined forces with 150 companies in 1987 to form an organization called the Concerned Alliance of Responsible Employers (CARE). This organization lobbied intensely against parental legislation and turned the tide against what looked like certain passage (*Business Week*, 1987).

Market competitiveness is seen as being jeopardized by the costs associated with replacing an employee absent on parental leave. The U.S. Chamber of Commerce first maintained that it would cost U.S. companies $16 billion annually to underwrite replacement and training costs for workers on unpaid parental leave (Kovach, 1987). The U.S. Government Accounting Office disagreed with this estimate, pointing out that the Chamber's assumption that all employees would take the leave was an unfounded one, since most could not afford to take it even if they should need it. The GAO also maintained that companies usually postpone or reassign a worker's duties in the event of a temporary absence rather than train a new employee. Small companies may also cope by training people to do multiple jobs, so they can take over during any particular employee's absence (Doherty, 1990). Most of the cost of unpaid parental leave would therefore be the continuation of health insurance benefits, which would be mandated by the new law. The GAO estimated that legislation granting ten weeks of parental leave would cost employers $90 million annually (McEntee, 1989). The Institute for Women's Policy Studies has pointed out that the *lack* of national parental leave leads to much greater economic costs, $715 million in lost income taxes and in costs of public assistance to workers who are forced to leave their jobs (Spalter-Roth and Hartmann, 1988).

The U.S. Chamber of Commerce has also argued that parental leave would result in a loss of productivity. However, an academic study funded by a national association of women office workers, 9 to 5, found that the economic growth rate is up 21% in those states which have passed parental leave in comparison to other states judged to be good climates for business growth (9 to 5, 1988). Moreover, numerous capitalist countries, where productivity is no less a concern than in the U.S., now offer paid or unpaid leave. For example, Canada allows mothers and fathers to share six months of unpaid leave, France grants workers of both sexes in firms with over one hundred employees two years of unpaid leave, West Germany allows fathers or mothers eighteen months of child care leave (at a very modestly paid level) and in Italy either parent can take up to six months of partially paid parental leave (Mathews, 1989).

Another economic obstacle to paid parental leave in the U.S. derives from Americans' suspicion of government. The provision of parental leave will call for federal involvement in employer–employee relationships, if the Swedish model is followed, and there is considerable reluctance in the U.S. to have such federal involvement (Malo and Murray, 1986). The National Association of Manufacturers (which represents many larger businesses), as well as the U.S. Chamber of Commerce, is strongly opposed to the government's mandating any additional benefits or labor standards (*U.S. News and World Report*, 1986). Companies are afraid that if the government starts to tell them what employee benefits to provide, the list will just grow longer and longer. In a classic statement, the "Congressional Alert" column of the magazine *Nation's Business* (1988:87) stated:

> If this bill [parental leave] is enacted, Congress will likely impose other, equally detrimental requirements on business. . . . mandated health insurance, mandated catastrophic health-care coverage, minumum-wage increases, mandatory notice of plant closings and layoffs, occupational-disease notification—all loom on the horizon. Each would increase the cost of doing business, intrude on an employer's right to manage, reduce flexibility to adapt to changing global markets and specific work-force concerns.

Acceptance of permeability between government, business, and family spheres, which allows the Swedish government to mandate policies like parental leave and to win general acceptance for them, is thus noticeably absent in the U.S. Because of this, advocates of parental leave will need to "sell" parental leave as being in companies' self-interest (Clay and Feinstein, 1987). Some companies have come to see programs like parental leave as good for business. For example:

> Merck has recognized that lifestyles and family patterns have changed significantly over recent years . . . We believe the cor-

> poration can benefit from helping employees balance the demands of the family and the demands of the workplace." (Bernstein, 1986:50)

In an article titled "June Cleaver Would Need Help Today," *Business Week* stated that "companies simply cannot afford to discourage qualified women from becoming employees" (1987:90). The magazine was opposed to federally mandated parental leave, but an appreciation of the benefits of company-provided parental leave was shown:

> studies are showing that those costs [involving temporary replacements for workers] are more than offset by the expense of recruiting and training permanent replacements. The loss of expertise of workers forced to quit, and the reduced productivity of workers worried they will lose their jobs if they have children, also imposes costs on employers. Experience suggests that companies ought to adopt parental leave policies in their own enlightened self-interest.

A study of American corporations revealed that company managers are aware of growing interest in men's greater involvement in child care and family life because of women's increased participation in the labor market, and that workplace policies need to take into account potential strains men can experience in assuming dual roles (Friedman, 1987).

Some social scientists have maintained that a powerful labor union movement facilitates improvement in women's employment opportunities and in the development of workplace policies designed to help workers combine work and family roles (Kamerman, Kahn, and Kingston, 1983; Ruggie, 1984). Sweden and the United States are radically different when it comes to the status of labor unions. In Sweden, over 80% of workers belong to labor unions (Milner, 1989), and labor unions have been strong, albeit belated, supporters of full equality between men and women. In the U.S., unions represent a minority of workers (19%), and this percentage dwindles with each passing year (down from 35% in 1944) (Laber, 1986). In contrast to Sweden, where women make up almost half of union membership, American women tend not to belong to labor unions (comprising only 28% of membership) (Laber, 1986).

Until recently, American labor unions were not particularly interested in women's issues. This may be changing, however;

studies show that 41% of women would like to be represented by a labor union, in contrast to 27% of men (Gladstone, Williams, and Belous, 1985). Half of all the new members of unions since 1966 have been women (Laber, 1986). This suggests that American unions could increase their strength by recruiting more women into their ranks. One way to do this would be to support policies which help mothers stay employed. This support seems to have begun. The AFL-CIO was one of the main sponsors of a 1987 national conference on work and family issues and is one of the supporters of national parental leave legislation. Some individual unions have fought for pay equity for women, child care and parental leave (Sweeney, 1986), but the over-all impact is still limited. One survey found that unionized employers were more likely than nonunion employees to have access to job-protected leaves of at least eight weeks (York, 1991). However, another study found that unionized workers in the U.S. were no more likely than nonunionized ones to enjoy parental leaves (Gladstone, Williams, and Belous, 1985).

Ideological Reasons

In Sweden, there is a noticeable lack of ideological opposition to the concept of gender equality. No traditionally minded organizations or strong fundamentalist religious sentiments stand in the way. In the U.S., on the other hand, there has developed strong ideological opposition to the concept of gender equality, in the form of the New Right. Emerging in the late 1970s and enjoying its heyday during the Reagan administration, this group is made up of religious fundamentalists and political conservatives who believe strongly that

> A man's responsibility to his family is best met by his success in the labor market, his ability as a wage earner to support his wife and children; a woman's worth is measured by her dedication to her role as wife and mother. (Cohen and Katzenstein, 1988:26–27)

A gender-based division of labor in the family is seen as biologically natural and divinely ordained (Andersen, 1988; Falwell,

1980). Some conservative social scientists have also declared it to be functional, helping to perpetuate capitalism and democracy (Berger and Berger, 1983). These conservatives oppose public policies which would make motherhood more voluntary (e.g., abortion) or would help women combine work and family roles (e.g., daycare, parental leave). They have also condemned programs that would make marriage more optional—e.g., battered women's shelters, spouse abuse legislation, no-fault divorce laws, and equal employment opportunity legislation (Cohen and Katzenstein, 1988; Hess, 1984). The New Right's agenda on family policy was only partially realized during the Reagan years, however. They were successful in defeating the Equal Rights Amendment, eliminating a tax credit for dual-earner couples, reducing access to abortion for poor women and teenagers, and discouraging government subsidies for child care. However, other efforts failed—a constitutional amendment banning abortion was not successful, domestic violence legislation was passed, scores of battered women's shelters were established, and a "Family Protection Act," which would have restricted women's reproductive and educational rights and required schools to teach the traditional family model as the only right one, died in committee (Hess, 1984; Sapiro, 1986).

While conservative organizations have undoubtedly impeded progress so far on legislation such as parental leave, the liberal perspective on family policy, which advocates the development of programs designed to assist working parents, has gradually gained popularity. This was evident at a 1987 government-sponsored conference in Washington, D.C., titled "Work and Family: Seeking a New Balance." High-level government officials, business representatives, and labor union leaders met with social scientists to discuss which reforms were needed in order to help single parents and dual-earner families combine work and family responsibilities. That such reforms were needed was taken for granted. Liberal rhetoric was apparent in the speeches and panel discussions, as was concern for the economic costs of not implementing new policies. Acceptance of the trends leading to diverse family lifestyles, such as the rise in mothers' employment and the high incidence of divorce, was particularly noticeable. No one suggested that the answer to families' problems would lie in the conservative solution of a return to the traditional family.

Another ideological reason for the slow progress of parental leave relates to attitudes toward children in the United States. Societies with family policy care about the quality of life for families with children (Kamerman, 1983). The U.S. does not seem to be a very "child-friendly" society; children's welfare is not a high priority (Edelman, 1987). The sanctity of the family has held sway over society's regard for the well-being of children in ways that Swedes would find unacceptable. Parental leave in Sweden is partially justified because of its potential benefits for children; it is seen as giving children the opportunity to be breastfed and to develop close bonds with both parents early in life, as well as to enjoy economic security. In the U.S., social scientists and childbearing experts have argued that parental leave is necessary for children's sake, but this position has not been acknowledged to any significant degree by policymakers (Brazelton, 1989; Hopper and Zigler, 1988). The original eighteen-week paid parental leave first recommended in 1985 was designed to be that length because experts such as Dr. T. Berry Brazelton said children and parents needed four months alone together to form a secure basis for their relationships. In response to business opposition, the proposal has been reduced to twelve weeks, much less than that advocated by childrearing experts. That political and economic concerns could take such precedence over the needs of children would be unthinkable in Sweden.

Conclusion

It seems unlikely that the United States will adopt a parental leave program similar to Sweden's in the near future. Substantial political, economic, and ideological obstacles stand in the way of the development of family policy in general and of lengthy paid parental leave for both mothers and fathers in particular. Unlike Sweden, the United States has a tradition of individualism and suspicion of government, as well as a decentralized political process, based on disconnected reforms, that has tended to excluded women. These obstacles have up to now prevented the development of national consensus concerning the need for government policies which would promote full equality between men and women.

On the other hand, the same pressures that led Sweden to enact parental leave legislation are mounting today in the United States. Among these are concern about a declining birth rate and what this will mean for the economy, recognition of the important economic role women play in families and in the society at large, and interest in liberating men from the confines of the traditional breadwinner role and in involving them more in the lives of children. Work and family issues are finally appearing on the American political agenda, in the form of proposals for subsidized child care for poor families and short unpaid family leaves (Radigan, 1988). A 1988 *Newsweek* article declared: "Mom, Dad, and the kids seem to be gaining a new prominence on the national agenda, right alongside arms control and the deficit" (Kantrowitz, 1988:60). The 1990s just might see the United States gradually move toward the development of a family policy, now in place in over a hundred other nations, and such a policy could include parental leave.

POSSIBLE CONSEQUENCES OF A U.S. PARENTAL LEAVE POLICY

The United States may someday have a nationally mandated parental leave program. Meanwhile, some states and companies offer modest versions of parental leave to employees. A study of the Swedish parental leave program can show us whether or not men are likely to take parental leave and suggest what types of parental leave programs might be most attractive to American men. The study can also be used to predict what factors might prevent American men from taking leave, and to predict how men will fare while on leave. Finally, the consequences of American men's leavetaking for the division of the labor in the family can also be anticipated.

Usage of Parental Leave

The Swedish experience suggests that it takes a long time to involve men in a parental leave program. After fifteen years of operation, less than one-half of Swedish fathers take leave. Those who take leave use only a small percentage (an average of 19%) of all days taken by parents. If parental leave became national policy in the United States, we would also expect that the majority of fathers would not take advantage of the program, particularly in its earliest years, and that few fathers would elect to take as much leave as mothers.

This prediction is confirmed by what little data we have about American men's current participation in the few parental leave programs that exist. While many men (maybe even a majority) take advantage of vacation or personal leave to be with their newborn children for a short time (Pleck, 1990), less than 10% use any existing leave policies which allow longer leave. (See Chapter 3 for a review of this literature.)

The Swedish government has undertaken extensive information campaigns to encourage fathers to take leave. There is no doubt that policymakers consider parental leave an important way to increase men's overall responsibility for child care. Such a strong national commitment to the concept of equal parenthood does not exist in the United States, or elsewhere in the world for that matter. The "sex-neutral" national legislation which has been proposed seems motivated out of a desire to prevent the legislation from being ruled discriminatory by the courts and hence invalid (Clay and Feinstein, 1987). Without a major emphasis on the importance of fatherhood, a U.S. parental leave program would be unlikely to attract even as many men as the Swedish program does. Evidence for this point comes from other Nordic countries which allow but do not especially encourage fathers to take paid leave—few fathers take advantage of their rights to stay home.

It is clear from the Swedish case that financial reimbursement for leave is crucial to men's willingness to take the leave. Men seldom take the lowly paid portion of leave. Even fewer take advantage of the part-time leave available to preschoolers' parents whereby they can work a six-hour versus an eight-hour day, with a corresponding loss a wages. Pleck's (1990) report on American fathers' use of formal unpaid parental leave and informal paid leave is interesting in this regard. A very small percentage of fathers are reported to use the unpaid leave policies available at some workplaces. On the other hand, a majority of fathers seem to take paid time off at childbirth by taking vacation or sick days or through rearranging their work schedules. We could therefore expect the unpaid leave that would result from the Family and Medical Leave Act would not be used by many fathers. Yet prospects for a paid leave for American fathers seems dim. A majority of parents surveyed said they opposed a law which would give a three-month leave with 75% pay to both mothers and fathers (Shapiro et al., 1987).

The study shows that Swedish fathers take more advantage of shorter leaves than they do longer ones. Nine in ten take the two paid weeks off after childbirth or adoption offered especially to fathers, and over two-fifths take leave to care for sick children. When fathers take parental leave, they tend to take it for a relatively short period, an average of one and one-half months. These findings suggest that shorter leaves might be effective ways of involving men in child care in the United States.

On the other hand, extending parental leave beyond the prescribed time of breastfeeding (six months) had the effect of increasing Swedish fathers' participation in parental leave. Restricting parental leave to immediately after childbirth would presumably reduce the likelihood that American fathers would take it. With this in mind, it might be best to expand the period in which parental leave is available as long as possible, for example through the child's first two years.

One of the disadvantages of the Swedish parental leave program is that it makes women and men competitors for the leave available, since only one parent can stay home at a time. Evidence suggests that mothers tend to monopolize the leave and that support from the mother is a prerequisite of men's taking leave. One feature of the American proposal for parental leave is that parents can choose to stay home on leave without affecting their spouses' access to the leave. Women would therefore not lose any leave if men should take some.

In summary, survey results in Sweden can be used to speculate about what type of parental leave program might be most attractive to American fathers. Unfortunately, the type of program that exists in Sweden and that attracts at least a sizable minority of men—paid, well-advertised, based on a strong commitment to equal parenthood, and available over an extended period of time—is not yet envisioned for the United States. Consequently, we might assume that a parental leave program as it is likely to be developed in the United States—particularly one that is unpaid and based mainly on a desire to secure women's employment rights—will not succeed in attracting many men.

Barriers to Fathers' Use of Leave

The previous section described possible barriers to American fathers taking parental leave which were inherent in program rules and restrictions. This section describes potential obstacles that arise instead out of social psychological and social structural forces. A study of the Swedish parental leave program can be helpful in increasing our understanding of what social forces may operate to keep American men from participating fully in a program designed to involve them in early child care.

One set of barriers to fathers' use of parental leave is social psychological in character. Some of these relate to traditional gender-role attitudes and lack of egalitarian role models in women's families of origin. Swedish women were found to be generally lukewarm toward their partners' taking leave, and when women were less supportive, men took less leave. Such social psychological barriers are difficult to overcome quickly. We might assume that traditional gender role attitudes would prevent American couples from sharing leave as well. While it is difficult to locate comparable data, it appears that Swedes hold more egalitarian viewpoints on gender roles than do Americans (Haas, 1986; Sandqvist, 1987a). If men's leavetaking rights were independent of their partners', we might assume that mothers' social psychological states might be less an obstacle to their leavetaking than they are in Sweden. On the other hand, fathers would undoubtedly still need the strong support of their wives, since taking leave would be a major violation of traditional social norms.

While Swedish fathers' lack of participation in parental leave was related to their partners' lack of willingness to share, it is important to keep in mind how structural factors outside the family can affect women's interest in sharing child care with fathers. The Swedish results suggest that a gender-segregated labor market, in which women work for less pay at less attractive jobs, may lead women to monopolize child care as a source of self-esteem. The U.S. labor market is sex-segregated like Sweden's, and women earn even less, compared to men, than they do in Sweden (Horrigan and Markey, 1990). Therefore, lack of employment opportunities for women may serve as an even more formidable barrier to sharing parental leave in the U.S. than it appears to do in Sweden.

Another structural barrier uncovered in the Swedish study is the opposition men encounter in the workplace. Employers, supervisors, and co-workers did not usually give positive support to the concept of fathers' taking leave, and lack of support affected men's leavetaking. Negative attitudes were most prevalent in the private sector. The workplace would probably be an even thornier barrier in the U.S., as the private sector employs more workers than in Sweden (85% vs. 62%) (Standard and Poor, 1990; Statistiska Centralbyrån, 1986a). One study found that two-thirds of U.S. companies do not believe there is a need for parental leave for fathers (Catalyst, 1986). If workplace support is lacking in Sweden, we can imagine how difficult it will be to convince American employers of the importance of parental leave. Such convincing would most likely need to appeal to the economic interests of U.S. employers, while Swedish employers seem to be swayed at least somewhat by ideological concerns, such as the well-being of children. American employers will need hard evidence that parental leave will improve economic productivity and contribute positively to the welfare of the next generation of workers. As Kingston (1990) points out, such evidence is so far sparse.

Governmental influence in the media is also strong in Sweden. Two of the four television channels are government-owned and allow only public service announcements, including those associated with parental leave. It is thus easier in Sweden for governmental policy on parental leave to permeate the mass media. While independent from government influence, the mass media in the United States might still be a powerful tool to expose men to the concept of parental leave, particularly through popular talk shows and news segments on family life.

In summary, the impediments to men's taking an equal share of parental leave in Sweden seem likely to be even more difficult to overcome in the American setting. Traditional gender role attitudes, sex discrimination in the labor market, workplace opposition, and a lack of social support serve as important obstacles to parents' sharing early child care. All inhibiting factors seem more in evidence in the U.S. than in Sweden.

Experiences with Leave

The Swedish study found that men who elected to take parental leave enjoyed the leave and experienced few problems with it. The structural supports for men's taking leave in Sweden, as well as the popularity of the concept of equal parenthood, probably contribute considerably to this. Fathers who take leave in the United States might be less likely to experience positive outcomes, for several reasons.

The most common problem reported by Swedish men on leave was related to the family budget, and the experience of such problems reduced men's enjoyment of leave. If getting "only" 90% of salary (up to a certain ceiling) could cause family budget problems for Swedish men, we can imagine that American men who typically have access to only unpaid leaves would find leave an even more financially stressful situation. Only providing paid leave would help to alleviate this.

When Swedish men reported that their leavetaking had caused problems at the workplace, they were less likely to say they enjoyed leave. American employers are undoubtedly more opposed to men's taking parental leave than Swedish employers, as witnessed by the successful campaign on the part of an employer coalition to prevent the Family and Medical Leave Act from becoming law during 1985–1990. We might therefore expect that American employers would not take measures to reduce workplace disruptions caused by parental leave. Congressional testimony during the hearings on the Family and Medical Leave Act suggested that they might even not hire employees likely to take leave in the first place (Motley, 1989). Since American men would likely experience more problems in the workplace than Swedish men do, we would anticipate that this would dampen American men's enjoyment of parental leave.

American men also seem more likely to be absorbed by the breadwinner role than Swedish men and thus would be more likely to report problems with missing the job. In contrast to Sweden, a movement to encourage both sexes to have well rounded personalities and to share domestic roles is generally lacking in the U.S. Studies of men who were at home full-time (i.e., househusbands) report that men typically report that the loss of work status is a problem for them (Russell and Radin, 1983).

The Swedish findings show that parental leave is enjoyed by women even more than by men. In the U.S., plans to make leave available to individuals rather than families might keep women from monopolizing all of the leave. On the other hand, if parental leave ever became as generous in the U.S. as it is in Sweden, men may not feel it is necessary for them to stay home at all when their wives have been home during the child's first crucial year. In several respects, American women have less employment opportunities than Swedish women. A lack of meaningful alternatives to full-time housewifery might be a big obstacle to American women's wanting to share early child care with men.

Consequences of Men's Taking Leave

Sweden's parental leave program was explicitly designed as a tool for undoing the traditional gender-based stratification system in society. In particular, it was intended to increase men's involvement in child care and to equalize the sexes' involvement and status in the labor market. State and private parental leave programs and the proposed national policy in the United States have up to now not had such lofty goals. Nevertheless, results from the Swedish study can give us some ideas about how effective parental leave might be as a policy to promote gender equality in the U.S.

Swedish fathers' participation in parental leave did lead to men's greater involvement in child care after the leave was over. Swedish fathers are strongly encouraged to be involved in child care. Parental leave might not have such positive effects on child care sharing in a society like the U.S., which lacks such encouragement.

Women remained more involved in child care, however, unless their partners had taken a high proportion of the leave and both worked full-time. Swedes are interested in promoting men's involvement in parental leave, and to a lesser extent, there is interest in a reduced work week (of thirty hours) for all workers. Both of these are very unlikely developments in the U.S. This suggests that the conditions under which men's participation in parental leave would be likely to lead to equal parenthood in the United States are absent. The greater tendency of American women to work full-time, however, may pressure men already interested in child care through taking parental leave to participate in child care more after the leave is over. Four-fifths of American women in the labor force work full-time, compared to only about two-fifths (43%) of Swedish women (Pettersson, 1989; U.S. Department of Labor, 1990).

Swedish men are encouraged to curtail their involvement in the labor force when they have young children, through policies such as the six-hour day for parents of preschoolers, leave for sick children, and parental leave. Not surprisingly, taking leave had the effect of modestly reducing men's absorption in occupational achievement. Given American businesses' emphasis on short-term productivity and economic profit, it seems highly unlikely that American men will receive similar encouragement to reduce their labor force involvement in the childrearing years, as women traditionally have done.

Sharing parental leave with men tended to improve slightly Swedish women's labor market position and also to reduce gender inequality in work involvement. Nevertheless, parental leave policy did not seem to contribute much to the government's goal of gender equality in the labor market. American women's labor market position would seem even less likely to change because of parental leave. In Sweden, women's traditional absorption in the motherhood role, discriminatory pay policies, and inadequate day care seem to be likely explanations for why parental leave has not lived up to its promise. These barriers are even more intractable in the United States. Full-time working American women, for example, earn 65% of what full-time men earn, which is considerably less than the 73%–91% earned by Swedish women workers (depending on sector of employment—see Chapter 2). Almost half (45%) of Swedish children are in government-subsidized child care facilities (Swedish Institute, 1987). No comparable statistics could be found in the United States, but there is no doubt that the figure is dramatically lower.

The results of the Swedish study suggest that social policy needs to be developed in the U.S. in several areas simultaneously in order to reduce gender inequality in the family and in society. These include:

education - for promoting the equality model and building occupational skills and interests in both sexes

health care - for building support systems for prospective and new parents contemplating leave and while home on leave

labor market - for reducing disruptions and negative effects of parental leave on employment and for improving women's employment and pay potential

unions - for securing rights to parental leave for workers, for easing the transition to and from parental leave

day care - for improving the quality and supply of places, especially for the youngest children, so that working parents can look forward to adequate care after parental leave is over

political institutions - for ensuring an adequate financial base for work-family programs and for developing a national commitment to the needs of children and working parents

While increasing attention is being paid in the United States to the needs of working parents, no concerted or organized policy efforts are underway that would compare to the ones launched in Sweden. If it has taken Sweden so long to come only this far, we can expect that it will take a long time indeed for reformist policies to take hold in the United States.

8

CONCLUSION: EQUAL PARENTHOOD AND SOCIAL POLICY

Until very recently, social policies directed toward families have sought to maintain "the idea that women are the guardians of the home and the primary nurturers of children . . ." (Newland, 1980:33). The role mothers play in the labor market, as well as the role fathers might play in nurturing and caring for their children, has been virtually ignored.

This situation appears to be changing, however. It has become increasingly obvious that mothers in industrial societies are in the labor market to stay. According to Kamerman (1983:28), the central new family policy question is

> What is to be the nature of the relationship between work and family life, when adults, regardless of gender, are increasingly likely to be in the labor force during the same years that they are at the peak of their childbearing and child-rearing responsibilities? What should be the role of government, and of the private sector, in addressing the issue?

She maintains that more support needs to be given for "fathers in their nurturant and caretaking roles and for mothers in their economic roles" if the well-being of children is to be ensured (1983:24).

Sweden is the society that has done the most to acknowledge that both mothers and fathers have economic and caretaking roles. For over twenty years, Swedish policymakers have recognized that equality for women cannot be realized unless the roles and responsibilities of men are transformed. Accordingly, social policy in Sweden is based on the premise that both fathers and mothers should be equally responsible for meeting children's economic, physical, and psychological needs.

The particular social program that most typifies Sweden's commitment to the concept of equal parenthood is parental leave. With job security and nearly full income compensation, Swedish mothers and fathers have the opportunity to share a full year of leave from employment to take care of their babies. (An additional three months of leave is also available with slight income compensation.) Sweden was the first society to extend parental leave to fathers (as early as 1974) and maintains the most generous and flexible leave system available to working parents in the world. Parental leave is designed to provide both parents the opportunity to develop close relationships with offspring and become proficient at child care at the same time as they are allowed and encouraged to maintain a continued attachment to the labor force.

Sweden provides, therefore, a unique opportunity to investigate two important questions, relevant to many other postindustrial societies today. First, can social policy—in particular, parental leave—be used effectively to bring about the goal of equal parenthood? Second, does it seem likely that the goal of equal parenthood will be realized in the near future, in Sweden and elsewhere? To answer these questions, the findings presented in the preceding analysis are reconsidered in this chapter.

EFFECTIVENESS OF SOCIAL POLICY

Historically, Swedes have been optimistic that governmental policies can be used to realize the two most important goals of a social democracy: social welfare and social equality. Over fifty years of welfare programs have resulted in the virtual elimination of poverty and in the reduction of social class differences in opportunities and lifestyles. For twenty-five years, social equality has been defined as including the concept of equal parenthood, whereby both mothers and fathers are responsible for children's well-being through active involvement in nurturing tasks as well as income-earning. Programs like parental leave have been developed to further this goal. Is the parental leave program effective in realizing the goal of equal parenthood?

How Parental Leave Is Effective

The Swedish program of parental leave can be judged to be very effective, according to several important criteria.

1. *The program was explicitly designed to realize a specific goal of social policy.* A program would be less likely to lead to social change if program developers did not have a clear vision of a new society in mind. The specifically stated policy goal Swedes have in mind is equal parenthood, part of a larger vision of *jämställdhet* or equality between the sexes. This vision was first clearly articulated in a 1968 report to the United Nations and was used soon after as justification for the establishment of a government commission to reform existing maternity leave legislation to include men. In contrast, the Family and Medical Leave Act being considered by the U.S. Congress, as well as various parental leave programs throughout the world, are not explicitly tied to the specific social policy goal of equal parenthood. They are intended to provide job security for women whose companies now force them to quit after childbirth. Without any loftier goal being envisioned, making parental leave available to men seems unlikely to lead to such a radical change as fathers' greater participation in early child care.

2. *The Swedish commitment to equal parenthood and the program for parental leave are based on a realistic analysis of contemporary social trends.* Swedes became interested in the goal of equal parenthood as a way to deal with obvious and important economic concerns. The Swedish economy, as well as the financial stability of individual Swedish families, depends heavily on the permanent attachment of mothers to the labor force. Encouraging men to become more active in childrearing does seem a reasonable measure to take in order to give women more freedom to participate in productive activity outside the home. Results from the 1986 Gothenburg survey suggest that early participation of fathers in child care—as in parental leave—does indeed improve women's attachment to, and position in, the labor market.

The Swedish economy also depends upon a continued supply of good workers. A labor shortage could develop if the low birth rate continues. Parental leave is designed to allow parents to combine paid employment with childbearing and childrearing. Because parental leave allows parents to be home full-time during babies' crucial months of development, babies may be ensured a good start in life, eventually leading to their becoming more productive workers. While it is not possible to confirm a direct connection between the development of parental leave policy and the birth rate, the recent upturn in birth rates in Sweden seems likely to be at least partly due to the comprehensiveness of social programs (like parental leave) to aid working parents.

In their attempt to increase women's attachment to the labor force, Swedish policymakers realized that any drastic change in women's roles needs to be simultaneously accompanied by a transformation in men's roles. Accordingly, programs like parental leave were designed to involve men more in child care. In other societies policymakers have sought to encourage women to be more permanently attached to the labor force without suggesting that men should be more involved in the domestic sphere. The result has been severe role overload for women and a declining birth rate.

3. *The policy goal and social program are in general accordance with prevailing social values and social institutions, rather than in severe conflict with them.* Social policy, almost by definition, calls for social change, but if the change called for is an odd departure from the status quo, the prospects for success are limited. Parental leave is designed to realize a larger goal of *jämställdhet* or equality between the sexes, and this goal in turn fits in well with the value of social equality, the cornerstone of social democracy in Sweden since the 1930s. Parental leave is also designed to promote the well-being of Swedish children, itself an important social value.

Sweden is already characterized by an unusual amount of permeability between government and private sector economic activity. While the economy remains basically capitalist in nature, powerful labor unions have negotiated contracts and lobbied for laws that give workers more rights than perhaps anywhere else in the world. Parental leave in many respects fits in well with other programs that restrict the rights of employers and provide for improvements in working conditions, job security, and income compensation in order to realize the goals of a social democracy. In the U.S., by contrast, the prerogatives of private employers are much greater and widely recognized, making a generous and extensive paid parental leave program an unlikely development.

4. *Both the goal of equal parenthood and the parental leave program are widely accepted by the population.* Survey results show that the vast majority of Swedes support the parental leave program and agree with the idea that mothers and fathers should be equally responsible for child care. The emergence of such a consensus is promoted by a unique legislative process (*remiss*) that over several years allows a wide spectrum of individuals and groups to comment on, and help change, legislative proposals; as well as by an unusual amount of propaganda spread toward individuals through the mass media, schools, and trade unions.

5. *The policy serves to build consensus rather then social conflict.* An enduring policy would seem to be one that did not become a political bone of contention or yield benefits disproportionately to one group over another. Parental leave is accepted and promoted by all political parties. This appears to be due to the unusually high representation of women among the activists of all political parties, as well as to party competition for the votes of working parents. Furthermore, there is virtually no political dissension about any component of the welfare state already established in Sweden, and in many respects parental leave is seen as just another program among many that guarantee a high quality of life to Swedes.

Parental leave, as it has been developed, is not designed to benefit one sex more then the other. Both mothers and fathers are entitled to take the leave; in fact, a certain portion of the leave is formally reserved for each parent, who has to officially sign over rights to it if it is to be given to the other partner. The general policy of equal parenthood is presented as one that would benefit women and men to equal degrees. It also places equal value on the activities women and men have traditionally been responsible for—domestic work and productive labor. Men have the opportunity to develop close relationships with children, as well as the parts of their personalities associated with emotion and caring. Women have the opportunity to seek self-fulfillment in occupational activities outside of the home. The family unit is seen as growing stronger, with two incomes for economic stability and two active parents for children's emotional security.

The parental leave program links together what have been two different types of social policy in Sweden: labor market policy and family (or social) policy. It therefore serves an integrative function, perhaps reducing the likelihood of competition between the two areas for government attention and setting an example for the future for other possible social programs that would enhance individuals' opportunities for self-fulfillment in the home and in the labor market.

6. *Other social programs exist to complement the parental leave program, making the realization of the over-all policy goal of equal parenthood more likely.* A program that exists in isolation would seem unlikely to have a significant impact on social behavior. In addition to parental leave, working parents in Sweden are entitled to a generous amount of time off with pay in order to take care of sick children and to visit children's day care and school facilities. Fathers are entitled to two weeks off from work, with pay, immediately after childbirth. Until their child turns seven and starts first grade, parents can elect to reduce their workday to six hours. Heavily subsidized high-quality daycare and after-school programs make it easier for parents to combine employment with child care responsibilities.

Swedes are also interested in preparing individuals for equal parenthood before children are actually born. Accordingly, a national school curriculum mandates that the equal parenthood model be taught and that both boys and girls receive instruction in child care skills. Girls are admonished to prepare themselves for a lifetime in the labor force, and they receive special counseling to encourage them to consider lucrative fields traditionally dominated by men. Voluntary parental education (with paid time off from work) is also offered to prospective parents.

7. *The program attracts a growing number of clients.* Fifteen years ago when the parental leave program first began, less than 3% of fathers took any leave at all. Presently, over 40% of

fathers take some leave, for an average of over one and one-half months. About half of fathers express interest in taking leave in the future.

8. *When fathers take advantage of the parental leave program, couples come closer to realizing the ideal of equal parenthood.* Results of the study showed that in families where the father took parental leave, parents were more likely to share equally in child care after the leave was over. Gender differences in several aspects of employment attitudes and behavior were also reduced or eliminated.

How the Program Is Not Effective

Despite these impressive accomplishments, the Swedish parental leave program is ineffective in many important respects.

1. While the program has been developed generally in accordance with prevailing social values and institutions, *policymakers have not paid sufficient attention to how the structure of the labor market impedes progress toward the goal of equal parenthood.* The labor market still appears to be structured on the premise that women are more responsible for the nurturing of small children, while men are more responsible for providing economically for small children. This is manifested in several ways.

First, employers and supervisors, though obligated to release employees for parental leave, still look unfavorably upon the involvement of men in the program. This decreases men's participation in the program and lessens their enjoyment of leave when they do take it. While generally more favorable toward women's taking parental leave, employers and supervisors tend to assign them less satisfying tasks upon their return from leave, which may reduce their interest in employment.

Second, dating from the 1960s, the jobs women traditionally have filled tend to be available on a part-time basis (most often thirty hours a week), while jobs that have traditionally attracted men are not. When mothers are home more, it is easier for couples to justify the mother's retaining primary responsibility for child care. Lower earning women are also in a weak position to press for change in the domestic division of labor. Feminist proposals to reduce the work week to thirty hours for all workers have met with opposition from male leaders of political parties as well as from employers.

Third, while unions have joined the government and mass media in launching propaganda campaigns to encourage men to take parental leave, they have not done much else to reduce the resulting disruptions at the workplace or to smooth the reentry process for either male or female workers. Nor have they supported proposals for a reduced work week for all workers.

The Swedish labor market remains sex-segregated, which reduces women's job opportunities. Women's access to jobs that might better suit their interests and abilities is therefore limited. Traditionally female jobs pay less than male jobs, although the discrepancy is less in Sweden than elsewhere, due to exceptional efforts made by labor unions to lessen overall wage differentials.

Women remain economically dependent on their male partners. They are not equal parents when it comes to providing for their children financially. It is not all that surprising that the majority of Swedish mothers remain more oriented to motherhood than employment, and that they are not especially interested in having men take half of all parental leave days available.

2. While the goal of equal parenthood is designed to encourage consensus rather than conflict between women and men, *program rules actually force competition between mothers and fathers in regard to fully paid days of leave taken.* While a certain portion of parental leave days is reserved for each parent, the system is set up in such a way that fathers' taking leave reduces the time mothers can stay home. Since the vast majority of mothers want to stay home and enjoy it very much (even those holding androgynous views toward gender roles), this makes it difficult for men to gain access to parental leave.

3. While the program attracts an increasing number of fathers, *only a minority of those eligible take advantage of the program.* More than one-half of Swedish fathers take no leave at all. Of those who do, less than 10% take an equal portion of the leave. Study results suggest several reasons for this.

As mentioned above, the labor market remains structured along traditional lines. Men fear that workplace disruptions would ensue if they took leave. They perceive their employers and supervisors as not being positive toward their taking parental leave.

Program rules also create financial disincentives for some fathers. Those working in the private sector who were entitled to only 90% of their regular pay were found to participate in parental leave less than public sector employees who generally receive 100% compensation. Because of an income ceiling on benefits, higher earning men had more to lose by taking leave, and, not surprisingly, took fewer leave days.

Another reason so few fathers take leave is that they lack *strong* social support for doing so. Positive reinforcement may be necessary for them to make a radical departure from social tradition, but fathers reported mostly neutral attitudes toward the possibility of their taking parental leave, on the part of family members, friends, and co-workers. While generally supportive of the concept of fathers' participation, only a small minority of Swedish parents felt strongly that fathers *should* take parental leave or that the leave should be *equally* shared by mothers and fathers

A crucial person to provide support for a father's decision was the child's mother. Yet mothers in general registered low levels of interest in the concept of equal parenthood, unless they themselves had working mothers as role models or had high-status occupations with considerable income potential. Improving women's economic opportunities may thus be a prerequisite for increasing mothers' interest in sharing parental leave with fathers.

4. *The effects of parental leave in terms of accomplishing the goal of equal parenthood are to date only modest.* In general, mothers remain more responsible for child care after fathers take leave. Significant gender differences in employment patterns, particularly in terms of hours worked and income earned, persist even among couples who shared leave. While early involvement of fathers in child care, as during parental leave, appears to be a useful tool in realizing the goal of equal parenthood, it clearly is not sufficient in itself.

The limited effectiveness of the Swedish parental leave program as a way to realize the goal of equal parenthood confirms an observation made by feminist theorist Janet Chafetz. She states:

> Systems of gender stratification are higher resistant to substantial change toward greater equality. The elements that support such systems are many. . . . Such mechanisms exist at all levels, from the intrapsychic to the highest macro-social levels. (1988:129)

5. Following Risman and Schwartz (1989), *social policy which aims to bring about gender equality should go beyond encouraging men to participate in early child care; it should expect men to do so.* To enable both men and women to escape gender constraints, structural changes in society must occur. The rules of the parental leave program allow fathers to take parental leave, and information campaigns coax men to do so. Still, no serious attempt has been made to require or provide strong financial incentives for men to take leave. Given women's lesser absorption and status in the labor market, it thus becomes easier for couples to let mothers take all or most of the leave. In turn, women's occupational position can suffer, as they (not fathers) are forced to adjust work demands to family life. Gender inequality thus becomes reinforced, rather than eliminated.

PROSPECTS FOR EQUAL PARENTHOOD

What does a study of Sweden tell us about the future of equal parenthood? For one thing, it is obvious that the complete elimination of the gender-based division of labor for child care will take a long time. In response to a question about why more Swedish men do not take parental leave, and architect who was interviewed for the study because she and her husband had shared parental leave fairly equally made the following comment:

> It is still a relatively new program and it takes a long time to change values. . . . It takes a little nerve to break the old pattern. It is irritating that it takes so long, but people must voluntarily go along.

It has taken fifteen years for usage of parental leave by fathers to arrive at the present level of 44%. Optimistically expecting an increase of 2% a year, it will take almost thirty years, or a whole generation, for the percentage of Swedish fathers who take parental leave to approach 100%. When asked what would increase the number of Swedish men who took parental leave, and auto assembly line worker noted this snail's pace by saying, "It's a generational question—the models and ideology must change."

Equal parenthood seems not only to take a long time but to come in stages. In examining what types of child care fathers were more likely to share equal responsibilities for, it was found that fathers tended first to spend more time around children and to be involved in emotional caregiving tasks (like playing), then they took up direct physical caretaking tasks (like feeding), and finally indirect domestic tasks associated with children (like laundry). Men were more likely to develop confidence in their parenting ability and progress further in terms of these stages when they had taken parental leave, particularly when they had taken lots of it. This suggests that solo responsibilities for parenting, which occurs during the Swedish parental leave program, may be a necessary prerequisite for men's becoming equal parents.

Taking parental leave during a child's first year or so is, of course, only one possible manifestation of equal parenthood. As we have seen, this does not necessarily lead to the father's remaining equally involved in nurturance of small children. The latter depends on whether the mother is as involved as the father in gainful employment and whether the father took a substantial percentage of the couple's total leave. These conditions proved to be rare in the sample of Swedish parents studied, but when they did occur, equal sharing of parental responsibilities was extremely common. The prospects for equal parenting, then, may rest on the prospects for equalizing women's and men's employment (for example, through a thirty-hour work week), and for encouraging men to take an equal amount of parental leave (perhaps through financial incentives).

It will require dramatic changes in the structure of work if equal parenthood is to flourish. According to Newland (1984:109):

> [T]he most effective thing a government can do to encourage equality in private life is to enforce equality in the public sphere of employment.

As long as women's and men's job situations remain different, with women being channeled into part-time, low-status, and lower-paying jobs, women will remain uninterested in relinquishing their monopoly over child care. In addition, as long as employers see men as less dispensable than women, consider women to be responsible for early child care, and value short-term profit over long-term productivity gains, men will be discouraged from reducing their involvement in paid employment to be more involved in active child care. Roos (1985:161) claims we need to "encourage the recognition that men's work life should be responsive to . . . family life."

The structure of the labor market may change in the not too distant future in Sweden and elsewhere, as the importance of women's labor power gains recognition and more deliberate efforts are forthcoming to make employment attractive to women. The latter would include shortening the work week for everyone and reducing the amount of gender segregation in the labor market. In many countries, substantial efforts to ensure equal pay for comparable work will also be necessary. Not only will employment have to be made attractive to women, but ways for women to combine employment with childbearing must be found, if a serious decline in the birth rate is to be avoided. As awareness that employment reduces women's childbearing potential increases, policymakers seem likely to respond with more programs designed to help parents combine employment and family roles.

Equal parenthood is still rare. Couples who practice it serve as pioneers in uncharted territory. Nevertheless, the study suggests strongly that the few fathers who do embark on a career of equal parenthood serve as important role models for others who are interested in adopting this lifestyle. When asked what could be done to increase the number of Swedish men who take parental leave, a preschool teacher who was interviewed made this comment: "We can be an example, tell other people how positive it has been." Knowing men who had taken parental leave and reading about others in the mass media helped fathers make the decision to take leave in the first place, and contributed to their greater satisfaction with taking the leave. The increasing number of Swedish men who take parental leave can be seen as a force for social change. Risman and Schwartz (1989:8) state:

> [W]hen individuals collectively choose to defy current expectation and to organize new agendas, they eventually change the social structure itself.... When social structural forces are in flux—when individuals face conflicting options, opportunities, and expectations, their choices shape, mold, and create the structural forces that future generations will take for granted.

The results of the study, therefore, suggest that a cautious optimism in regard to the future of equal parenthood is in order. In the meantime, Sweden remains the only model of a society committed to this goal. The lessons of Sweden's ambitious attempt to realize this goal provide a useful guide in designing similar programs in other settings and clarify the role social policy can play in bringing about men's equal responsibility for child care.

Appendix A
Methodology of the Study

THE MAIL SURVEY

Chapters 3 through 6 of the book are based largely on findings from a 1986 mail survey of parents conducted in Gothenburg, Sweden. Located on the western coast of Sweden, Gothenburg (Göteborg in Swedish) is a city of half a million inhabitants. It is the second largest city in Sweden, next to Stockholm, the country's capital. Gothenburg contains many of the major industries of Sweden (including its auto factories) and is the largest port in Scandinavia. Choosing a sample of parents from an urban setting seemed appropriate since the topic was gender-role change and since historically such change has been known to come first to cities (Shorter, 1976).

Securing a sample for the survey became, unexpectedly, a very complicated affair. The original aim was to sample randomly among all couples who had had a child in Gothenburg in 1984. The year 1984 was picked because at least one year would have passed since the couple would have completed taking parental leave, and studying the consequences of fathers taking parental leave was one of the aims of the study. Bernhardt (1985) found that most Swedish parents return to the labor market within one year of childbirth.

The national insurance office was approached for permission to go through the records of the sixteen local insurance offices in Gothenburg (each of which represented a specific geographic area), to gather names of couples for the survey. This procedure had been used by a team of Swedish and American researchers for an earlier study of parental leave (Lamb et al., 1982a). However, a new privacy law protecting citizens from having their records examined by nonauthorized persons had recently become law, and the national insurance office was reluctant to grant permission for the study. With the help of Swedish colleagues, permission was finally granted, but two major restrictions were made which kept the research study from being conducted in the most scientific way. Limits were placed on which parents could be approached and on the number of times parents could be contacted.

Permission was obtained to sample from only two of the sixteen local offices. I was allowed to pick which two offices, and so two were chosen that seemed to reflect the diversity of the Gothenburg population in terms of social class, ethnicity, and social environment. The choice was made after examining census data on the different areas and after consulting colleagues at the university. One area was more middle-class, with about half of the mothers from this area holding professional or managerial jobs. Forty percent of the sample came from this area. The other district was more working-class, with two-thirds of the mothers who had had children in 1984 in this district holding jobs which were not professional or managerial. The remaining 60% of the sample came from this area. The two areas had similar rates for fathers' participation in parental leave (23% and 21% respectively).

Since the sample was not actually generated randomly (being a list of all those registered at only two insurance offices instead of a random list of those registered at all city offices), it was important to check for any potential sampling bias. This could be done by comparing known characteristics of the sample obtained from social insurance records with published data on parents in Sweden in general and in Gothenburg in particular. Census data on the Gothenburg population were available only on a limited basis from published reports, so it was necessary to commission a statistician at the Bureau of Statistics in Stockholm to collect and compute some of the figures needed.

The sample and the population of Gothenburg parents were identical in a very important respect: the percentage of couples where the father had taken some parental leave (22%). Two other similarities concerned family structure and family size.

Forty-five percent of children born in all of Gothenburg in 1984 were first-borns, compared to 44% in the sample. While the sample tended to be somewhat more likely than Gothenburg couples as a whole to be cohabiting or living together outside of marriage (16% vs. 12%), the difference was not statistically significant.

Given the sampling strategy of choosing two districts mainly on social class characteristics, the class heterogeneity and representativeness of the sample was a major concern. Specific data on the occupations of Gothenburg women were not available, although data on Swedish women in general were. In 1984, one-third (32%) of Swedish women held jobs that fell into census categories for professional, technical, and administrative work. The sample picked for the study contained slightly more women with jobs in these categories (38%), but the difference was not statistically significant (according to z-tests). (Comparative data for the city and country were obtained from Göteborgs Stadskansli, 1986; Riksförsäkringsverket, 1985; and Statistiska Centralbyrån, 1986b.)

When the names and addresses of all those who had received parental leave compensation from either of the two insurance offices were compiled, the list contained 1,210 families. Certain cases were then excluded from the study if they met any of the following conditions:

—twins or adopted children were involved. Parental leave lengths were longer for twins, and eligibility periods varied depending on the date of adoption. It was feared that this might complicate the analysis. Two percent of the original sample was eliminated for this reason.

—the father did not live with the mother at the time of the birth *or* at the time of the study. This was determined by checking computerized address records for mothers and fathers. This excluded 13% of the original sample.

—the couple had moved outside the Gothenburg metropolitan area by the time of the study. This constituted 9% of the original sample.

—one or both partners were not employed for pay immediately before the birth of the child. This excluded 16% of the original sample.

The latter stipulation was made because of the nature of the insurance regulations in force in 1984–85. At that time, a father could not stay home to take care of the newborn and receive 90–100% of his usual pay unless he *and* the mother of the child had been employed for pay the six months preceding the birth. He could still stay home, but he would get only $8 a day, a substantial disincentive for fathers' participation in infant care. (Regulations were changed in 1986 so that father's eligibility depended only on his own attachment to the labor force.) The sample was thus restricted to couples where the father had a genuine choice to stay home on parental leave, without a severe economic penalty. Two copies of an identical survey were then mailed to the remaining 740 couples in the survey, along with a stamped return envelope and a cover letter explaining the goals of the study. A reminder letter was sent two weeks after the initial mailing. (The questionnaire appears in Appendix B, in both the original Swedish version and in translation). More reminders and additional copies of the questionnaire could not be sent out (as would be typical mail survey research practice), because permission could not be obtained for this from the national insurance office. Nineteen of these couples were later ruled ineligible for the survey. Three had separated since the original mailing, three had left no forwarding address, one had had twins that had not been noticed on the insurance records, and twelve had not met the employment requirements of parental leave even though they had somehow managed to receive benefits.

In all, a 44% response rate was obtained. (319 couples returned questionnaires out of an eligible number of 721.) In 90% of the cases, both parents returned questionnaires. A 50% response rate in a mail survey is considered typical and acceptable, as long as no response bias exists (Babbie, 1985). A comparison was made between the group of actual respondents and the original sample to whom questionnaires were mailed. Although the responding group tended to have a slightly higher proportion of fathers who had taken parental leave (27%) than had occurred in the sample (22%), the difference was not statistically significant. The responding group was also found to be quite similar to the sample in terms of social class, with 40% of the women in the responding group holding professional, technical, or administrative jobs compared to 38% of women in the original sample. Family structure was also similar, with 15% of those responding living in cohabiting arrangements, compared to 16% of the original sample. At first, it appeared that there might have been significant differences between the two groups in terms of family size. While the child born in 1984 was the only child for 44% of couples in the sample, this was true for only 31% of the responding group. However, between one and two years had elapsed since the birth of the child in 1984, and many of the responding group (as well as the nonresponding couples in the sample) had had another child in the interim. (Swedish children tend to be very closely spaced, partly due to parental leave regulations that allow mothers to take parental leave for the second child without returning to the workforce if the time period has not exceeded two years.) From the interviews with nine couples, it was found that three had had another child since 1984. If that same percentage (33%) held for the original sample as a whole, then the abovementioned discrepancy in the figures for family size would be accounted for.

There was one respect in which the sample and responding groups were found to differ. The responding group tended to have a higher proportion of individuals who worked in the public sector. For example, about one-fourth (24%) of Gothenburg men work in the public sector, compared to 41% of the responding group. As mentioned in the text, considerable propaganda concerning fathers taking parental leave is aimed at government workers, who are given additional incentives to take leave by receiving 100% (vs 90%) of their usual pay while on leave. Such workers seem likely to be more attentive to the discussion about parental leave, and more inclined to return questionnaires on the subject than other workers who have not been so targeted.

In summary, despite the low response rate and potential sampling bias, the 319 couples who responded to the survey remained a group worthy of study, likely to be fairly representative of those who received questionnaires and of the population of parents in Gothenburg.

IN-PERSON INTERVIEWS

In addition to the mail survey, in-person interviews were conducted with nine couples where the father had taken two or more months of parental leave. These couples were recruited via the mail survey. Thirty-seven couples had shared parental leave fairly equally (defined as the father having taken two or more months of leave), according to social insurance office records. These were sent a special postcard, along with their questionnaires, which requested that they consider being interviewed in person. Nine couples returned this postcard agreeing to be interviewed, which was about one-fourth of those who had been asked.

All but one of the interviews took place in the couples' homes with both partners present. (In one case, only the mother was interviewed, at a downtown coffeeshop.) The interviews took about one and one-half hours each and were conducted in Swedish. The questions were general, designed to elicit more details about couples' motivations for sharing leave and the benefits and problems associated with fathers taking leave. (The protocol for the interview is included in Appendix B.)

All but one of the couples were middle class, with at least one partner holding a professional, technical, or administrative job. Their jobs were in government service, education, and health care for the most part. Five of the nine worked for the same organization. Fathers took an average of 3½ months of leave.

These couples provided many useful insights into the parental leave program that are included in the book, particularly in regard to obstacles to fathers' sharing parental leave and the benefits and problems associated with fathers' leavetaking. The quotes from the interviews that appear in the text are translations of responses given originally in Swedish.

Below is a brief sketch of each of these couples.

Marie (nurse) and Ove (teacher) lived in an apartment in central Gothenburg with their two-year-old daughter. He stayed home five months. He said he took leave because he had the chance and it was easy to arrange it in his job. Marie said it was important for him to stay home because daughters need contact with their dads and because he would have a good relationship with her when she is older.

Christina (office manager) and Erling (government administrator) lived with their two sons, ages two and three, in a two-family house in the central city. He stayed home three months. Erling said he took leave because he wanted to see what it was like, wanted to develop a good relationship with the baby, wanted his wife to get to be out in "real life", and saw it as a way to live up to his political ideals. Since he earned far more than she, he was home less long. The time he was home was a compromise between two conflicting goals: his desire to be at home and the family's economy. Christina said it was natural for him to be at home. She liked being at home but wanted him to build a relationship with the child and not to miss out on that important time.

Elisabet (nurse) and Peter (psychiatric nurse) lived with their daughter in a new apartment in a new suburb. He stayed home for three months. She made up her mind not to stay home the whole time, but it didn't seem as if she had to pressure him. Being thrilled about having a child and not particularly enamored of work, he was very interested in staying home.

Karin and Kid (both gym teachers) lived with their daughter, aged two, and infant son, four months, in a new row house in an affluent new suburb thirteen kilometers south of Gothenburg. He stayed home 5½ months with the two year old, but was planning to stay home only three months with the second because a new boss was being difficult. Both said it was "obvious" that they would share parental leave. Kid said, however, that maybe it would have been different if Karin had wanted to be home the whole time.

Christina (preschool teacher) and Lars (computer consultant) lived with their two children, ages two years and three months, in a house they shared with Christina's sister's family. He took one month of full-time leave, and three months of part-time leave (stretching it to six months). She had asked him if he wanted to stay home and was glad he did.

Kirsti and Lars (both auto assembly line workers) lived in an apartment in a working-class suburb near the city with their two preschoolers. Lars stayed home six months with each child. He insisted that "if one has children together, the care should be shared" and that he wanted to participate in their upbringing. She also indicated that she believed couples should share equally in all domestic tasks and that she didn't want to be home all the time.

Maria and husband (both physicians) lived in a house in the country with their two sons, two and one years old. He stayed home six months with the first but was grateful when she didn't pressure him to stay home the second time. He declined to be interviewed.

Ulla and Stefan (both architects) lived in a house with their daughter, aged two. He was home five months. They had shared all domestic tasks before, and felt it was natural to extend equality to child care.

Christina (a pharmacy worker) and Nils (a professor) lived in a row house in a suburb at the far edge of the county. They had three children, aged thirteen, nine, and two. He stayed home two months with the youngest. The last child was unplanned, and it seemed fairer that the early care should be shared; he also planned to make use of the time off for his research.

Appendix B

QUESTIONNAIRE
(English-language translation)*

Instructions: All questions concern only your child born in 1984. Place a cross or fill in the appropriate answer. Only one answer should be given per question unless indicated otherwise.

A. *YOUR JOB BEFORE THE CHILD'S BIRTH*

1. Were you employed before the child was born in 1984?
   [ ] yes, I was employed
   [ ] yes, I was employed but I was on leave
   [ ] no, I was not employed

   ↓

   NOTE! Continue with the next section on this page.

2. What type of job did you have? ______________________________

3. How many hours did you work on the average per work week? ______

4. Were you:
   [ ] employed in the private sector
   [ ] employed by the national government
   [ ] employed by the city government
   [ ] a business owner
   [ ] something else

5. How long had you worked at this job? ______

*The original Swedish-language version immediately follows.

6. In general, how good was the job you had, compared with the job which you really wanted to have? Was your job:
   [ ] precisely like the job you wanted to have
   [ ] very much like it
   [ ] somewhat like it
   [ ] not especially like it
   [ ] not at all like it

7. In which of these categories did your monthly pay fall into, after taxes?
   [ ] less than 5000 crowns a month
   [ ] 5000–5999 crowns a month
   [ ] 6000–6999 crowns
   [ ] 7000–7999 crowns
   [ ] 8000–8999 crowns
   [ ] 9000 or more crowns

8. Who had the most responsibility for earning your family's income, before the child was born?
   [ ] the man mostly
   [ ] the man a little more
   [ ] the man and the woman equally
   [ ] the woman a little more
   [ ] the woman mostly

B. *PARENTAL LEAVE*

1. Did you receive regular parental leave or special parental leave benefits from the Social Insurance Office for the child born in 1984? (Do *not* count the 10 days which the father takes at the time of delivery.)
   [ ] yes→Around how many days at the regular benefit level? ____
   Around how many days at the guarantee level? ________
   [ ] no

2. Do you pay any attention to the discussion about fathers taking parental leave which goes on in the daily newspapers, on TV, etc.?
   [ ] yes, a lot [ ] yes, a little [ ] no

3. How many men do you know personally who have taken parental leave? ______

4. In most families the mother uses all the parental leave or more days than the father. If this happened in your case, what were the most important reasons for this? (Place a cross in front of the answers which apply.)
   [ ] the man's work situation
   [ ] the man could not manage caring for an infant
   [ ] the family income

[ ] breastfeeding of the child
[ ] the man was not interested
[ ] the mother wanted to stay at home
[ ] something else (What? ______________________________)
[ ] inapplicable

5. How did the following people react when you went on parental leave? (If you did not take leave, how do you believe the people mentioned below would have reacted if you had taken parental leave?)

	Mostly positively	Neither postively nor negatively	Mostly negatively	Don't know	NA
a. your employer	[ ]	[ ]	[ ]	[ ]	[ ]
b. your supervisor	[ ]	[ ]	[ ]	[ ]	[ ]
c. your male co-workers	[ ]	[ ]	[ ]	[ ]	[ ]
d. your female co-workers	[ ]	[ ]	[ ]	[ ]	[ ]
e. your friends	[ ]	[ ]	[ ]	[ ]	[ ]
f. your mother	[ ]	[ ]	[ ]	[ ]	[ ]
g. your father	[ ]	[ ]	[ ]	[ ]	[ ]
h. your partner (i.e., your spouse or person you live with)	[ ]	[ ]	[ ]	[ ]	[ ]

6. Do you wish you and your partner had shared parental leave equally?
[ ] yes [ ] partly [ ] no [ ] inapplicable

7. If you were to have another baby, would you choose to take parental leave?
[ ] yes [ ] don't know [ ] no

8. Indicate how important you think it is that the following reforms be enacted in the near future in regard to parental leave.

	Very important	Rather important	Not so important	Not at all important
a. lengthening of parental leave with full pay from 9 to 12 months	[ ]	[ ]	[ ]	[ ]
b. a lengthening of parental leave for those couples where the woman and man take turns staying at home	[ ]	[ ]	[ ]	[ ]
c. obligatory equal division of leave between the parents	[ ]	[ ]	[ ]	[ ]

C. *FOR THOSE WHO TOOK PARENTAL LEAVE*

If you did not take parental leave for the child born in 1984, skip this section and continue with the next.

1. What were the consequences for your workplace when you took parental leave?
   [ ] no difficulties at the workplace
   [ ] problem-free for the most part
   [ ] some difficulties
   [ ] great difficulties ensued
   [ ] don't know
   [ ] inapplicable

2. Was your family income adversely affected by your being on leave for child care purposes?
   [ ] yes, rather a lot [ ] yes, a little [ ] no

3. How well did you get along in general when you were home and caring for the child?
   [ ] very well
   [ ] rather well
   [ ] neither well nor badly
   [ ] rather badly
   [ ] very badly

4. Indicate if the following statements applied to your leave:

	Very true	Rather true	Not especially true	Not at all true
a. I felt lonely	[ ]	[ ]	[ ]	[ ]
b. I liked caring for the child.	[ ]	[ ]	[ ]	[ ]
c. It was boring.	[ ]	[ ]	[ ]	[ ]
d. It felt good not to be working for awhile.	[ ]	[ ]	[ ]	[ ]
e. It was hard work and stressful.	[ ]	[ ]	[ ]	[ ]

D. *CHILD CARE*

1. Did you have practical experience concerning child care, before you became a parent?
   [ ] yes, a lot [ ] yes, a little [ ] no
2. How good do you think that you are at caring for a child now?
   [ ] very good [ ] rather good [ ] not so good
3. How good do you think that your partner is at caring for a child?
   [ ] very good [ ] rather good [ ] not so good
4. Who has main responsibility for the care and upbringing of the child born in 1984?
   [ ] the woman mostly
   [ ] the woman a little more
   [ ] the woman and the man equally
   [ ] the man a little more
   [ ] the man mostly
5. Which of you can best comfort the child?
   [ ] the mother [ ] the father [ ] both equally
6. How many hours approximately do you take care of or are you together with your child on a day when you work?
   _____ hours [ ] not presently employed
7. How many hours appproximatley does your partner take care of or is your partner together with your child on a day when s/he works?
   _____ hours [ ] not presently employed
8. How many hours approximately do you take of or are you together with your child on a day when you are not working? _____ hours

9. How many hours approximately does your partner take care of or is your partner together with your child on a day when s/he is not working? _____ hours

10. Which of you does the following things in your family?

	Woman mostly	Woman more	Both equally	Man more	Man mostly	Inapplicable
a. buy food for child	[ ]	[ ]	[ ]	[ ]	[ ]	[ ]
b. prepare child's food	[ ]	[ ]	[ ]	[ ]	[ ]	[ ]
c. feed child	[ ]	[ ]	[ ]	[ ]	[ ]	[ ]
d. change diapers	[ ]	[ ]	[ ]	[ ]	[ ]	[ ]
e. put child to bed	[ ]	[ ]	[ ]	[ ]	[ ]	[ ]
f. buy child's clothes	[ ]	[ ]	[ ]	[ ]	[ ]	[ ]
g. wash child's clothes	[ ]	[ ]	[ ]	[ ]	[ ]	[ ]
h. arrange child care	[ ]	[ ]	[ ]	[ ]	[ ]	[ ]
i. play with child	[ ]	[ ]	[ ]	[ ]	[ ]	[ ]
j. read books to child	[ ]	[ ]	[ ]	[ ]	[ ]	[ ]
k. teach child to do something new	[ ]	[ ]	[ ]	[ ]	[ ]	[ ]
l. comfort the child when s/he is sick or tired	[ ]	[ ]	[ ]	[ ]	[ ]	[ ]
m. take child to doctor	[ ]	[ ]	[ ]	[ ]	[ ]	[ ]
n. get up at night	[ ]	[ ]	[ ]	[ ]	[ ]	[ ]

11. How long did the mother breastfeed full-time? ______
    part-time? ______ [ ] did not breastfeed

12. How many siblings does the child have? ______

13. When was your child born? Day: ______ Month: ______

E. *YOUR JOB NOW*

1. What would you rather do now:
   [ ] work full-time [ ] work part-time [ ] be at home

2. How important is employment to you just now in comparison with your other interests and activities? Would you say it is:
   [ ] the main interest in your life
   [ ] a main interest, buy not the only interest in your life
   [ ] one of several important interests in your life
   [ ] a less important interest in your life
   [ ] not at all important compared with your other interests

3. Are you employed at the present time?
   [ ] no→Indicate the reason: ______
   Note! Continue with section F.
   [ ] yes

4. Have you the same employer as before the child's birth?
   [ ] yes
   [ ] no→What type of job do you have now? ______
   [ ] inapplicable

5. Have you the same work assignments as you had before the child's birth? [ ] yes [ ] partly [ ] no

6. How many *days* do you work on the average per work week? ______

7. How many *hours* do you work on the average per work week? ______

8. Can you vary your work times?
   [ ] yes, usually [ ] yes, sometimes [ ] no

9. Compared to the time before the child's birth, have your chances for advancement on the job:
   [ ] improved [ ] worsened [ ] stayed the same

10. In general, how good is the job which you now have, compared to the job which you really would rather have? Is your job:
    [ ] precisely like the job you really want to have

[ ] very much like it
[ ] somewhat like it
[ ] not especially like it
[ ] not at all like it

11. In which of these categories does your monthly pay after tax fall?
[ ] less than 5000 crowns a month
[ ] 5000–5999 crowns
[ ] 6000–6999 crowns
[ ] 7000–7999 crowns
[ ] 8000–8999 crowns
[ ] 9000 or more crowns

F. *YOUR OPINIONS*

Do you think the following statements are right or not?

	Yes, absolutely	Yes, sometimes	No, not usually	No, not at all	Don't know
1. Women can be as interested in employment as in children.	[ ]	[ ]	[ ]	[ ]	[ ]
2. If the woman works full-time, the man and woman ought to share equally in child care.	[ ]	[ ]	[ ]	[ ]	[ ]
3. A father can be as close emotionally to his child as a mother.	[ ]	[ ]	[ ]	[ ]	[ ]
4. A man can become as capable as a woman at child care if he has the chance to learn.	[ ]	[ ]	[ ]	[ ]	[ ]

	Yes, absolutely	Yes, sometimes	No, not usually	No, not at all	Don't know
5. The man is the one who should be the family's primary breadwinner.	[ ]	[ ]	[ ]	[ ]	[ ]
6. Success on the job ought to be a man's main goal in life.	[ ]	[ ]	[ ]	[ ]	[ ]
7. A father ought to take parental leave in order to take care of a child.	[ ]	[ ]	[ ]	[ ]	[ ]
8. Parental leave ought to be shared equally between fathers and mothers.	[ ]	[ ]	[ ]	[ ]	[ ]

G. *YOURSELF*

1. In what year were you born? ______

2. How many years did you go to school (count also technical and postsecondary school). ______

3. Did your own mother (or female caregiver) work outside the home when you were growing up?
   [ ] yes, full-time [ ] yes, part-time [ ] no

4. Who had the main responsibility for your care and upbringing when you were growing up?
   [ ] mother mostly (or female caregiver)
   [ ] mother a little more
   [ ] mother and father (or male caregiver) shared equally
   [ ] father a little more
   [ ] father mostly
   [ ] inapplicable (caregiver was single)

5. Are you:
   [ ] a Swedish citizen, born in Sweden
   [ ] a Swedish citizen, born abroad
   [ ] foreign citizen

6. Are you: [ ] married [ ] cohabiting

7. Are you a: [ ] woman [ ] man

THE QUESTIONNARIES SHOULD BE RETURNED IN THE ENVELOPE PROVIDED. MANY THANKS FOR YOUR HELP!

FRÅGEFORMULÄR

Anvisningar: Alla frågor gäller bara barn födda 1984. Sätt kryss eller fyll i lämpligt svarsalternativ. Endast ett svar skall avges per fråga om ej annat anges.

A. *DITT ARBETE FÖRE BARNETS FÖDELSE*

1. Hade Du anställning innan barnet föddes 1984?
   - ☐ ja, hade arbete
   - ☐ ja, hade arbete men var tjänst- eller havandeskapsledig
   - ☐ nej, hade ej arbete → OBS! FORTSÄTT MED NÄSTA AVSNITT.

2. Vad hade Du för arbete? ______________________

3. Hur många timmar arbetade Du i genomsnitt per arbetsvecka? ______________________

4. Var Du:
   - ☐ privat anställd
   - ☐ statligt anställd
   - ☐ kommunalt anställd
   - ☐ egen företagare
   - ☐ något annat

5. Hur länge hade Du arbetat på detta jobb? ______________________

6. Över huvud taget, hur bra var det jobb som Du hade, jämfört med det jobb som Du verkligen ville ha? Var Ditt jobb:
   - ☐ precis likt det jobb som Du verkligen ville ha
   - ☐ väldigt mycket likt det
   - ☐ något likt det
   - ☐ inte särskilt likt det
   - ☐ inte alls likt det

7. I vilken av dessa kategorier föll vanligen Din månadslön *efter* skatt?
   - ☐ mindre än 5000 kronor i månaden
   - ☐ 5000–5999 kronor i månaden
   - ☐ 6000–6999 kronor i månaden
   - ☐ 7000–7999 kronor i månaden
   - ☐ 8000–8999 kronor i månaden
   - ☐ 9000 eller mer kronor

8. Vem bar det största ansvaret för Din familjs ekonomi, innan barnet föddes?
   - ☐ mannen mest
   - ☐ mannen lite mer
   - ☐ mannen och kvinnan lika mycket
   - ☐ kvinnan lite mer
   - ☐ kvinnan mest

B. *FÖRÄLDRALEDIGHET*

1. Fick Du föräldrapenning eller särskild föräldrapenning från Försäkringsassan för barnet fött 1984? (Räkna *ej* de 10 dagar som pappan tar barnets födelse.)
   - ☐ ja → Ungefär hur många dagar med sjukpenningsbelopp? (Räkna om den ledigheten till hela arbetsdagar.) ____
     → Ungefär hur många dagar med garantibelopp? ______
   - ☐ nej

2. Ägnar Du någon uppmärksamhet åt debatten om pappaledighet som förekommer i dagspressen, i TV, osv?
   ☐ ja, mycket ☐ ja, lite ☐ nej

3. Hur många män känner Du personligen som har tagit föräldraledighet? ______________________________

4. I de flesta familjer tar mamman ut alla föräldralediga dagar eller flera än pappan. Om det hände i Ert fall, vilka var de viktigaste orsakerna till det? (Sätt ett kryss framför de svarsalternativ som är lämpliga.)
   - ☐ mannens arbetsförhållande
   - ☐ mannen kunde inte klara att ta hand om ett spädbarn
   - ☐ familjens ekonomi
   - ☐ amningen av barnet
   - ☐ mannen ej intresserad
   - ☐ mamman ville stanna hemma
   - ☐ något annat (vad? ______________________________)
   - ☐ ej tillämpligt

5. Hur reagerade nedanstående personer när Du var föräldraledig? (Om Du inte var föräldraledig, hur tror Du att nedanstående personer skulle ha reagerat om Du hade varit föräldraledig?)

	Positivt i stort sett	Varken positivt eller negativt	Negativt i stort sett	Vet ej	Ej tillämpligt
a. Din arbetsgivare	☐	☐	☐	☐	☐
b. Din närmaste chef	☐	☐	☐	☐	☐
c. Dina manliga arbetskamrater	☐	☐	☐	☐	☐
d. Dina kvinnliga arbetskamrater	☐	☐	☐	☐	☐
e. Dina vänner	☐	☐	☐	☐	☐
f. Din mama	☐	☐	☐	☐	☐
g. Din pappa	☐	☐	☐	☐	☐
h. Din partner (dvs Din make/ maka eller samboende)	☐	☐	☐	☐	☐

6. Önskar Du att Din partner och Du hade delat föräldraledighten lika?
☐ ja ☐ delvis ☐ nej ☐ ej tillämpligt

7. Om det blev aktuellt, skulle Du vilja vara föräldraledig i framtiden?
☐ ja ☐ vet ej ☐ nej

8. Ange hur viktigt Du anser det är att man inom en nära framtid genomför följande reformer i föräldraledigheten.

	Mycket viktigt	Ganska viktigt	Inte så viktigt	Inte alls viktigt
a. en förlängning av föräldraledighten med sjukpenningsbelopp från f.n. 9 till 12 månader	☐	☐	☐	☐
b. en förlängning av föräldraledighten för de par där båda kvinnan och mannen turas om att stanna hemma med barnet	☐	☐	☐	☐
c. obligatoriskt lika uppdelning av ersättningstiden mellan föräldrarna	☐	☐	☐	☐

C. *FÖR DE SOM TOG FÖRÄLDRALEDIGHET*

Om Du *inte* var föräldraledig med barnet fött 1984, hoppa över detta avsnitt och fortsätt med det nästa.

1. Vilka blev konsekvenserna för Din arbetsplats när Du var föräldraledig?
   - ☐ inga svårigheter på arbetsplatsen
   - ☐ problemfritt i stort sett
   - ☐ en del svårigheter
   - ☐ kraftiga störningar uppstod
   - ☐ vet ej
   - ☐ ej tillämpligt

2. Påverkades Din familjs ekonomi av att Du var ledig för att vårda barnet?
   ☐ ja, ganska mycket ☐ ja, lite ☐ nej

3. Hur trivs Du i allmänhet med att vara hemma och passa barn?
   - ☐ mycket bra
   - ☐ ganska bra
   - ☐ varken bra eller dåligt
   - ☐ ganska dåligt
   - ☐ mycket dåligt

4. Ange vad Du anser om följande påståenden beträffande Din ledighet:

	Mycket sant	Ganska sant	Inte särskilt sant	Inte alls sant
a. Jag kände mig ensam.	☐	☐	☐	☐
b. Jag tyckte om att vårda barnet.	☐	☐	☐	☐
c. Det var tråkigt.	☐	☐	☐	☐
d. Det kändes bra att inte förvärvsarbeta under en tid.	☐	☐	☐	☐
e. Det var jobbigt och stressigt.	☐	☐	☐	☐

D. *BARNAVÅRD*

1. Hade Du praktisk erfarenhet av hur man tar hand om barn, innan Du blev förälder?
   ☐ ja, mycket ☐ ja, lite ☐ nej

2. Hur bra tycker Du att Du är på att sköta barn nu?
   ☐ mycket bra ☐ ganska bra ☐ inte så bra

3. Hur bra tycker Du att Din partner är på att sköta barn?
   ☐ mycket bra ☐ ganska bra ☐ inte så bra

4. Vem har huvudansvaret för vård och uppfostran av barnet fött 1984?
   ☐ kvinnan mest
   ☐ kvinnan lite mer
   ☐ kvinnan och mannen lika mycket
   ☐ mannen lite mer
   ☐ mannen mest

5. Vilken av Er kan bäst trösta barnet?
   ☐ mamman ☐ pappan ☐ lika bra

6. Hur många timmar ungefär tar Du hand om eller är Du tillsammans med Ditt barn en dag när Du förvärvsarbetar?
   _____ timmar ☐ förvärvsarbetar ej

7. Hur många timmar ungefär tar Din partner hand om eller är tillsammans med Ert barn en dag när hon/han förvärvsarbetar?
   _____ timmar ☐ förvärvsarbetar ej

8. Hur många timmar ungefär tar Du hand om eller är Du tillsammans med Ditt barn en dag när Du *inte* förvärvsarbetar? _____ timmar

9. Hur många timmar ungefär tar Din partner hand om eller är tillsammans med Ert barn en dag när hon/han *inte* förvärvsarbetar? _____ timmar

10. Vilken av Er gör följande saker in Din familj?

	Kvinnan mest	Kvinnan lite mer	Lika mycket	Mannen lite mer	Mannen mest	Ej tillämpligt
a. köper mat till barnet	☐	☐	☐	☐	☐	☐
b. lagar mat till barnet	☐	☐	☐	☐	☐	☐
c. matar barnet	☐	☐	☐	☐	☐	☐
d. byter blöjor	☐	☐	☐	☐	☐	☐
e. badar barnet	☐	☐	☐	☐	☐	☐
f. köper barnkläder	☐	☐	☐	☐	☐	☐
g. tvättar barnkläder	☐	☐	☐	☐	☐	☐
h. ordnar barnvakt	☐	☐	☐	☐	☐	☐
i. leker med barnet	☐	☐	☐	☐	☐	☐
j. läser böcker för barnet	☐	☐	☐	☐	☐	☐
k. lär barnet att göra något nytt	☐	☐	☐	☐	☐	☐
l. tröstar barnet när det är sjukt eller trött	☐	☐	☐	☐	☐	☐

	Kvinnan mest	Kvinnan lite mer	Lika mycket	Mannen lite mer	Mannen mest	Ej tillämpligt
m. tar barnet till Barnavårdcentralen	☐	☐	☐	☐	☐	☐
n. tar upp barnet när det skriker pä natten	☐	☐	☐	☐	☐	☐

11. Hur länge ammade mamman helt? _____ delvis? _____ ☐ ammade ej

12. Hur många syskon har Ditt barn? _____

13. När är Ditt barn Född? Dag: _____ Månad _____

E. *DITT ARBETE NU*

1. Vad skulle Du helst vilja göra nu:
   ☐ arbeta heltid ☐ arbeta deltid ☐ vara hemmarbetande

2. Hur viktigt är det att jobba för Dig just nu jämfört med Dina andra intressen och aktiviteter? Skulle Du säga att arbete är:
   ☐ det huvudsakliga intresset i Ditt liv
   ☐ ett huvudintresse, men inte det enda intresset i Ditt liv
   ☐ en av flera viktiga intressen i Ditt liv
   ☐ ett mindre viktigt intresse i Ditt liv
   ☐ inte alls viktigt jämfört med Dina andra intressen

3. Förvärvsarbetar Du för närvarande?
   ☐ nej ⟶ Ange orsaken till det: ____________________
   Obs! Fortsätt med avsnitt.
   ☐ ja

4. Har Du samma arbetsgivare som före barnets födelse?
   ☐ ja
   ☐ nej ⟶ Vad har Du nu för arbete? ____________________
   ☐ ej tillämpligt

5. Har Du samma arbetsuppgifter som Du hade före barnets födelse?
   ☐ ja ☐ delvis ☐ nej

6. Hur många *dagar* arbetar Du i genomsnitt per arbetsvecka? _____

7. Hur många *timmar* arbetar Du i genomsnitt per arbetsvecka? _____

8. Kan Du variera Dina arbetstider?
   ☐ ja, vanligen ☐ ja, ibland ☐ nej

9. Jämfört med tiden före barnets födelse, har Dina chanser till avancemang i jobbet:
   ☐ förbättrats
   ☐ försämrats
   ☐ inte förändrats

10. Över huvud taget, hur bra är det jobb som Du nu har, jämfört med det jobb som Du verkligen skulle vilja ha? Är Ditt jobb:
   ☐ precis likt det jobb som Du verkligen vill ha
   ☐ väldigt mycket likt det
   ☐ något likt det
   ☐ inte särskilt likt det
   ☐ inte alls likt det

11. I vilken av dessa kategorier faller vanligen Din månadslön *efter* skatt?
   ☐ mindre än 5000 kronor i månaden
   ☐ 5000–5999 kronor i månaden
   ☐ 6000–6999 kronor i månaden
   ☐ 7000–7999 kronor i månaden
   ☐ 8000–8999 kronor i månaden
   ☐ 9000 eller mer kronor i månaden

F. *DINA ÅSIKTER*

Anser Du att följande påståenden är riktiga eller inte?

	ja, absolut	ja, i vissa fall	nej, knappast	nej, inte alls	vet ej
1. Kvinnor kan bli lika intresserade av yrkesarbete som av barn.	☐	☐	☐	☐	☐
2. Om kvinnan förvärvsarbetar på heltid, bör mannen och kvinnan dela lika på skötseln av barnet.	☐	☐	☐	☐	☐

	ja, absolut	ja, i vissa fall	nej, knappast	nej, inte alls	vet ej
3. En pappa kan känslomässigt stå lika nära sitt barn som en mamma.	☐	☐	☐	☐	☐
4. En man kan, om han får lära sig, bli lika bra som en kvinna på att sköta barn.	☐	☐	☐	☐	☐
5. Mannen är den som i första hand skall vara familjeförsörjare.	☐	☐	☐	☐	☐
6. Framgång på jobbet borde vara en mans huvudmål i livet.	☐	☐	☐	☐	☐
7. En pappa borde ta ledigt från sitt arbete med ersättning från Försäkringskassan för att passa barn.	☐	☐	☐	☐	☐
8. Föräldraledighet borde fördelas jämnt mellan pappor och mammor.	☐	☐	☐	☐	☐

G. *DU SJÄLV*

1. Vilket år är Du född? ____

2. Hur många år har Du sammanlagt gått i skolan (dvs inräknat ev yrkes och högskola)? ____

3. Förvärvsarbetade Din egen mor (eller kvinnlig vårdnadshavare) när Du växte upp?
   ☐ ja, heltid ☐ ja, deltid ☐ nej

4. Vem hade huvudansvaret för Din vård och uppfostran när Du växte upp?
   - ☐ mamma (eller kvinnlig vårdnadshavare) mest
   - ☐ mamma lite mer
   - ☐ mamma och pappa (eller manlig vårdnadshavare) delade lika
   - ☐ pappa lite mer
   - ☐ pappa mest
   - ☐ ej tillämpligt (t.ex. vårdnadshavare var ensamstående)

5. Är Du:
   - ☐ svensk medborgare, född i Sverige
   - ☐ svensk medborgare, född utomlands
   - ☐ utländsk medborgare

6. Är Du: ☐ gift ☐ sammanboende

7. Är Du: ☐ kvinna ☐ man

FORMULÄREN ÅTERSÄNDS I KUVERT SOM HAR BIFOGATS.
HJÄRTLIGT TACK FÖR HJÄLPEN!

INTERVIEW PROTOCOL*
English-language version

[Note: These questions were used as a guide in a semi-structured interview situation.]

Introduction—Duscuss my professional postition, desire to know more about how parents share parental leave and what happens when they take parental leave, how they were chosen.

I. *Participation in parental leave*

Did the mother take parental leave first? For how long? Whole days? When did the father take leave? How old was the child? How long did he take leave? Whole days?
Why did they decide to take leave in this way? (Why did the father take leave?)
Who wanted the father to take leave more - the mother or the father?

II. *Reactions*

How did the mother's employer and supervisor react when they knew that she would take parental leave?
How did you know what they thought? Did they say something special? Was she influenced by their opinions? How?

How did the father's employer and supervisor react when they knew that he would taken parental leave?
How did he know what they thought? Did they say something special? Was he influenced by their opinions? How?

How did the mother's co-workers react . . . ?
Father's co-workers . . . ?

How did your relatives and friends react when they knew that the father would stay home with the child?
How did you know what they thought? Did they say something special? Were you influenced by their opinions? How?

III. *Experiences with leave*

Did it go well for the mother when she was home with the child? Why (why not)?

---

*The original Swedish-language version follows.

What did she like about the leave? What didn't she like?
How did she feel when it was the father's turn to stay home?

Did it go well for the father when he was home with the child? Why (why not)?
What did he like about the leave? What didn't he like?

I have read that it sometimes happens that the father doesn't like staying home in the beginning but after a while it became more pleasant. Did this happen in your case?

How did the child react when it became dad instead of mom who stayed at home?

What were advantages of the father staying at home for the child? for the father himself? for the mother?

What types of problems occurred when the father was at home? How did you manage them?

Do you wish that the father could have stayed home longer? Why (why not)? Why did he not?
If the opportunity came up, would the father take leave again? Why (why not)?

IV. *The job after the leave was over*

Did the mother go back to the same job after her leave was over? (If not, why not?)
Was it difficult or easy for her to go back to work? (Why?)
Does she feel the same about work after taking leave? (How?)

Did the father go back to the same job after his leave was over? (If not, why not?)
Was it difficult or easy for him to go back to work? (Why?)
Does he feel the same about work after staying home? (How?)

Is it difficult or easy for you two to combine employment and parenthood? How? What helps you be able to combine both? What could be done so that it would be easier for you to combine both?

V. *Child care*

After the leave was over, how did you arrange child care? And now? (If the mother works part-time: Why is it that the mother works part-time?)

Who has primary responsibility for the child now—the mother or the father? Why?

Is the father's relationship with the child the same as the mother's or different? How?

What type of person would you wish your child to become when s/he has grown up? What type of education and occupation would you wish s/he would have?

VI. *Recommendations*

Why do you think that so few men in Sweden take parental leave? What would increase the numbers of men who take leave?

INTERVJU FRÅGOR

Introduktion—Jag ville veta mer om hur föräldrar delar på ledighet och vad som händer när de tar föräldraledighet. Jag frågade par där pappan hade tagit åtministone två månader ledighet om de skulle ställa up för en intervju.

I. *Medverkan i föräldraledighet*

Tog mamman föräldraledighet först? Hur länge? Hela dagar? När tog pappan föräldraledighet? Hur gammal var barnet då? Hur länge? Hela dagar?

Varför beslutade ni att ta ledigt på det här sättet? (Varför tog pappan ledighet?)
Vem ville att pappan skulle ta ledigt mer—mamman eller pappan?

II. *Reaktioner*

Hur reagerade mammans arbetsgivare och närmaste chef när de visste att hon skulle bli föräldraledig?
Hur visste Du vad de tyckte? Sa de något särskilt?
Blev Du påverkade av deras åsikter? Hurså?

Hur reagerade pappans arbetsgivare och närmaste chef när de visste att han skulle bli föräldraledig?
Hur visste Du vad de tyckte? Sa de något särskilt?
Blev Du påverkade av deras åsikter? Hurså?

Hur reagerade mammans arbetskamrater när de visste att hon skulle bli föräldraledig?
Hur visste Du vad de tyckte? Sa de något särskilt?
Blev Du påverkade av deras åsikter? Hurså?

Hur reagerade pappans arbetskamrater när de visste att han skulle bli föräldraledig?
Hur visste Du vad de tyckte? Sa de något särskilt?
Blev Du påverkade av deras åsikter? Hurså?

Hur reagerade Era släktingar och bekanta när de visste att pappan skulle stanna hemma med barnet?
Hur visste Du vad de tyckte? Sa de något särskilt? Blev Du påverkade av deras åsikter? Hurså?

III. *Upplevelser med ledighet*

Trivdes mamman med att stanna hemma med barnet? Varför (inte)?
Vad var det som hon gillade om sin ledighet?

Vad var det som hon inte gillade?
Hur kändes det när det var pappans tur att stanna hemma med barnet?

Trivdes pappan med att stanna hemma med barnet? Varför (inte)?
Vad var det som han gillade om sin ledighet?
Vad var det som han inte gillade?
Jag har läst att det händer ibland att pappan inte trivs bra med att stanna hemma i början men efter en stund blir det trivsammare. Hände det i Ditt fall?

Hur reagerade barnet när det blev pappan i stället för mamman som stannade hemma?
Vilka var fördelarna med att pappan var hemma för barnet? pappan själv? mamman?

Vad för slags problem uppstod när pappan var hemma? Hur klarade Ni dem?

Önskar Ni att pappan kunde ha stannat hemma längre? Varför (inte)?
Om det blev aktuellt, skulle pappan ta föräldraledighet igen? Varför (inte?)

IV *Arbete efter ledighet*

Gick mamman tillbaka till samma jobb efter ledigheten var slut? (Varför inte?)
Var det svårt eller lätt för mamman att gå tillbaka till jobbet? (Varför?)
Känner mamman det samma om arbete efter att hon hade tagit föräldraledighet? Hurså?

Gick pappan tillbaka till samma jobb efter ledigheten var slut? (Varför inte?)
Var det svårt eller lätt för pappan att gå tillbaka till jobbet? (Varför?)
Känner pappan det samma om arbete efter att han hade tagit föräldraledighet? Hurså?

Är det svårt eller lätt för Er att förena förvärvsarbete och föräldraskap? Hurså?
Vad hjälper Er att göra det?
Vad kunde göras så att det skulle bli lättare för Er att förena arbete och föräldraskap?

V. *Barnavård*

Efter ledigheten tog slut, hur ordnade Ni barnpassning? Och nu? (Om mamman arbetar deltid: Varför är det så att bara mamman arbetar deltid?)

Vem har huvudsansvaret för barnets vård nu—mamman eller pappan? Varför?

Är pappans kontakt med barnet samma som mammans eller annorlunda? Hurså?

Vad för slags människa skulle ni vilja att barnet ska bli när det har vuxit upp? Vad för slags utbildning och yrke skulle Ni vilja att det ska ha?

VI. *Rekommendationer*

Varför tycker Ni att så få män i Sverige tar föräldraledighet? Vad skulle öka antalet män som tar ledighet?

References

Adamo, Amelia. 1980. " 'Year of the Child' Provides New Rights for Sweden's Kids and Parents." *Social Change in Sweden*, #19. New York: Swedish Information Service.

Adams, Carolyn and Kathryn Winston. 1980. *Mothers at Work—Public Policies in the United States, Sweden, and China.* New York: Longman.

Agassi, Judith. 1989. "Theories of Gender Equality: Lessons from the Israeli Kibbutzim." *Gender and Society* 3:160–186.

Allen, Joseph. 1988. "European Infant Care Leaves: Foreign Perspectives on the Integration of Work and Family Roles." Pp. 245–275 in *The Parental Leave Crisis—Toward a National Policy,* edited by Edward Zigler and Meryl Frank. New Haven, CT: Yale University Press.

Andersen, Margaret. 1988. *Thinking about Women—Sociological Perspectives on Sex and Gender.* New York: Macmillan.

Anonymous. 1976. "Jag Klarar Inte Den Nya Rollen" [I can't manage the new role]. *Dagens Nyheter* [Stockholm's daily newspaper], October 28, p. 21.

Arbetsgruppen om Mansrollen [Work group on the male role]. 1985. *Mannen i förändring* [The Changing Man]. Stockholm: Tiden/Arbetsmarknadsdepartementet [Department of Labor].

Arbetsmarknadsstyrelsen [National Labor Market Board]. 1977. *Equality in the Labour Market—Programme Adopted by the Labour Market Board.* Solna, Sweden: National Labor Market Board.

Babbie, Earl. 1985. *The Practice of Social Research.* Belmont, CA: Wadsworth.

Backett, Kathryn. 1982. *Mothers and Fathers: A Study of the Development and Negotiation of Parental Behavior.* London: Macmillan.

Barnett, Rosalind and Grace Baruch. 1987. "Determinants of Father's Participation in Family Work." *Journal of Marriage and the Family* 49:29–40.

Barry, Herbert and Leonora Paxson. 1971. "Infancy and Early Childhood: Cross-Cultural Codes 2." *Ethnology* 10:466–508.

Baude, Annika. 1979. "Public Policy and Changing Family Patterns in Sweden: 1930–1977." Pp. 145–176 in *Sex Roles and Social Policy,* edited by Jean Lipman-Blumen and Jessie Bernard. Beverly Hills: Sage.

Beer, William. 1983. *Househusbands.* New York: Praeger.

Belsky, Jay. 1979. "Mother-Father-Infant Interaction: A Naturalistic Observational Study." *Developmental Psychology* 15: 601–607.

Bengtsson, Margot and Jonas Frykman. 1987. *Om Maskulinitet-Mannen som Forskningsprojekt* [On Masculinity—The Man as Research Subject]. Rapport 11. Stockholm: Delegationen för Jämställdhetsforskning [Delegation for Equality Research].

Benokraitis, Nijole. 1985. "Fathers in the Dual-earner Family." Pp. 243–268 in *Dimensions of Fatherhood*, edited by Shirley Hanson and Frederick Bozett. Beverly Hills: Sage.

Berger, Birgitte and Peter Berger. 1983. *The War Over the Family.* New York: Anchor Press.

Bernard, Jessie. 1974. *The Future of Marriage.* New York: Bantam.

———. 1981. "The Good-Provider Role—Its Rise and Fall." *American Psychologist* 36:1–12.

Bernhardt, Eva. 1985. "Women's Home Attachment at First Birth: The Case of Sweden." Stockholm: Department of Demography, University of Stockholm.

Bernheim, Nicole. 1970. "Sweden's Men and Women Learn to Share and Share Alike." *Atlas* 19:31–32.

Bernstein, Aaron. 1986. "Business Starts Tailoring Itself to Suit Working Women." *Business Week,* October 6, pp. 50–54.

Bird, Gloria, Gerald Bird, and Marguerite Scruggs. 1984. "Determinants of Family Task Sharing: A Study of Husbands and Wives." *Journal of Marriage and the Family* 46:345–356.

Blau, Francine and Anne Winkler. 1988. "Women in the Labor Force: An Overview." Pp. 265–286 in *Women: A Feminist Perspective,* edited by Jo Freeman. Mountain View, California: Mayfield.

Booth, Alan and John Edwards. 1980. "Fathers: The Invisible Parent." *Sex Roles* 6:445–456.

Bosanquet, Helen. 1906. *The Family.* New York: Macmillan.

Bozhkov, O. B. and V. B. Golofast. 1988. "The Division of Labor in the Urban Family." *Soviet Sociology* 26:82–95.

Bradley, Robert. 1985. "Fathers and the School-Age Child." Pp. 141–169 in *Dimensions of Fatherhood,* edited by Shirley Hanson and Frederick Bozett. Beverly Hills: Sage.

Brandth, Berit and Elin Kvande. 1989. "Like Barn Deler Best." Trondheim, Norway: Institutt for Industriell Miljoforskning [Institute for Social Research in Industry].

———. 1990. *Pappa Kom Hem!* [Daddy, Come Home!] Trondheim: Institutt for Industriell Miljoforskning.

Branson, Meredith, Elaine Anderson and Leigh Leslie. 1987. "Childcare Responsibilities in Working Families." Paper presented at the annual meetings of the National Council on Family Relations, Atlanta.

Brazelton, T. Berry. 1988. "Issues for Working Parents." Pp. 36–54 in *The Parental Leave Crisis*, edited by Edward Zigler and Meryl Frank. New Haven, CT: Yale University Press.

———. 1989. Testimony, Hearing of the Subcommittee on Education and Labor, U.S. House of Representatives, Feb. 7.

Bronfenbrenner, Urie. 1986. "A Generation in Jeopardy." Testimony, Hearing of Senate Committee on Rules and Administration.

Bronstein, Phyllis. 1984. "Differences in Mothers' and Fathers' Behaviors Toward Children: A Cross-Cultural Comparison." *Developmental Psychology* 20:995–1003.

Brown, Charles and Shirley Wilcher. 1987. "Sex-Based Employment Quotas in Sweden." Pp. 271–296 in *Gender in the Workplace,* edited by Clair Brown and Joseph Pechman. Washington: Brookings.

Brown, Judith. 1970. "A Note on the Division of Labor by Sex." *American Anthropologist* 72:1073–1078.

Bureau of National Affairs. 1986. *Work and Family—A Changing Dynamic.* Washington, D.C.: Bureau of National Affairs.

Business Week. 1987. "June Cleaver Would Need Help Today." *Business Week*, August 31, p. 90.

Butler, Barbara and Janis Wasserman. 1988. "Parental Leave: Attitudes and Practices in Small Businesses." Pp. 223–234 in *The Parental Leave Crisis,* edited by Edward Zigler and Meryl Frank. New Haven, CT: Yale University Press.

Calleman, Catharina, Lena Lagercrantz, Ann Petersson, and Karin Widerberg. 1984. *Kvinnoreformer på Männens Villkor* [Women's Reforms on Men's Conditions]. Lund, Sweden: Studentlitteratur.

Caplan-Cotenoff, Scott. 1987. "Parental Leave." *American Journal of Law and Medicine* 13:71–104.

Catalyst. 1986. *Report on National Study of Parental Leaves.* New York: Catalyst.

Chafetz, Janet. 1988. "The Gender Division of Labor and the Reproduction of Female Disadvantage: Toward an Integrated Theory." *Journal of Family Issues* 9:108–131.

Childs, Marquis. 1980. *Sweden: The Middle Way on Trial.* New Haven, CT: Yale University Press.

Chodorow, Nancy. 1978. *The Reproduction of Mothering.* Berkeley: University of California Press.

Clarke-Stewart, K. Alison. 1978. "And Daddy Makes Three: The Father's Impact on Mother and Child." *Child Development* 49:466–478.

Clay, William and Frederick Feinstein. 1987. "The Family and Medical Leave Act: A New Labor Standard." *Industrial and Labor Relations Report* 25:28–33.

Cohen, Susan and Mary Katzenstein. 1988. "The War over the Family is Not over the Family." Pp. 25–46 in *Feminism, Children, and the New Families,* edited by Stanley Dornbusch and Myra Strober. New York: Guilford Press.

Cohen, Theodore. 1987. "Remaking Men." *Journal of Family Issues* 8:57–77.

Condran, John and Jerry Bode. 1982. "Rashomon, Working Wives, and Family Division of Labor: Middleton, 1980." *Journal of Marriage and the Family* 44:421–426.

Congressional Digest. 1988. "Family and Medical Leave Policy." *Congressional Digest* 67 (May):129–160.

Coverman, Shelley. 1985. "Explaining Husbands' Participation in Domestic Labor." *Sociological Quarterly* 26:81–97.

Dahlström, Edmund. 1971. "Analysis of the Debate on Sex Roles." Pp. 170–206 in *The Changing Roles of Men and Women,* edited by Edmund Dahlström. Boston: Beacon Press.

Day, Randal and Wade Mackey. 1989. "An Alternate Standard for Evaluating American Fathers." *Journal of Family Issues* 10:401–408.

Demos, John. 1982. "The Changing Faces of Fatherhood: A New Exploration in American Family History." Pp. 425–445. in *Father and Child: Developmental and Clinical Perspectives*, edited by Stanley Cath, Alan Gurwitt, and John Ross. Boston: Little, Brown.

DiLeonardi, Joan and Patrick Curtis. 1988. *What to Do When the Numbers Are In.* Chicago: Nelson-Hall.

Doherty, Kathleen. 1990. "Parental Leave: Strategies in the 1990s." *Business and Health* 8 (January):21–23.

Dowd, Nancy. 1989. "Envisioning Work and Family: A Critical Perspective on International Models." *Harvard Journal of Legislation* 26:311–348.

Dumon, Wilfried and Joan Aldous. 1979. "European and U.S. Political Contexts for Family Policy Research." Journal of *Marriage and the Family* 41:497–505.

Easterbrooks, M. Ann and Wendy Goldberg. 1984. "Toddler Development in the Family: Impact of Fathers' Involvement and Parenting Characteristics." *Child Development* 55:740–752.

Edelman, Marian. 1987. *Families in Peril.* Cambridge, MA: Harvard University Press.

Eduards, Maud. 1988. "Gender Politics and Public Policies in Sweden." Paper prepared for a Conference on Gender Politics and Public Policy, New York.

Ehrensaft, Diane. 1983. "When Women and Men Mother." Pp. 237–244 in *Mothering: Essays in Feminist Theory,* edited by Joyce Trebilcot. Totowa, NJ: Rowman & Allenheld.

———. 1985. *Parenting Together.* New York: Free Press.

Eidem, Rolf. 1981. "Erkänn att Pappaledigheten Hotar Ditt Karriärtänkande" [Admit That Parental Leave Threatens Your Careermindedness]. *Dagens Nyheter*, July 11, p. 1.

Eisenstein, Zillah. 1984. *Feminism and Sexual Equality.* New York: Monthly Review Press.

Ellingsaeter, Anne Lise. 1990. *Fathers Working Long Hours: Trends, Causes and Consequences.* Oslo: Institute for Social Research.

Ericsson, Ylva and Ranveig Jacobsson. 1985. *Side by Side—A Report on Equality Between Women and Men in Sweden.* Stockholm: Gotab.

Fagerström, Eva. 1976. *Barn-En Sammanfattning av Barnmiljöutredningen* [Children—Recommendations from the Commission on Children's Environment]. Stockholm: LiberFörlag.

Falkenberg, Eva. 1990. *Far till 100%* [100% Father]. Stockholm: Tjänstemännens Centralorganisation.

Falwell, Jerry. 1980. *Listen America.* Garden City, NY: Doubleday.

Familjepolitiska Kommittén [Family Politics Committee]. 1969. "Jämställdhet Mellan Män och Kvinnor inom Sjukförsäkring [Equality Between Men and Women in Sick Leave Insurance]". Stockholm: Socialdepartementet [Ministry of Social Affairs].

Farmer, Helen. 1983. "Career and Homemaking Plans for High School Youth." *Journal of Consulting Psychology* 30:40–45.

Fasteau, Marc Feigen. 1976. "Men as Parents." Pp. 60–65 in *The 49% Majority—The Male Sex Role,* edited by Deborah David and Robert Brannon. Reading, MA: Addison-Wesley.

Fein, Robert. 1974. "Men and Young Children." Pp. 54–62 in *Men and Masculinity*, edited by Joseph Pleck and Jack Sawyer. Englewood Cliffs, N.J.: Prentice-Hall.

Feldman, S. Shirley, Sharon Nash, and Barbara Aschenbrenner. 1983. "Antecedents of Fathering." *Child Development* 54:1628–1636.

Ferree, Myra. 1988. "Negotiating Household Roles and Responsibilities." Paper presented at the conference "Gender Roles Through the Life Course," Ball State University, Muncie, Indiana.

Field, Tiffany. 1978. "Interaction Behaviors of Primary Vs. Secondary Caretaker Fathers." *Developmental Psychology* 14:183–184.

Flanagan, Robert. 1987. "Efficiency and Equality in Swedish Labor Market Relations." Pp. 125–184 in *The Swedish Economy*, edited by Barry Bosworth and Alice Rivlin. Washington: The Brookings Institute.

Fleming, Jeanne. 1988. "Public Opinion on Change in Women's Rights and Roles." Pp. 47–66 in *Feminism, Children, and the New Families,* edited by Sanford Dornbush and Myra Strober. New York: Guilford Press.

Försäkringskassan [Social Insurance Office]. 1987. *Föräldraförsäkring* [Parental Insurance]. Stockholm: Försäkringskasseförbundet.

Forsberg, Mats. 1984. *The Evolution of Social Welfare Policies in Sweden.* Stockholm: The Swedish Institute.

Frank, Meryl and Robyn Lipner. 1988. "History of Maternity Leave in Europe and the United States." Pp. 3–22 in *The Parental Leave Crisis—Toward a National Policy,* edited by Edward Zigler and Meryl Frank. New Haven, CT: Yale University Press.

Fredriksson, Ingrid. 1987. Jämstalldhet—Om Könideologin [Equality—About Gender Role Ideology]. Stockholm: Tidens Förlag.

Friedl, Ernestine. 1975. *Women and Men: An Anthropologist's View.* New York: Holt, Rinehart and Winston.

Friedman, Dana. 1985. *Corporations and Families: Changing Practices and Perspectives.* New York: The Conference Board.

———. 1987. *Family-Supportive Policies: The Corporate Decision-making Process.* New York: The Conference Board.

Frykman, Jonas and Orvar Löfgren. 1987. *Culture Builders—A Historical Anthropology of Middle Class Life.* New Brunswick, NJ: Rutgers University Press.

Gainer, William. 1989. Testimony at the Hearing of the Subcommittee on Labor Market Relations, Committee on Education and Labor, U.S. House of Representatives, Feb. 7.

Genevie, Louis and Eva Margolies. 1987. *The Motherhood Report.* New York: Macmillan.

Gerson, Kathleen. 1985. *Hard Choices—How Women Decide about Work, Career, and Motherhood.* Berkeley: University of California Press.

Gilbert, Lucia. 1985. *Men in Dual-Career Families.* Hillsdale, N.J.: Lawrence Erlbaum.

Giveans, David and Michael Robinson. 1985. "Fathers and the Preschool-Age Child." Pp. 115–140 in *Dimensions of Fatherhood, edited by Shirley Hanson and Frederick Bozett. Beverly Hills: Sage.*

Gladstone, Leslie, Jennifer Williams and Richard Belous. 1985. *Maternity and Parental Leave Policies: A Comparative Analysis.* Report No. 85–148, Congressional Research Service. Washington, D.C.: Government Printing Office.

Glenn, Evelyn. 1986. "Gender and the Family." Pp. 348–380 in *Analyzing Gender,* edited by Beth Hess and Myra Marx Ferree. Newbury Park, CA: Sage.

Grimberg, Carl. 1935. *A History of Sweden.* Rock Island, IL: Augustana.

Grossman, Frances, William Pollack, and Ellen Golding. 1988. "Fathers and Children," *Developmental Psychology* 24:82–91.

Grubb, Norton and Marvin Lazerson. 1984. "Gender, Roles and the State." Pp. 247–254 in *Women in the Workplace,* edited by Kathryn Borman. Norwood, N.J.: Ablex.

Grønseth, Erik. 1978. "Work-Sharing: A Norwegian Example." Pp. 108–121 in *Working Couples,* edited by Rhona Rapoport and Robert Rapoport. New York: Harper and Row.

Grönvik, Monica, Eva Sellström, and Göran Swedin. 1988. "Mot ett Jämställdt Föräldraskap? Erfarenheter av Delad Föräldraledighet hos 419 Förstagångsföräldrar i Jämtlands Län [Toward an Equal Parenthood? Experiences of Shared Parental Leave by 419 First-time Parents in Jämtland's County]." Östersund, Sweden: Jämtlands Läns Landsting.

Gustafsson, Siv. 1979. "Women and Work in Sweden." *Working Life in Sweden* #15. New York: Swedish Information Service.

———. 1983. "Equal Employment Policies in Sweden." Stockholm: Arbetslivcentrum [Center for Working Life].

Gustafsson, Siv and Petra Lantz. 1985. *Arbete och Löner—Ekonomika Teorier och Fakta omkring Skillnader mellan Kvinnor och Män* [Work and Pay—Economic Theories and Facts Concerning Differences between Women and Men]. Stockholm: Almqvist and Wiksell.

Göteborgs Stadskansli [Municipal Office of Gothenburg]. 1986. *Statistiska Årsbok-Göteborg* [Statistical Yearbook for Gothenburg].

Haas, Linda. 1980. "Role-Sharing Couples: A Study of Egalitarian Marriages." *Family Relations* 29:289–296.

———. 1981. "Domestic Role-Sharing in Sweden." *Journal of Marriage and the Family* 43:957–967.

———. 1982. "Parental Sharing of Childcare Tasks in Sweden." *Journal of Family Issues* 3:389–412.

———. 1986. "Wives' Orientation toward Breadwinning: Sweden and the United States." *Journal of Family Issues* 7:358–381.

———. 1988. "Understanding Father's Participation in Childcare." Paper presented at the annual meeting of the National Council on Family Relations, Philadelphia.

Haavio-Mannila and Kaisa Kaupinnen. 1990. "Women's Lives and Women's Work in the Nordic Countries." Unpublished manuscript.

Hadenius, Stig. 1985. *Swedish Politics During the 20th Century.* Stockholm: The Swedish Institute.

Hagberg, Jan and Lena Johansson. 1986. *Kvinnors and Mäns Löner* [Women's and Men 's Wages]. Report #3, Information om Arbetsmarkaden [Information on the Labor Market]. Stockholm: Statistiska Centralbyrån.

Hamrin, Björn, Agneta Nilsson, and Claes-Otto Sörman. 1983. *Att Dela På Föräldraledigheten* [Sharing Parental Leave]. Stockholm: Socialstyrelsen.

Hatje, Ann-Katrin. 1974. *Befolkningsfrågan och Välfärden* [The Population Question and Welfare]. Stockholm: Allmänna Förlaget.

Heath, Douglas. 1976. "What Meaning and Effects Does Fatherhood Have for the Maturing of Professional Men?" *Merrill-Palmer Quarterly* 24:265–277.

Hedvall, Barbro. 1975. *Kvinnan i Politiken* [The Woman in Politics]. Stockholm: Trevi.

Hernes, Helga. 1988. "The Welfare State Citizenship of Scandinavian Women." Pp. 187–213 in *The Political Interests of Gender,* edited by Kathleen Jones and Anna Jónasdóttir. London: Sage.

———. 1987 *Welfare State and Woman Power.* Oslo: Norwegian University Press.

Herzog, A. Regula and Jerold Bachman. 1982. *Sex Role Attitudes among High School Seniors.* Ann Arbor. MI: University of Michigan Institute of Social Research.

Hess, Beth. 1984. "Protecting the American Family: Public Policy, Family and the New Right." Pp. 11–21 in *Families and Change.* New York: Praeger.

Hiller, Dana and William Philliber. 1986. "The Division of Labor in Contemporary Marriage: Expectations, Perceptions, and Performance." *Social Problems* 33:191–201.

Hirdman, Yvonne. 1988. "The Swedish Social Democrats and the Importance of Gender—Another Approach to the History of the Swedish Welfare State." Paper prepared for presentation at the New Sweden 1988 Seminars on Women and Power.

Ho, David. 1987. "Fatherhood in Chinese Culture." Pp. 227–246 in *The Father's Role—Cross-Cultural Perspectives,* edited by Michael Lamb. Hillsdale, NJ: Lawrence Erlbaum.

Hochschild, Arlie. 1989. *The Second Shift.* New York: Viking.

Hodgson, Susan. 1979. "Childrearing Patterns." Pp. 126–172 in *The Child in the City, Volume 2,* edited by William Michelson, Saul Levine, and Anna-Rose Spina. Toronto: University of Toronto Press.

Hoem, Britta and Jan Hoem. 1989. "The Impact of Women's Employment on Second and Third Births in Modern Sweden." *Population Studies* 43:47–67.

Hoffman, Lois. 1983. "Increased Fathering: Effects on the Mother." Pp. 167–190 in *Fatherhood and Family Policy,* edited by Michael Lamb and Abraham Sagi. Hillsdale, NJ: Lawrence Erlbaum.

Hofstede, Geert. 1984. *Culture's Consequences.* Beverly Hills: Sage.

Hood, Jane. 1983. *Becoming a Two-Job Family.* New York: Praeger.

Hood, Jane and Susan Golden. 1979. "Beating Time/Making Time: The Impact of Work Scheduling on Men's Family Roles." *Family Coordinator* 28:575–582.

Hopper, Pauline and Edward Zigler. 1988. "The Medical And Social Science Basis for a National Infant Care Leave Policy." *American Journal of Orthopsychiatry* 58:324–338.

Horna, Jarmila and Eugen Lupri. 1987. "Fathers' Participation in Work, Family Life, and Leisure—A Canadian Experience." Pp. 54–73 in *Reassessing Fatherhood,* edited by Charlie Lewis and Margaret O'Brien. London: Sage.

Horrigan, Michael and James Markey. 1990. "Recent Gains in Women's Earnings." *Monthly Labor Review*, July, pp. 11–17.

Huber, Joan. 1976. "Toward a Sociotechnical Theory of the Women's Movement." *Social Problems* 23:371–388.

Huber, Joan and Glenda Spitze. 1983. *Sex Stratification.* New York: Free Press.

Hunt, Janet and Larry Hunt. 1987. "Male Resistance to Role Symmetry in Dual-Earner Households." Pp. 192–203 in *Families and Work*, edited by Naomi Gerstel and Harriet Gross. Philadelphia: Temple University Press.

Hwang, C. Philip. 1985. *Småbarnspappor* [Fathers of Small Children]. Pp. 15–38 in *Faderskap* [Fatherhood], edited by C. Philip Hwang. Stockholm: Natur och Kultur.

———. 1987. "The Changing Role of Swedish Fathers." Pp. 115–138 in *The Father's Role—Crossing-Cultural Perspectives*, edited by Michael Lamb. Hillsdale, NJ: Lawrence Erlbaum.

Hwang, C. Philip, Görel Eldén, and Christer Fransson. 1984. "Arbetsgivares och Arbetskamraters Attityder till Pappaledighet [Employers' and Co-workers' Attitudes toward Fathers Taking Parental Leave]." Gothenburg, Sweden: Göteborgs Universitet, Psykologiska Institutionen, Rapport 31.

Jalakas, Anne. 1986. "Svenskt Babyrecord" [Swedish Baby Record]. *Arbetet* [Social Democratic daily newspaper], May 30, p. 16.

Jalmert, Lars. 1983. *Om Svenska Män* [About Swedish Men]. Stockholm: Arbetsmarknadsdepartementet [Ministry of Labor].

———. 1984. *Den Svenska Mannen* [The Swedish Man]. Stockholm: Tiden.

Jancar, Barbara. 1978. *Women Under Communism.* Baltimore: Johns Hopkins Press.

Jones, L. Collette. 1985. "Father-Infant Relationships in the First Year of Life." Pp. 92–114 in *Dimensions of Fatherhood*, edited by Shirley Hanson and Frederick Bozett. Beverly Hills: Sage.

Jump, Teresa and Linda Haas. 1987. "Fathers in Transition: Dual-Career Fathers Participating in Childcare." Pp. 98–114 in *Changing Men—New Directions in Research on Men and Masculinity*, edited by Michael Kimmel. Newbury Park, CA: Sage.

Kagan, Sharon, Edgar Klugman, and Edward Zigler. 1983. "Shaping Child and Family Policies." Pp. 415–438 in *Children, Families and Government*, edited by Edward Zigler. New York: Cambridge University Press.

Kalleberg, Arne and Rachel Rosenfeld. 1990. "Work in the Family and in the Labor Market: A Cross-National, Reciprocal Analysis." *Journal of Marriage and the Family* 52:331–346.

Kälvemark, Ann-Sofie. 1980. *More Children of Better Quality?—Aspects on Swedish Population Policy in the 1930s.* Stockholm: Almqvist and Wiksell International.

Kamerman, Sheila. 1983. "Fatherhood and Social Policy: Some Insights from a Comparative Perspective." Pp. 23–37 in *Fatherhood and Family Policy*, edited by Michael Lamb and Abraham Sagi. Hillsdale, NJ: Lawrence Erlbaum.

———. 1985. "Time Out for Babies—A Look at Maternity Leave Policies around the World." *Working Mother,* September, pp. 80–81.

———. 1989. "Childcare, Women, Work and the Family: An International Overview of Childcare Services and Related Policies." Pp. 93–110 in *Caring for Children,* edited by Jeffrey Lande, Sandra Scarr, and Nina Gunzenhauser. Hillsdale, NJ: Lawrence Erlbaum.

Kamerman, Sheila and Alfred Kahn. 1978. *Family Policy: Government and Families in Fourteen Countries.* New York: Columbia University Press.

———. 1987. *The Responsive Workplace.* New York: Columbia University Press.

Kamerman, Sheila, Alfred Kahn and Paul Kingston. 1983. *Maternity Policies and Working Women.* New York: Columbia University Press.

Kantrowitz, Barbara. 1988. "The Clamor to Save the Family." *Newsweek,* February 29, pp. 60–61.

———. 1989. "Parental Leave Cries to be Born." *Newsweek,* June 5, p. 65.

Katsh, Beverly. 1981. "Fathers and Infants: Reported Caregiving and Interaction." *Journal of Family Issues* 2:275–96.

Katz, Mary and Melvin Konner. 1981. "The Role of the Father: An Anthropological Perspective." Pp. 155–186 in *The Role of the Father in Child Development,* 2nd edition, edited by Michael Lamb. New York: Wiley.

Kaul, Hjordis and Berit Brandth. 1988. *Lov og Liv—En Sammenlikning av Omsorgspermisjoner i Norden* [Leaves and Lives—A Comparison of Child Care Leaves in the Nordic Countries]. Trondheim, Norway.

Kauppinen, Kaisa and Elina Haavio-Mannilla. 1989. "A Nordic Perspec tive: How Women's Employment Affects Women's Well-Being and Life Satisfaction," unpublished paper.

Kimmel, Michael. 1987. "Rethinking 'Masculinity' ". Pp. 9–24 in *Changing Men—New Directions in Research on Men and Masculinity,* edited by Michael Kimmel. Newbury Park, CA: Sage.

Kingston, Paul. 1990. "Illusions and Ignorance about the Family-Responsive Workplace." *Journal of Family Issues* 11:438–454.

Kjellman, Kalle and Tore Wizelius. 1983. *Pappa Kom Hem* [Daddy Came Home]. Stockholm: Wahlström and Widstrand.

Konsumentverket [Consumer Affairs Agency]. 1982. *Svenska Folkets Tidsanvändning 1981* [Swedish People's Time Use 1981]. Stockholm: Allmänna Byrån/Liber.

Kotelchuk, M. 1976. "The Infant's Relationship to the Father." In *The Role of the Father in Child Development,* edited by Michael Lamb. New York: Wiley.

Kovach, Kenneth. 1987. "Creeping Socialism or Good Public Policy: The Proposed Parental and Medical Leave Act." *Labor Law Journal* 38:427–432.

Kugelberg, Clarissa. 1987. *Allt eller Inget—Barn, Omsorg och Förvärvsarbete* [Everything or Nothing—Children, Child Care and Employment]. Stockholm: Carlssons.

Laber, Pamela. 1986. "The U.S. Labor Movement and Working Women: An Alliance for the Future." Pp. 179–186 in *Family and Work—Bridging the Gap,* edited by Sylvia Hewlett, Alice Ilchman, and John Sweeney. Cambridge, MA: Ballinger.

Lamb, Michael. 1981. "Fathers and Child Development: An Integrative Review." Pp. 1–71 in *The Role of the Father in Child Development,* edited by Michael Lamb. New York: Wiley.

———. 1983. "Introduction." Pp. 1–7 in *Fatherhood and Family Policy,* edited by Michael Lamb and Abraham Sagi. Hillsdale, NJ: Lawrence Erlbaum.

Lamb, Michael and M. Ann Easterbrooks. 1981. "Individual Differences in Parental Sensitivity." Pp. 127–154 in *Infant Social Cognition,* edited by Michael Lamb and Lonnie Sherrod. Hillsdale, NJ: Lawrence Erlbaum.

Lamb, Michael, Ann Frodi, Majt Frodj, and Carl-Philip Hwang. 1982a. "Characteristics of Maternal and Paternal Behavior in Traditional and Nontraditional Swedish Families." *International Journal of Behavioral Development* 5:131–141.

Lamb, Michael, Ann Frodi, Carl-Philip Hwang, Majt Frodi, and Jamie Steinberg. 1982b. "Mother- and Father-Infant Interaction Involving Play and Holding in Traditional and Nontraditional Swedish Families." *Developmental Psychology* 19:215–221.

Lamb, Michael, Majt Frodi, Carl-Philip Hwang, and Ann Frodi. 1983. "Effects of Paternal Involvement on Infant Preferences for Mothers and Fathers." *Child Development* 54:450–458.

Lamb, Michael, Carl-Philip Hwang, Anders Broberg, Fred Bookstein, Gunilla Hult, and Majt Frodi. 1988. "The Determinants of Paternal Involvement in Primiparous Swedish Families." *International Journal of Behavioral Development* 11:433–449.

Lamb, Michael and James Levine. 1983. "The Swedish Parental Insurance Policy: An Experiment in Social Engineering." Pp. 39–51 in *Fatherhood and Social Policy,* edited by Michael Lamb and Abraham Sagi. Hillsdale, NJ: Lawrence Erlbaum.

Lamb, Michael, Joseph Pleck, Eric Charnow, and Jim Levine. 1985. "Paternal Behavior in Humans." *American Zoologist* 25:883–894.

Lamb, Michael, Graeme Russell, and Abraham Sagi. 1983. "Summary and Recommendations for Public Policy." Pp. 247–258 in *Fatherhood and Family Policy,* edited by Michael Lamb and Abraham Sagi. Hillsdale, NJ: Lawrence Erlbaum.

Landsorganisationen i Sverige [LO]. 1976. *Fackföreningsrörelsen och Familjepolitiken* [The Trade Union Movement and Family Policy]. Stockholm: Prisma.

Lapidus, Gail. 1978. *Women in Soviet Society.* Berkeley: University of California Press.

LaRossa, Ralph. 1988. "Fatherhood and Social Change." *Family Relations* 37:451–457.

LaRossa, Ralph and Maureen LaRossa. 1981. *Transition to Parenthood.* Beverly Hills, CA: Sage.

Leijon, Anna-Greta. 1968. *Swedish Women—Swedish Men.* Stockholm: The Swedish Institute.

Lein, Laura. 1979. "Male Participation in Home Life." *Family Coordinator* 28:489–496.

Levine, James. 1976. *Who Will Raise the Children?* New York: Lippincott.

Lewis-Beck, Michael. 1980. *Applied Regression.* Beverly Hills: Sage.

Liljeström, Rita, Gunilla Mellström and Gillan Svensson. 1975. *Sex Roles in Transition—A Report on A Pilot Program in Sweden.* Stockholm: The Swedish Institute.

Liljeström, Rita, Gillan Svensson and Gunilla Mellström. 1976. *Roller i Omvandling—En Rapport På Uppdrag av Delegationen för Jämställdhet mellan Män och Kvinnor* [Roles in Transition—A Report at the Request of the Delegation for Equality between Men and Women]. Stockholm: Justitiedepartementet.

Lindren, Gerd. 1989. "Kamrater, Kollegor och Kvinnor—En Studie av Könssegregeringprocessen [Comrades, Colleagues, and Women—A Study of the Process of Sex Segregation]." Sociologiska Institutionens Forskningsrapporter [Department of Sociology Research Reports]. University of Umeå.

Linnér, Birgitta. 1977. "No Illegitimate Children in Sweden." *Current Sweden* #157. Stockholm: The Swedish Institute.

Löfgren, Orvar. 1976. "Arbetsfördelning och Könsroller i Bondesamhället—Kontinuitet och Förändring" [Division of Labor and Gender Roles in Agricultural Society—Continuity and Change]. Lund, Sweden: Etnologiska Sällskapets Bokförmedling [Ethnological Society's Publication Office].

Lutwin, David and Gary Siperstein. 1985. "Househusband Fathers." Pp. 269–287 in *Dimensions of Fatherhood,* edited by Shirley Hanson and Frederick Bozett. Beverly Hills, CA: Sage.

Lyle, Gunhild and Gunnar Qvist. 1974. *Kvinnorna i Mannens Samhälle* [Women in a Man's Society]. Stockholm: Esselte Studium.

McCrea, Joan. 1979. "Equality of the Sexes in Sweden Under a New Government." *Labour and Society* 4:309–324.

McEntee, Gerald. 1989. Testimony at the Hearing of the Subcommittee on Labor—Market Relations, Committee on Education and Labor. House of Representatives, February 7.

McHale, Susan and Ted Huston. 1984. "Men and Women as Parents." *Child Development* 55:1349–1361.

Mackey, Wade. 1986. *Fathering Behaviors.* New York: Plenum.

McNeely, R. L. and Barbe Fogarty. 1988. "Balancing Parenthood and Employment: Factors Affecting Company Receptiveness to Family—Related Innovations in the Workplace." *Family Relations* 37:189–295.

Makuen, Kathleen. 1988. "Public Servants, Private Parents: Parental Leave Policies in the Public Sector." Pp. 195–210 in *The Parental Leave Crisis—Toward a National Policy,* edited by Edward Zigler and Meryl Frank. New Haven, CT: Yale University Press.

Malo, Annemarie and Mary Anne Murray. 1986. "HR 4300—Maternity Leave: Helping or Hurting, the Viability of the Family?" *Family Policy Insights* 4:1–8.

Margolis, Maxine. 1985. *Mothers and Such.* Berkeley: University of California Press.

Mathews, Iola. 1989. "A Parental Leave Test Case—Background Information." Australian Council of Trade Unions, January.

Meisenheimer, Joseph. 1989. "Employer Provisions for Parental Leave." *Monthly Labor Review,* October, pp. 20–24.

Melsted, Lillemor. 1988. "Swedish Family Policy and the Election This Autumn." *Current Sweden* #361. Stockholm: The Swedish Institute.

Milner, Harry. 1989. *Sweden: Social Democracy in Practice.* Oxford: Oxford Press.

Ministry of Health and Social Affairs. 1979. "Financial Assistance to Families with Children." Stockholm: Ministry of Health and Social Affairs.

Mintz, Steven and Susan Kellogg. 1988. *Domestic Revolutions—A Social History of American Family Life.* New York: Free Press.

Mitchell, Juliet. 1971. *Woman's Estate.* London: Pelican Books.

Moberg, Eva. 1962. *Kvinnor och Män* [Women and Men]. Stockholm: Bonnier.

Moen, Phyllis. 1989. *Working Parents.* Madison: University of Wisconsin Press.

Morgan, David. 1990. "Issues of Critical Sociological Theory: Men in Families." Pp. 67–106 in *Fashioning Family Theory,* edited by Jetsey Sprey. Newbury Park, CA: Sage.

Morgan, Robin. 1984. *Sisterhood is Global.* Garden City, NY: Anchor.

Moss, Peter and Julia Brannen. 1987. "Fathers and Employment." Pp. 36–53 in *Reassessing Fatherhood,* edited by Charlie Lewis and Margaret O'Brien. London: Sage.

Motley, Gerald. 1989. Testimony at the Hearing of the Subcommittee on Labor Market Relations, Committee on Education and Labor, House of Representatives, February 7.

Myrdal, Alva. 1938. "Swedish Women in Industry and at Home." *Annals of the American Academy of Political and Social Sciences* 197:216–223.

Myrdal, Alva and Gunnar Myrdal. 1934. *Kris i Befolkningsfrågan* [Crisis in the Population Question]. Stockholm.

Näsman, Elisabet. 1986. "Work and Family—A Combination Made Possible by Part-time Work and Parental Leaves?" Stockholm: Arbetslivcentrum [Center for Working Life].

Näsman, Elisabet and Eva Falkenberg. 1990. "Parents' Rights in the Work and Family Interface." Stockholm: Arbetslivcentrum.

Näsman, Elisabet, Kristin Nordström, and Rut Hammarström. 1983. *Föräldrars Arbete och Barns Villkor* [Parents' Work and Children's Conditions]. Report #41, Arbetslivcentrum. Stockholm: LiberTryck.

National Social Insurance Board. 1989. Social Insurance Statistics—Facts. Stockholm: National Social Insurance Board.

Nation's Business. 1988. "Congressional Alert." *Nation's Business*, February, p. 87.

Nätti, Jouko. 1990. "A Comparison of Part-time Work in the Nordic Countries." Paper presented at the annual meeting of the World Congress of Sociology, Madrid.

Nelson, Richard. 1988. "State Labor Laws: Changes During 1987." *Monthly Labor Review* 111:38–61.

Nettelbladt, Per. 1984. *Men Pappa Då?* [What about Daddy?] Lund, Sweden: Studentlitteratur.

New, Rebecca and Laura Benigni. 1987. "Italian Fathers and Infants." Pp. 139–168 in *The Father's Role—Cross-Cultural Perspectives*, edited by Michael Lamb. Hillsdale, NJ: Lawrence Erlbaum.

Newland, Kathleen. 1980. "Women, Men and the Division of Labor." *Worldwatch Paper* #37. Washington, D.C.: Worldwatch Institute.

———. 1984. "The Symmetrical Family." Pp. 106–109 in *Families and Change*, edited by Rosalie Genovese. New York: Praeger.

Nickel, Horst and Ellen Köcher. 1987. "West Germany and the German-Speaking Countries." Pp. 89–114 in *The Father's Role—Cross-Cultural Perspectives*, edited by Michael Lamb. Hillsdale, NJ: Lawrence Erlbaum.

Nine to Five. 1988. "New Workforce Policies and the Small Business Sector: Is Family Leave Good for Business?" Cleveland: Nine to Five, National Association of Working Women.

Nock, Steven and Paul Kingston. 1988. "Time with Children: The Impact of Couples' Work—Time Commitments." *Social Forces* 67:59–85.

Nordic Council of Ministers. 1988. *Kvinnor och Män i Norden— Fakta om Jämställdheten* [Women and Men in the Nordic Countries—Facts about Equality]. Stockholm: Nordic Council of Ministers.

Norgren, Jill. 1988. "In Search of a National Child-Care Policy." Pp. 168–189 in *Women, Power, and Policy*, edited by Ellen Boneparth and Emily Stoper. New York: Pergamon Press.

Oakley, Ann. 1974. *Woman's Work*. New York: Vintage.

Oakley, Stewart. 1966. *A Short History of Sweden*. New York: Praeger.

Olofsson, Anita. 1986. *Kvinnor och Män på Arbetsmarknaden* [Women and Men in the Labor Market]. Information om Arbetsmarknaden #2 [Report #2 on Information on the Labor Market]. Stockholm: Statistiska Centralbyrån.

Palkovitz, Rob. 1984. "Parental Attitudes and Fathers' Interactions with their Five-Month Old Infants." *Developmental Psychology* 20:1054–1060.

Parke, Ross and Barbara Tinsley. 1981. "The Father's Role in Infancy." Pp. 429–457 in *Role of the Father in Child Development,* edited by Michael Lamb. New York: Wiley.

Parseval, Genevieve and Francois Hurstel. 1987. "Paternity á la Française." Pp. 59–88 in *The Father's Role—Cross-Cultural Perspectives,* edited by Michael Lamb. Hillsdale, NJ: Lawrence Erlbaum.

Paulsen, Marit, Sture Andersson, and George Sessler. 1975. *Rätten att Vara Människa* [Right to be Human]. Stockholm: Rabén and Sjögren.

Pettersson, Gisela. 1989. "Working Hours in Sweden." *Current Sweden,* #368, June. Stockholm: The Swedish Institute.

Pettersson, Gunnar. 1990. "Is the Swedish Welfare Model Dead?" *Scandinavian Review* 78 (Autumn):14–20.

Piccirillo, Mary. 1988. "The Legal Background of a Parental Leave Policy and Its Implications." Pp. 293–315 in *The Parental Leave Crisis—Toward a National Policy,* edited by Edward Zigler and Meryl Frank. New Haven, CT: Yale University Press.

Pleck, Joseph. 1983. "Husbands' Paid Work and Family Roles: Current Research and Issues." Pp. 251–333 in *Research in the Interweave of Social Roles, volume 3,* edited by Helena Lopata and Joseph Pleck. Greenwich, CT: JAI Press.

———. 1985. "Paternity Leave." Working paper #157, Wellesley College Center for Research on Women.

———. 1986. "Employment and Fatherhood: Issues and Innovative Policies." Pp. 385–412 in *The Father's Role—Applied Perspectives,* edited by Michael Lamb. New York: Wiley.

———. 1987. "The Theory of Male Sex-Role Identity: Its Rise and Fall, 1936 to the Present." Pp. 21–38 in *The Making of Masculinities,* edited by Harry Brod. Boston: Allen and Unwin.

———. 1988. "Fathers and Infant Care Leave." Pp. 177–191 in *The Parental Leave Crisis—Toward a National Policy,* edited by Edward Zigler and Meryl Frank. New Haven, CT: Yale University Press.

———. 1990. "Family-Supportive Employer Policies: Are They Relevant to Men?" Paper presented at the 98th Annual Meeting of the American Psychological Association, Boston.

Pogrebin, Letty Cottin. 1982. "A Feminist in Sweden." *Ms. Magazine* 67:69–70, 82–88.

Polatnick, M. Rivka. 1983. "Why Men Don't Rear Children: A Power Analysis." Pp. 21–39 in *Mothering,* edited by Joyce Trebilcot. Totowa, NJ: Rowman and Allanheld.

Popenoe, David. 1988. *Disturbing the Nest—Family Change and Decline in Modern Societies.* Hawthorne, NY: Aldine de Gruyter.

Pruett, Kyle. 1987. *The Nurturing Father.* New York: Warner Books.

Qvarfort, Anne-Marie, Joan McCrae, and Pauline Kolunda. 1988. "Sweden's National Policy of Equality Between Men and Women." Pp. 161–193 in *Cultural Constructions of Women,* edited by Pauline Kolenda. Salem, WI: Sheffield.

Qvist, Gunnar. 1980. "Policy Towards Women and the Women's Struggle in Sweden." *Scandinavian Journal of History* 5:51–74.

Qvist, Gunnar, Joan Acker, and Val Lorwin. 1984. "Sweden." Pp. 261–285 in *Women and Trade Unionism in Industrialized Countires,* edited by Alice Cook, Val Lorwin, and Arlene Daniels. Philadelphia: Temple University Press.

Radigan, Anne. 1988. *Concept and Compromise—The Evolution of Family Leave Legislation in the U.S. Congress.* Washington, D.C.: WREI.

Radin, Norma. 1982. "Primary Caregiving and Role-Sharing Fathers of Preschoolers." Pp. 173–204 in *Nontraditional Families,* edited by Michael Lamb. Hillsdale, NJ: Lawrence Erlbaum.

———. 1988. "Primary Caregiving Fathers of Long Duration." Pp. 127–143 in *Fatherhood Today,* edited by Phyllis Bronstein and Carolyn Cowan. New York: Wiley.

Ratner, Ronnie. 1980. "The Policy and Problem: Overview of Seven Countries." Pp. 1–52 in *Equal Employment Policy for Women,* edited by Ronnie Ratner. Philadelphia: Temple University Press.

Rhoadie, Eschel. 1989. *Discrimination Against Women—A Global Survey.* Jefferson, N.C.: McFarland.

Ricks, Shirley. 1985. "Father-Infant Interactions: A Review of the Empirical Literature." *Family Relations* 34:505–512.

Riksförsäkringsverket [National Social Insurance Board]. 1984. "Föräldraförsäkringen 1983 [Parental leave 1983]." Statistisk Rapport #9. Stockholm: Matematisk-Statistiska Byrån.

———. 1985. "Föräldraledighet i Samband med Barns Födelse-Barn Födda 1978–1982 [Parental Leave in Connection with Childbirth, for Children Born 1978–1982]." Statistisk Rapport #4. Stockholm: Matematisk-Statistiska Byrån.

———. 1989a. "Föräldraförsäkringen 1986 [Parental Leave 1986]." Statistisk Rapport #8. Stockholm: Matematisk-Statistiska Byrån.

———. 1989b. "Tillfällig Föräldrapenning för Vård av Barn 1987 [Temporary Parental Leave for Care of Children in 1987]." Statistisk Information, #26, October 16.

———. 1990. "Uttag av Föräldrapenning med Anledning av Barns Födelse under Barnets Första Levnadsår [Use of Parental Leave During Child's First Year]." Statistisk Information, #16, September 20.

Risman, Barbara. 1989. "Can Men 'Mother'? Life as a Single Father." Pp. 155–164 in *Gender in Intimate Relationships—A Microstructural Approach,* edited by Barbara Risman and Pepper Schwartz. Belmont, CA: Wadsworth.

Risman, Barbara and Pepper Schwartz. 1989. "Being Gendered: A Microstructural View of Intimate Relationships." Pp. 1–9 in *Gender in Intimate Relationships—A Microstructural Approach,* edited by Barbara Risman and Pepper Schwartz. Belmont, CA: Wadsworth.

Robinson, Bryan and Robert Barret. 1985. *The Developing Father.* New York: Guilford Press.

Röcklinger, Anna-Stina. 1987. "Hur Används Föräldraförsäkringen? [How Is Parental Insurance Used?]" Pp. 85–99 in *Barnfamiljerna och Arbetslivet* [Families with Children and Worklife], edited by Socialdepartementet Stockholm: Socialdepartementet/Gotab.

Rössel, James. 1970. *Kvinnorna och Kvinnorörelsen i Sverige 1850–1950* [Women and the Women's Movement in Sweden 1850–1950]. Stockholm.

Rollén, Berit. 1978. "Gently Towards Equality." *Working Life in Sweden,* #5. New York: Swedish Information Service.

Roos, Patricia. 1985. *Gender and Work.* Albany: State University of New York Press.

Rotundo, E. Anthony. 1985. "American Fatherhood—A Historical Perspective." *American Behavioral Scientist* 29:7–25.

———. 1987. "Patriarchs and Participants: A Historical Perspective on Fatherhood." Pp. 64–80 in *Beyond Patriarchy,* edited by Michael Kaufman. Toronto: Oxford University Press.

Ruggie, Mary. 1984. *The State and Working Women—A Comparative Study of Britain and Sweden.* Princeton, NJ: Princeton University Press.

Russell, Graeme. 1982. *The Changing Role of Fathers.* St. Lucia, Australia: Queensland University Press.

———. 1987. "Fatherhood in Australia." Pp. 331–358 in *The Father's Role—Cross-Cultural Perspectives,* edited by Michael Lamb. Hilldale, NJ: Lawrence Erlbaum.

Russell, Graeme and Norma Radin. 1983. "Increased Paternal Participation: The Fathers' Perspective." Pp. 139–165 in *Fatherhood and Social Policy,* edited by Michael Lamb and Abraham Sagi. Hillsdale, NJ: Lawrence Erlbaum.

Sandlund, Maj-Britt. 1971. "The Status of Women in Sweden—Report for the United Nations 1968." Pp. 290–302 in *The Changing Roles of Men and Women,* edited by Edmund Dahlström. Boston: Beacon Press.

Sandqvist, Karen. 1987a. *Fathers and Family Work in Two Cultures.* Stockholm: Almqvist and Wiksell International.

———. 1987b. "Swedish Family Policy and the Attempt to Change Paternal Roles." Pp. 144–160 in *Reassessing Fatherhood—New Observations on Fathers and Mothers in the Modern Family,* edited by Charlie Lewis and Margaret O'Brien. London: Sage.

———. 1989. Private communication.

Sapiro, Virginia. 1986. "The Women's Movement, Politics and Policy in the Reagan Era." Pp. 122–139 in *The New Women's Movement,* edited by Drude Dahlerup. Hillsbury Park. CA: Sage.

Scanzoni, John. 1983. *Shaping Tomorrow's Families—Theories and Policy in the 21st century.* Beverly Hills, CA: Sage.

Schönnesson, Lena Nilsson. 1986. "Föräldraskap–Delad Föräldraledighet–Jämställdhet [Parenthood–Shared Parental Leave–Equality]." Stockholm: Delegationen för Jämställdhetsforskning [Delegation for Research on Equality].

Schorr, Alvin. 1979. "Views of Family Policy." *Journal of Marriage and the Family* 41:465–467.

Schroeder, Patricia. 1988. "Parental Leave: The Need for a Federal Policy." Pp. 326–332 in *The Parental Leave Crisis—Toward a National Policy,* edited by Edward Zigler and Meryl Frank. New Haven, CT: Yale University Press.

Sciabarrasi, Paula and Kendall Johnson. 1988. "Family and Medical Leave is Necessary for Working Parents." *Civil Liberties*, Winter, p. 8.

Scott, Hilda. 1982. ***Sweden's Right to be Human—Sex Role Equaltiy: The Goal and the Reality.*** London: Allison and Busby.

Selbyg, Arne. 1989. "Why Are Women in Power in the Nordic Countries but Not in the U.S.?" *Scandinavian Review* 77 (4):20–26.

Sellström, Eva and Göran Swedin. 1987. "Mot ett Jämställdt Föräldraskap?—EnStudie över Nyblivna Förstagångsföräldrars Planering inför Föräldraledigheten [Toward Equal Parenthood?—A Study of Prospective First-time Parents' Planning for Parental Leave]." Studier för Vårdutveckling [Studies for Progress in Caregiving] #12. Östersund, Sweden: Vårdhögskolan Östersund [Östersund's College for Caregiving].

Shapiro, Robert, Kelly Patterson, Judith Russell, and John Young. 1987. "Employment and Social Welfare." *Public Opinion Quarterly* 51:268–271.

Shaw, Susan. 1988. "Gender Differences in the Definition and Perception of Household Labor." *Family Relations* 37:333–337.

Shehan, Constance and John Scanzoni. 1988. "Gender Politics in the U.S.," *Family Relations* 37:444–480.

Shorter, Edward. 1976. *The Making of the Modern Family.* London: Collins.

Shreve, Anita. 1987. *Remaking Motherhood.* New York: Viking.

Sidel, Ruth. 1986. *Women and Children Last.* New York: Viking.

Skard, Torild and Elina Haavio-Mannila. 1984. "Equality Between the Sexes—Myth or Reality in Norden." *Daedalus* 113:141–167.

Smith, Audrey and William Reid. 1986. *Role-Sharing Marriage.* New York: Columbia University Press.

Sorrentino, Constance. 1990. "The Changing Family in International Perspective." *Monthly Labor Review,* March, pp. 41–58.

Spakes, Patricia. 1983. *American Family Policy and the Development of Family Impact Analysis.* Cambridge, Mass.: Schenkman.

Spalter-Roth, Roberta and Heidi Hartmann. 1988. *Unnecessary Losses: Costs to Americans of the Lack of Family and Medical Leave.* Washington, D.C.: Institute of Women's Policy Research.

Standard and Poor. 1990. *Standard and Poor's Statistical Service,* November, p. 9. New York: Standard and Poor.

Statens Offentliga Utredningar [Official Government Reports]. 1978. *Föräldraförsäkringen—Betankande av Familjestödsutredningen* [Parental Insurance—Thoughts by the Commission for the Support of Families]. Rapport #39. Stockholm: Gotab.

———. 1979. *Kvinnans Arbete—En Rapport från Jämställdhetskommittén* [Woman's Work—A Reform from the Committee on Equality]. Rapport #89. Stockholm: Gotab.

———. 1982a. *Förvärvsarbete och Föräldraskap* [Employment and Parenthood]. Arbetsmarknadsdepartement [Labor Department]. Rapport #18. Stockholm: Gotab.

———. 1982b. *Enklare Föräldraförsäkring* [Simpler Parental Insurance]. Report #36. Stockholm: Gotab.

Statistiska Centralbyrån [Central Bureau of Statistics]. 1980. *Levnadsförhållanden—Hur Jämställda är Vi?* [Living Conditions—How Equal Are We?] Report #20. Stockholm: Modintryck.

———. 1986a. *Kvinno- och Mans Världen* [The World of Women and Men]. Stockholm, Statistiska Centralbyrån.

———. 1986b. Private communication.

———. 1987. *På Tal om Kvinnor och Män* [Talking about Women and Men]. Stockholm: Statistiska Centralbyrån.

———. 1988. *Statistisk Årsbok 1989* [Statistical Yearbook for 1989]. Stockholm: Statistiska Centralbyrån.

———. 1990. *På Tal om Kvinnor och Män* [Talking about Women and Men]. Stockholm: Statistiska Centralbyrån.

Swedish Institute. 1987. "Childcare in Sweden." *Facts Sheets on Sweden.* Stockholm: The Swedish Institute.

———. 1988. "General Facts on Sweden." *Facts Sheets on Sweden.* Stockholm: The Swedish Institute.

———. 1989a. "Equality between Men and Women in Sweden." *Fact Sheets on Sweden,* September. Stockholm: The Swedish Institute.

———. 1989b. "Facts and Figures about Youth in Sweden." *Fact Sheets on Sweden,* September. Stockholm: The Swedish Institute.

———. 1989c. "Religion in Sweden." *Fact Sheets on Sweden,* March. Stockholm: The Swedish Institute.

———. 1989d. "The Swedish Population." *Fact Sheets on Sweden,* November. Stockholm: The Swedish Institute.

Sweeney, John. 1986. "Collective Bargaining's Role in the Determination of Family Policy." Pp. 17–22 in *Family and Work—Bridging the Gap,* edited by Sylvia Hewlett, Alice Ilchman, and John Sweeney. Cambridge, MA: Ballinger.

Tiller, Per. 1971. "Parental Role Division and the Child's Personality Development." Pp. 79–104 in *The Changing Roles of Men and Women,* edited by Edmund Dahlström. Boston: Beacon.

Tjänstemannens Centralorganisationen (TCO) [Central Organization of Salaried Employees]. 1976. *Familjepolitiskt Program* [Program for Family Policy]. Stockholm: TCO.

Török, Pal. 1990. "Forskning Bekräftar Fördomar om Föräldraledighet [Research Concerning Prejudices Regarding Parental Leave]." *Lag & Avtal* [Law and Contract], #5: 15–16.

Trost, Jan. 1983a. *Mäns Åsikter om Ledighet från Arbete* [Men's Views Concerning Leave from Work]. Familjerapporter #3. Uppsala: University of Uppsala.

———. 1983b. "The Changing Role of Swedish Women in Family and Society." Pp. 225–242 in *The Changing Position of Women in Family and Society—A Cross-National Comaprison,* edited by Eugen Lupri. Leiden: E. J. Brill.

Uddenberg, Nils. 1982. *Den Urholkade Fadern* [The Hollowed Out Father]. Stockholm: Wahlström and Widstrand.

U.S. Department of Labor. 1989. *Employment and Earnings* 36:38.

———. 1990. *Bureau of Labor Statistics Update,* Winter.

U.S. News and World Report. 1986. "Require Firms to Give 'Family Leave?' " *U.S. News and World Report,* July 28, pp. 63–64.

Ve, Hildur. 1989. "The Male Gender Role and Responsibility for Child Care." Pp. 249–261 in *Changing Patterns of European Family Life,* edited by Katja Boh, Maren Bok, Cristine Clason, Maja Pankratova, Jens Qvortrup, Giovanni Sgritta, and Kari Waerness. London: Routledge.

Verney, Douglas. 1972. "Foundations of Modern Sweden." *Political Studies* 20:42–59.

Von Hall, Gunilla. 1989. "Pappan i Huvudrollen—Om Kvinnan Vill [The Father in the Primary Role—If the Woman Wants]." *Dagens Nyheter,* July 22, p. A2.

Wahlström, Björn. 1981. "Viktigare Ge Jobb än Ledighet [More Important to Give Jobs than Leaves]." *Dagens Nyheter,* July 15, p. 3.

Wall Street Journal. 1988. "People Patterns." *Wall Street Journal,* February 4, p. 1.

Warner, Rebecca. 1986. "Alternative Strategies for Measuring Household Division of Labor: A Comparison." *Journal of Family Issues* 7:179–198.

Weisner, Thomas and Ronald Gallimore. 1977. "My Brother's Keeper: Child and Sibling Caretaking." *Current Anthropology* 18:169–180.

Widerberg, Karin. 1978. "Social Change and the Law: The Example of Women's Legal and Social Position in Sweden 1750–1978." Paper presented at the World Congress of Sociology, Uppsala.

———. 1985. "Världens Bästa Reformer—En Fråga om Perspectiv? Den Svenska Föräldraledighets Lagstiftningen i Rampljuset [The World's Best Reforms—A Question of Perspective? The Swedish Parental Leave Legislation in the Limelight]." *Tidskrift för Rättsociologi [Journal of Legal Sociology]* 2:109–123.

Wisensale, Steven and Michael Allison. 1989. "Family Leave Legislation: State and Federal Initiatives." *Family Relations* 38:182–189.

Wistrand, Birgitta. 1981. *Swedish Women on the Move.* Stockholm: The Swedish Institute.

World Almanac. 1989. *The World Almanac and Book of Facts.* New York: Pharos.

Yogev, Sara. 1981. "Do Professional Women have Egalitarian Marital Relationships?" *Journal of Marriage and the Family* 43:865–872.

Yogman, Michael. 1984. "Competence and Performance of Fathers and Infants." Pp. 130–145 in *Progress in Child Health, volume 1,* edited by J. A. Macfarlane. Edinburgh: Churchill Livingstone.

Yogman, Michael, James Cooley and Daniel Kindlon. 1988. "Fathers, Infants, and Toddlers." Pp. 53–65 in *Fatherhood Today,* edited by Phyllis Bronstein and Carolyn Cowan. New York: Wiley.

York, Carolyn. 1991. "The Labor Movement's Role in Parental Leave and Child Care." Pp. 176–186 in Parental Leave and Child Care, edited by Janet Hyde and Marilyn Essex. Philadelphia: Temple University Press.

Zacur, Susan, Sue Greenfield, and Donald Drost. 1989. "Parental Leave: U.S. Employer Action is Inevitable." *Business and Public Affairs* 16:5–10.

Zigler, Edward and Meryl Frank. 1988. "Conclusion." Pp. 346–352 in *The Parental Leave Crisis—Toward a National Policy,* edited by Edward Zigler and Meryl Frank. New Haven, CT: Yale University Press.

Index

Acker, Joan, 39, 41, 282
Adamo, Amelia, 24, 265
Adams, Carolyn, 9, 11, 20, 23, 26, 27, 45, 46, 48, 51, 197, 198, 265
Agassi, Judith, 13, 265
Aldous, Joan, 198, 269
Allen, Joseph, 25, 50, 265
Allison, Michael, 191, 288
Andersen, Margaret, 204, 265
Anderson, Elaine, 2, 267
Andersson, Sture, 43, 281
Arbetsgruppen om Mansrollen, 42, 66, 265. *See also* Commission to study men's roles
Arbetsmarknadsstyrelsen, 27, 41, 265
Aschenbrenner, Barbara, 97, 270

Babbie, Earl, 234, 265
Bachman, Jerold, 85, 273
Backett, Kathryn, 25, 97, 154, 265
Barnett, Rosalind, 3, 97, 265
Barret, Robert, 89, 283
Baruch, Grace, 3, 97, 265
Barry, Herbert, 4, 266
Baude, Annika, 13, 27, 28, 33, 40, 42, 266
Beer, William, 135, 266
Belous, Richard, 188, 189, 204, 271
Belsky, Jay, 4, 266
Bengtsson, Margot, 43, 266
Benigni, Laura, 1, 280
Benokraitis, Nijole, 2, 10, 84, 97, 266
Berger, Birgitte, 205, 266
Berger, Peter, 205, 266
Bernard, Jessie, 10, 11, 266
Bernhardt, Eva, 231, 266
Bernheim, Nicole, 53, 266
Bernstein, Aaron, 189, 200, 203, 266
Bird, Gerald, 110, 266
Bird, Gloria, 110, 266
Birth rate: as a reason for maternity leave in Sweden, 19–23, 220; in the U.S., 192–93. *See also* Delayed parenthood
Blau, Francine, 9, 266
Bode, Jerry, 2, 268
Bookstein, Fred, 277
Booth, Alan, 1, 3, 266
Boredom: men's problems with, 131, 134; women's problems with, 143
Bosanquet, Helen, 5, 6, 266
Bozhkov, O. B., 1, 266
Bradley, Robert, 11, 267
Brandth, Berit, 12, 63, 93, 104, 105, 110, 111, 112, 267, 275
Brannen, Julia, 1, 12, 14, 279
Branson, Meredith, 2, 267
Brazelton, T. Berry, 196, 200, 206, 267
Breadwinner role: advantages of, 11; American attitudes toward, 213; development of, 6; disadvantages of, 10; encourage of Swedish women to take on, 37–38; effects of attitudes toward, on Swedish men's taking parental leave, 89–90, 97; policies which advocate

Breadwinner Role (*continued*)
sharing of, 12; Swedish attitudes toward, 90, 97
Breastfeeding: as a barrier to child care sharing, 7–8; as a determinant of fathers' taking parental leave, 64, 82, 115–18, 122–25; as a determinant of women's leave satisfaction, 148, 149; extent of, 117
Broberg, Anders, 277
Bronfenbrenner, Urie, 196, 267
Bronstein, Phyllis, 1, 267
Brown, Charles, 29, 267
Brown, Judith, 7, 267
Bureau of National Affairs, 14, 189, 267
Business Week, 201, 203, 267
Butler, Barbara, 200, 267

Calleman, Catharina, 175–77, 267
Caplan-Cotenoff, Scott, 188, 189, 267
Catalyst, 211, 268
Chafetz, Janet, 153, 226, 268
Charnow, Eric, 277
Child allowance, 23–24
Child care: difficulties with, 131, 133; dislike of, 131, 135, 138, 143; effects of industrialization on, 4–6; effects on women's employment, 2; growing interest in men's participation in, 8–9; impact of biology on, 3–8; as responsibility of women, 1–2; why men might not want to share, 11. *See also* Child care sharing; Equal parenthood; Parenting ability
Child care experience. *See* Parenting experience
Child care sharing: attitudes toward, 89; breastfeeding as obstacle to, 7–8; differences in Swedish mothers' and fathers' reports of, 158; disadvantages of, 11; effects of couples' sharing parental leave on, 158–64; effects of father's early involvement on, 154–55; effects of Swedish men's employment on, 163–64; effects of Swedish women's employment on, 164–65, 178; measures of, 156–58
Childhood socialization, 85–86, 95–96. *See also* Role models
Childrearing experts, 6
Children: American attitudes toward, 198, 206; and their capacity for developing relationships with both parents, 7; concern for well-being of, 9–10, 23, 25; and their need for mothers, 4; as reason for developing parental leave, 24–25; rights of, in Sweden, 24; status of, 5; Swedish attitudes toward, 24–25, 219, 220
Childs, Marquis, 48, 268
Chodorow, Nancy, 3, 268
Clarke-Stewart, K. Alison, 7, 268
Clay, William, 202, 208, 268
Cohabitation: as a determinant of couples' sharing parental leave, 114–15; Swedish incidence of, 53, 114; Swedish laws concerning, 37
Cohen, Susan, 204, 205, 268
Cohen, Theodore, 3, 85, 268
Commission to study men's roles, 42, 74. *See also* Arbetsgruppen
Condran, John, 2, 268
Congressional Digest, 200, 268
Cooley, James, 9, 10, 97, 288
Coverman, Shelly, 85, 268
Curtis, Patrick, 118, 268

Daddy days, 66
Dagens Nyheter, 103, 106, 265
Dahlström, Edmund, 39, 268
Daycare: cost effectiveness of, in Sweden, 50; development of, in Sweden, 28, 43; effects of limited access to, 176–77, 185; opposi-

tion to, in Sweden, 26; in the U.S., 205, 215
Day, Randal, 1, 268
Delayed parenthood, in Sweden, 114–15, 132
Demos, John, 6, 268
Determinants of Swedish fathers' participation in parental leave: family contextual, 113–18, 120, 122–25; mothers as, 90, 93, 95, 119, 123–26, 149; social psychological, affecting men, 84–92, 120, 122–25; social psychological, affecting women 92–98, 120, 122–25; social structural, affecting men, 98–108, 120, 122–25; social structural, affecting women, 109–13, 120, 122–25
DiLeonardi, Joan, 118, 268
Doctrine of separate spheres, 6, 26
Doherty, Kathleen, 200, 268
Domestic labor, 37, 44, 153
Dowd, Nancy, 174, 198, 269
Drost, Donald, 190, 194, 288
Dumon, Wilfried, 198, 269

Easterbrooks, M. Ann, 1, 9, 10, 269, 276
Economic productivity: and parental leave in Sweden, 49–50, 99; and parental leave in the U.S., 190; in Sweden, 25–26, 33, 43, 50; in the U.S., 194, 201, 211
Edelman, Marian, 206, 269
Eduards, Maud, 28, 41, 45, 47, 50, 51, 74, 88, 269
Education: as a determinant of leave satisfaction, 148; as a determinant of men's taking parental leave, 104; free, 24; women's 27, 54. *See also* Schools
Edwards, John, 1, 3, 266
Effects of Swedish father's participation in parental leave: on child care sharing, 154–66; on men's employment, 178–84; on women's employment, 166–71, 184, 185
Ehrensaft, Diane, 2, 9, 10, 269
Eidem, Rolf, 104, 269
Eisenstein, Zillah, 9, 153, 269
Eldén, Görel, 84, 101, 104, 110, 130, 132, 138, 274
Ellingsaeter, Anne Lise, 165, 269
Employer resistance to equal parenthood in Sweden, 49–50, 98, 99, 101, 103
Employment: effects of leavetaking on gender differences in, 171–74, 181, 185; effects of men's taking leave on women's, 166–77; effects of taking leave on men's, 98–106. *See also* Job type
Employment discrimination: in Sweden, 174–75; in U.S., 188, 194. *See also* Sex segregation
Equal parenthood: advantages of, for children, 9–10; advantages of, for men, 10; advantages of, for women, 9; American attitudes toward, 195; attitudes toward, 9, 11; definition of, 8; disadvantages of, for men, 11; extent of, in Sweden, 165; growing interest in 8–10; prospects for, 226–29; and social policy, 12; stages of, 227; Swedish attitudes toward, 40–41, 153, 218–20. *See also* Child care sharing
Ericsson, Ylva, 23, 24, 30, 31, 32, 35, 36, 37, 42, 183, 269
Experiences with parental leave: effects of leave length on, 137–38; effects of self-selection on, 139; effects of sharing on 147; family context correlates of, 136, 148; gender differences in, 144; men's, 130–35; social psychological correlates of, 136, 148; social structural correlates of, 136, 139, 148, 150; women's, 141–50. *See*

also Problems with taking parental leave; Satisfaction with parental leave

Fagerström, Eva, 110, 269
Falkenberg, Eva, 25, 36, 38, 61, 73, 269, 279
Falwell, Jerry, 204–205, 269
Familjepolitiska Kommittén, 269
Family and Medical Leave Act, 190–91, 209, 212, 219
Family contextual determinants of couples' sharing parental leave, 114–18, 120, 122
Family size, 23, 115–16
Farmer, Helen, 9, 269
Fasteau, Marc, 11, 270
Fatherhood, 6, 8, 11, 195–96
Fathers, 4, 55. *See also* Fathers' participation in parental leave Fathers' participation in parental leave: determinants of, in Sweden, 68, 83–128, 225; extent of , in Sweden, 60–66, 69, 73, 74, 120, 127–28, 224, 227; extent of, in the U.S., 207–12; factors related to Swedish attitudes toward, 78–81, 95; Swedish attitudes toward, 74–78, 95, 221. *See also* Experiences with parental leave; Problems with taking parental leave
Fein, Robert, 9, 270
Feinstein, Frederick, 202, 208, 268
Feldman, S. Shirley, 97, 270
Feminist movement: and interest in equal parenthood, 10; in Sweden, 45–47, 99; in the U.S., 188, 190, 196, 198–99
Ferree, Myra, 98, 269
Fertility rate. *See* Birth rate
Field, Tiffany, 4, 270
Flanagan, Robert, 37, 270
Fleming, Jeanne, 195, 270
Forsberg, Mats, 23, 24, 270
Frank, Meryl, 11, 22, 188, 189, 270, 288
Fransson, Christer, 84, 101, 104, 110, 130, 132, 138, 274
Fredrika Bremer Society, 45, 47, 74
Fredriksson, Ingrid, 32, 270
Friedl, Ernestine, 7, 270
Friedman, Dana, 190, 194, 203, 270
Frodi, Ann, 155, 276, 277
Frodj, Majt, 155, 276, 277
Frykman, Jonas, 5, 43, 55, 266, 270
Försäkringskassan, 73, 270

Gainer, William, 191, 271
Gallimore, Ronald, 4, 288
Gatekeepers, women as, 90, 93, 97–98, 149, 150. *See also* Determinants of fathers' participation in parental leave
Gender differences: in employment in Sweden, 171–73; in parenting, 1–3, 155
Gender role attitudes: as determinants of satisfaction with parental leave, 136, 148, 149; as determinants of Swedish couples' sharing parental leave, 87, 89–92, 96, 97, 104–105, 124–25; in Sweden, 88–89, 90, 96; Swedish debate on, 38
Genevie, Louis, 97, 271
Gerson, Kathleen, 92, 271
Gilbert, Lucia, 3, 271
Giveans, David, 10, 84, 271
Gladstone, Leslie, 188, 189, 204, 271
Glenn, Evelyn, 5, 271
Goldberg, Wendy, 1, 10, 269
Golden, Susan, 10, 256, 273
Golding, Ellen, 97, 271
Golofast, V. B., 1, 266
Gothenburg survey: in-person interviews in, 236; response bias in, 234–45; response rate in, 234; sampling for, 231–34; sampling bias in, 232–33
Government: American suspicion of, 197, 202; relationship with mar-

ket and family, 50, 202; Swedish trust in, 50
Greenfield, Sue, 190, 194, 288
Grimberg, Carl, 54, 271
Grossman, Frances, 97, 271
Grubb, Norton, 198, 271
Grønseth, Erik, 9, 10, 155–56, 271
Grönvik, Monica, 104, 110, 271
Gustafsson, Siv, 22, 27, 28, 29, 30, 32, 34, 35, 36, 50, 194, 271, 272
Göteborgs Stadskansli, 233, 272

Haas, Linda, 1, 3, 10, 11, 44, 89, 97, 178, 210, 272, 274
Haavio-Mannila, Elina, 12, 35, 54, 55, 272, 276, 285
Hadenius, Stig, 24, 272
Hagberg, Jan, 34, 35, 272
Hammarström, Rut, 44, 280
Hamrin, Björn, 84, 85, 93, 99, 101, 106, 107, 110, 116, 130, 132, 138, 141, 272
Hartmann, Heidi, 201, 285
Hatje, Ann-Katrin, 19, 21, 24, 272
Health care, in Sweden, 22–24
Heath, Douglas, 97, 272
Hedvall, Barbro, 44, 272
Hernes, Helga, 45, 46, 50, 272, 273
Herzog, A. Regula, 85, 273
Hess, Beth, 205, 273
Hiller, Dana, 2, 9, 97, 273
Hirdman, Yvonne, 20, 21, 26, 273
Ho, David, 13, 273
Hochschild, Arlie, 97, 165, 273
Hodgson, Susan, 10, 273
Hoem, Britta, 33, 273
Hoem, Jan, 33, 273
Hoffman, Lois, 9, 166, 273
Hofstede, Geert, 196, 273
Hood, Jane, 10, 97, 112, 156, 273
Hopper, Pauline, 206, 273
Horna, Jarmila, 1, 273
Horrigan, Michael, 241, 274
Housing subsidies, in Sweden, 22–24
Huber, Joan, 9, 274
Hult, Gunilla, 277
Hunt, Janet, 112, 274
Hunt, Larry, 112, 274
Hurstel, Francois, 1, 281
Huston, Ted, 97, 278
Hwang, C. Philip, 1, 4, 7, 84, 85, 86, 101, 104, 110, 117, 130, 132, 138, 155, 274, 276, 277

Income: as a determinant of leave satisfaction, 149, 150; as a determinant of Swedish men's taking parental leave, 68, 101, 103, 105–106, 111–12; effects of Swedish men's taking leave on men's, 180–82; effects of Swedish men's taking leave on women's, 168–71, 173; gender differences in, in Sweden, 54, 171, 173, 215; gender differences in, in the U.S., 193, 215; problems while on parental leave, 132, 138, 143, 145, 150; Swedish women's, 34–35, 54, 112. *See also* Wage solidarity policy
Individualism, 196–97, 200
Industrialization, 4–8
Information campaigns, in Sweden: effects of attentiveness to, on couples' sharing parental leave, 69, 73, 101, 113; men's attentiveness to, 107–108, 113; success of, 80; women's attentiveness to, 113, 149
Interview procedures, 236
Isolation. *See* Loneliness

Jacobsson, Ranveig, 23, 24, 30, 32, 35, 36, 37, 42, 183, 269
Jalakas, Anne, 23, 274
Jalmert, Lars, 7, 42, 75, 274
Jancar, Barbara, 13, 274
Job satisfaction: effects of men's taking leave on Swedish women's, 168–70; effects of taking leave on

Swedish men's, 169, 175–76, 179–80, 182; effects of taking leave on Swedish women's, 175; measure of, 167; sex differences in, 172
Johansson, Lena, 34, 35, 272
Johnson, Kendall, 200, 285
Jones, L. Collette, 1, 4, 274
Jump, Teresa, 11, 97, 178, 274

Kagan, Sharon, 192, 274
Kahn, Alfred, 12, 188, 189, 193, 194, 203, 275
Kalleberg, Arne, 34, 165, 275
Kamerman, Sheila, 11, 12, 14, 33, 188, 189, 193, 194, 203, 206, 217, 275
Kantrowitz, Barbara, 189, 191, 200, 207, 275
Katsh, Beverly, 1, 275
Katz, Mary, 1, 275
Katzenstein, Mary, 204, 205, 268
Kaul, Hjordis, 63, 275
Kaupinnen, Kaisa, 12, 35, 55, 272, 276
Kellogg, Susan, 5, 279
Kimmel, Michael, 97, 276
Kindlon, Daniel, 9, 10, 97, 288
Kingston, Paul, 3, 188, 190, 203, 211, 275, 276, 280
Kjellman, Kalle, 132, 134, 138, 276
Klugman, Edgar, 192, 274
Knowing men who took leave, 101, 107, 113
Kolunda, Pauline, 12, 23, 33, 51, 198, 282
Konner, Melvin, 1, 275
Konsumentverket, 44, 276
Kotelchuk, M., 2, 276
Kovach, Kenneth, 200, 201, 276
Kugelberg, Clarissa, 34, 276
Kvande, Elin, 12, 93, 104, 105, 110, 111, 112, 267
Källvemark, Ann-Sofie, 19, 20, 22, 275
Köcher, Ellen, 1, 280

Laber, Pamela, 203, 204, 276
Labor market status, 167–69, 214. *See also* Women's employment
Lagercrantz, Lena, 267
Lamb, Michael, 3, 4, 7, 9, 11, 12, 61, 66, 98, 155, 160, 231, 276, 277
Landsorganisationen i Sverige (LO), 30, 31, 36, 39–40, 41, 73, 277
Lantz, Petra, 27, 28, 32, 34, 35, 272
Lapidus, Gail, 12, 13, 277
LaRossa, Maureen, 97, 277
LaRossa, Ralph, 1, 2, 11, 97, 195, 277
Lazerson, Marvin, 198, 271
Leave to care for sick children, in Sweden, 41–42, 67
Leijon, Anna-Greta, 26, 37, 277
Lein, Laura, 107, 277
Length of parental leave: as a determinant of child care sharing, 165; as a determinant of satisfaction with leave, 137–38, 149; as a determinant of women's employment, 175
Leslie, Leigh, 2, 267
Levine, James, 9, 12, 61, 66, 277
Lewis-Beck, Michael, 118, 277
Liljeström, Rita, 44, 54, 277, 278
Lindgren, Gerd, 36, 278
Linnér, Birgitta, 24, 278
Lipner, Robyn, 22, 188, 189, 270
LO. *See* Landorganisationen i Sverige
Loneliness: men's problems with, 131–34, 138; women's problems with, 143, 145
Lorwin, Val, 39, 41, 282
Lupri, Eugen, 1, 273
Lutwin, David, 135, 278
Lyle, Gunhild, 45, 278
Löfgren, Orvar, 5, 54, 55, 270, 278

McCrae, Joan, 12, 23, 33, 51, 198, 282

McCrea, Joan, 29, 278
McEntee, Gerald, 190, 201, 278
McHale, Susan, 97, 278
Mackey, Wade, 1, 3, 4, 268, 278
Makuen, Kathleen, 191, 278
Male power, 153
Malo, Annemarie, 202, 278
Margolies, Eva, 97, 271
Margolis, Maxine, 4, 5, 6, 9, 279
Markey, James, 211, 274
Maternal instinct, 3–4
Maternity leave: in Sweden, 22, 32–33, 41; in the U.S., 188
Mathews, Iola, 14, 202, 279
Meisenheimer, Joseph, 189, 191, 279
Mellström, Gunilla, 44, 54, 277, 278
Melsted, Lillemor, 279
Men's crisis centers, 42–43
Men's employment: effects of child care sharing on, 178; effects of parental leave on, 172, 174, 178–83. *See also* Income; Promotion Opportunities; Work commitment; Work hours; Work hour preferences
Men's liberation: in Sweden, 38, 42–43; in the U.S., 195
Microstructural perspective, 97–98
Military: in Sweden, 52; in the U.S., 200
Milner, Harry, 203, 279
Ministry of Health and Social Affairs, 69, 73, 74, 279
Mintz, Steven, 5, 279
Mitchell, Juliet, 53, 279
Moberg, Eva, 38–39, 47, 55, 279
Moen, Phyllis, 50, 279
Morgan, David, 10, 195–96, 279
Morgan, Robin, 14, 279
Moss, Peter, 1, 12, 14, 279
Mothers' labor force participation: effects of Swedish fathers' taking parental leave on, 37–38; effects of Swedish social policy on, 20, 22, 26–32; and interest in child care sharing, 9; Swedish increase in, 26, 33; in the U.S., 191–93, 195
Mothers' participation in parental leave, in Sweden: 60–61, 63–66. *See also* Experiences with taking parental leave, Problems with taking parental leave
Motley, Gerald, 197, 200, 213, 279
Murray, Mary Anne, 202, 278
Myrdal, Alva, 20, 21, 22, 41, 54, 279
Myrdal, Gunnar, 20, 21, 22, 279

Nash, Sharon, 97, 270
National Labor Market Board, 27, 40. *See also* Arbetsmarknadsstyrelsen
National Social Insurance Board, 61, 111, 280
Nation's Business, 202, 280
Nelson, Richard, 191, 280
Nettelbladt, Per, 7, 280
New, Rebecca, 1, 280
Newland, Kathleen, 4, 9, 11, 13, 217, 227, 280
Newsweek, 207, 275
Nickel, Horst, 1, 12, 280
Nilsson, Agneta, 84, 85, 93, 99, 101, 105, 106, 107, 110, 116, 130, 132, 138, 141, 272
Nine to Five, 201, 280
Nock, Stephen, 3, 280
Nonsocialist parties in Sweden: and attitudes toward gender equality, 29, 30, 49; and support for parental leave, 41, 43; tax policy of, 28
Nontraditional jobs. *See* Job type; Sex segregation
Nordic Council of Ministers, 12, 14, 63, 280
Nordic countries: fathers' participation in parental leave in, 63, 208; interest in equal parenthood in, 12; parental leave programs in, 14; participation of women in politics in, 45, 46

Nordström, Kristin, 44, 280
Norgren, Jill, 192, 280
Näsman, Elisabet, 22, 24, 36, 44, 73, 176, 279, 280
Nätti, Jouko, 34, 67, 280

Oakley, Ann, 3, 6, 280
Oakley, Stewart, 47, 280
Olofsson, Anita, 34, 281

Pacifism. *See* Military
Palkovitz, Rob, 97, 281
Parenting ability: as a determinant of child care sharing, 3, 4, 85; as a determinant of Swedish men's sharing parental leave, 86, 87, 90, 96; as an effect of men's sharing parental leave, 159–64; measures of, 157–58; and men's work hours, 165; Swedish attitudes toward, 88–89, 96
Parenting experience: as a determinant of satisfaction with parental leave, 136, 148; as a determinant of Swedish fathers' taking parental leave, 86, 96; Swedish mothers' and fathers', 86, 90, 96
Parental leave in Sweden: attitudes toward reforms in, 74–76; basic rules for, 13–14; 209, 224; in comparison to other countries, 12, 14; compensation for, 13–14; financing of, 14, 43; flexibility of, 66; gender differences in use of, 63–64; percentage of workers using, 99; rule changes for, 43, 60, 66, 69, 73; use of paid vs. other, 65–66, 68, 208–209, 212. *See also* Experiences with parental leave; Fathers' participation in parental leave; Length of parental leave; Mothers' participation in parental leave; Problems with taking parental leave, Satisfaction with parental leave
Parental leave in the U.S.: attitudes toward, 190–96; company attitudes toward, 211–12; company programs for, 189–90, 203; costs of, 190, 201; development of, 187–91; economic obstacles to 200–204; ideological obstacle to, 204–206; in individual states, 191; length of, 189; parents' access to, 189-90; political obstacles to, 196–200; unpaid, 208–209, 212. *See also* Fathers' participation in parental leave, Mothers' participation in parental leave
Parental leave outside Sweden and the U.S., 14, 62–63, 202. *See also* Nordic countries
Parke, Ross, 4, 281
Parseval, Genevieve, 1, 281
Patterson, Kelly, 285
Paulsen, Marit, 43, 281
Paxson, Leonora, 4, 266
Petersson, Ann, 267
Pettersson, Gisela, 34, 35, 183, 214, 281
Pettersson, Gunnar, 25, 281
Philliber, William, 2, 9, 97, 273
Piccirillo, Mary, 189, 281
Pleck, Joseph, 3, 6, 9, 10, 61, 67, 85, 86, 98, 107, 156, 165, 178, 189, 208, 277, 281, 282
Pogrebin, Letty, 103, 282
Polatnick, M. Rivka, 11, 282
Politics: American, 196–200; American women's participation in, 198; Swedish, 45–47, 198; Swedish women's participation in, 44–45
Pollack, William, 197, 271
Poponoe, David, 53, 282
Population Committee, 21–22, 26
Pregnancy: and American women's employment rights, 188–89; Discrimination Act, 188–89, 199; leave in Sweden, 30, 64

Problems with taking parental leave in Sweden: as determinants of satisfactory leaves, 138; gender differences in, 144; types of, 131–35, 144–45
Professional and managerial jobs. *See* Job type
Promotion opportunities, effects of leavetaking on: men's, 172, 174–76, 180–82; women's 168, 172, 174–76
Pruett, Kyle, 9, 10, 282
Public sector employment: as a determinant of men's leavetaking, 101, 103, 109–110; development of, in Sweden, 26; gender differences in, 35; incomes in Swedish, 34–35

Qvarfort, Anne-Marie, 12, 23, 33, 51, 198, 282
Qvist, Gunnar, 39, 41, 45, 48, 54, 278, 282

Radigan, Anne, 190, 207, 282
Radin, Norma, 1, 10, 85, 97, 160, 178, 213, 282, 284
Ratner, Ronnie, 194, 282
Reid, William, 9, 10, 285
Religion: in Sweden, 53; in the U.S., 198, 204–205
Response bias in Gothenburg survey, 234–35
Response rate, in Gothenburg survey, 14, 234
Rhoadie, Eschel, 36, 37, 45, 282
Ricks, Shirley, 10, 282
Riksförsäkringsverket, 43, 61, 62, 63, 64, 66, 67, 68, 74, 111, 120, 233, 282, 283
Risman, Barbara, 84, 97, 226, 229, 283
Robinson, Bryan, 89, 283
Robinson, Michael, 10, 84, 271
Role bargaining, 93–95
Role models: as determinants of couples' sharing parental leave, 85–87, 95–96, 228, as determinants of men's experiences with parental leave, 136
Rollén, Berit, 37, 283
Roos, Patricia, 12, 228, 283
Rosenfeld, Rachel, 34, 165, 275
Rotundo, E. Anthony, 6, 283
Ruggie, Mary, 26, 28, 30, 37, 49, 54, 284
Russell, Graeme, 1, 9, 10, 85, 98, 135, 156, 178, 213, 277, 284
Russell, Judith, 285
Röcklinger, Anna-Stina, 61, 62, 283
Rössel, James, 54, 283

Sagi, Abraham, 11, 98, 277
Sampling, in Gothenburg survey, 17, 231–34
Sundlund, Maj-Britt, 27, 284
Sandqvist, Karin, 1, 44, 52, 68, 97, 199, 200, 210, 284
Sapiro, Virginia, 205, 284
Satisfaction with parental leave: correlates of Swedish men's, 138, 140; gender differences in, 142–43; Swedish men's, 130; Swedish women's, 142–43. *See also* Experiences with parental leave; Problems with parental leave
Scanzoni, John, 192, 193, 198, 284, 285
Schools, in Sweden, 27, 28, 30, 36, 40. *See also* Education
Schorr, Alvin, 196–98, 284
Schroeder, Pat, 193, 194, 284
Schwartz, Pepper, 226, 229, 283
Schönnesson, Lena Nilsson, 110, 284
Sciabarrasi, Paula, 200, 285
Scott, Hilda, 25, 31, 39, 40, 183, 285
Scruggs, Marguerite, 110, 266
Selbyg, Arne, 47, 54, 285
Sellström, Eva, 42, 75, 77, 101, 104, 110, 153, 271, 285

Sessler, George, 43, 281
Sex segregation of labor market: as a determinant of child care sharing in Sweden, 224; as a determinant of couples' sharing parental leave in Sweden, 105, 111; as a determinant of Swedish women's experience with parental leave, 148, 150; programs to combat, in Sweden, 27–28, 30, 36; reasons for, in Sweden, 35–36; in the U.S., 211
Shapiro, Robert, 190, 196, 209, 285
Shaw, Susan, 2, 285
Shehan, Constance, 192, 193, 285
Shorter, Edward, 231, 285
Shreve, Anita, 9, 285
Siblings, number of. *See* Family context; Family size
Sick children, days off to care for, 42, 67, 214
Sidel, Ruth, 14, 285
Siperstein, Gary, 135, 278
Six hour work day, in Sweden: availability of, 42; men's participation in, 44, 67; rules for, 67; as solution to gender stratifiction, 182–84; support for, 183, 214
Skard, Thorild, 54, 285
Small businesses, in the U.S., 200–201
Smith, Audrey, 9, 10, 285
Social Democratic Party: attitude toward six-hour day, 182–83; concern for children's welfare, 23; effects on gender policy, 48–49; loss of power of, 29; response to Myrdals' recommendations, 21–23, 41; support for parental leave, 43, 62; support for women's employment, 26, 30; tax policies of, 28; women's involvement in, 45
Social policy: and equal parenthood, 11–12, 217; criteria for effective, 219–26; development of, in Sweden, 47–48, 198; development of, in the U.S., 198
Social support, 101, 107, 112
Sorrentino, Constance, 192, 285
Spakes, Patricia, 198, 285
Spalter-Roth, Roberta, 201, 285
Spitze, Glenda, 9, 274
Standard and Poor, 211, 285
Statens Offentliga Utredningar, 13, 22, 24, 33, 42, 44, 67, 74, 75, 77, 84, 98, 105, 110, 111, 117, 155, 178, 286
Statistiska Centralbyrån, 13, 23, 28, 31, 33, 34, 35, 37, 44, 61, 68, 211, 233, 286
Steinberg, Jamie, 155, 277
Survey procedures, in Gothenburg survey, 17, 234
Svensson, Gillan, 44, 54, 277, 278
Sweden: definition of gender equality, 13; as first society to promote equal parenthood, 12, 217; status of women in, 37, 45, 53–55
Swedin, Göran, 42, 75, 77, 101, 104, 110, 153, 271, 285
Swedish Institute, 23, 30, 36, 37, 43, 45, 53, 114, 286
Sweeney, John, 204, 286
Sörman, Claes-Otto, 84, 85, 93, 99, 101, 105, 106, 107, 110, 116, 130, 132, 138, 141, 272

Tax policy: in Sweden, 28, 34, 36, 200; in the U.S., 196, 200, 205
TCO. *See* Tjänstemannens Centralorganisationen
Tiller, Per, 39, 287
Time off at childbirth. *See* Daddy days; Maternity Leave; Parental Leave
Temporary disability insurance, 189
Tinsley, Barbara, 4, 281
Tjänstemannens Centralorganisationen, 31, 39, 73, 287

Trade unions: Americans' participation in, 203; support for gender equality in American, 204, 215; support for gender equality in Swedish, 30–32, 39, 203; support for parental leave in American, 199, 203–204; support for parental leave in Swedish, 41, 224; and support for six-hour day, 183; Swedes' participation in, 31, 36–37, 203; Swedish women's leadership in 36–37
Trost, Jan, 44, 287
Török, Pal, 101, 104, 105, 132, 175, 176, 178, 287

Uddenberg, Nils, 93, 107, 287
U.S. Chamber of Commerce, 201–202
U.S. Department of Labor, 188, 193, 214, 287
U.S. News and World Report, 200, 202, 287

Ve, Hildur, 1, 18, 287
Verney, Douglas, 52, 287
Von Hall, Gunilla, 93, 98, 287

Wahlström, Björn, 104, 287
Wall Street Journal, 8, 193, 194, 287
Warner, Rebecca, 156, 287
Wasserman, Janis, 200, 267
Weissner, Thomas, 4, 288
Welfare state policies, in Sweden, 22–23, 51, 52
Widerberg, Karin, 54, 55, 175–77, 267, 288
Wilcher, Shirley, 29, 267
Williams, Jennifer, 188, 189, 204, 271
Winkler, Anne, 9, 266
Winston, Kathryn, 9, 11, 20, 23, 26, 27, 45, 46, 48, 51, 197, 198, 265
Wisendale, Steven, 191, 288
Wistrand, Birgitta, 27, 288
Wizelius, Tore, 132, 134, 138, 276
Women's employment: American attitudes toward, 188, 195; attitudes toward, 194–95; as a determinant of child care sharing, 160, 195; as a determinant of Swedish men's sharing parental leave, 109–12; effects of Swedish men's taking parental leave on, 166–70; 173–74; limits on American women's, 188; rates in Sweden, 25, 33, 54; rates in the U.S., 191–92, 193, 194; Swedish laws affecting, 22, 29–30; Swedish programs promoting, 27–33. *See also* Income; Promotion Opportunites; Work commitment; Work hours; Work hour preferences
Work commitment: effects of sharing child care on Swedish women's, 166–68; effects of Swedish men's taking leave on men's, 172, 174, 180–82; effects of Swedish men's taking parental leave on women's, 167–68, 170, 172, 174; measures of, 166–67; Swedish women's, 177
Work days, effects of men's leave taking: on men's, 172, 174, 179, 180, 182; on women's, 168, 170, 172, 174
Work hours: as a determinant of child care sharing, 161, 164, 165; effects of child care sharing on, 161–62, 164, 178; effects of children on parents', 178; effects of taking parental leave on men's, 172, 174, 178, 180, 182; effects of taking leave on women's, 168, 170, 173, 181, gender differences in, in Sweden, 37, 44, 67, 171; Swedish women's 33–34, 223
Work hour preferences: effects of leavetaking on men's, 179, 180,

182; effects of leavetaking on women's, 167–168, 170; gender differences, in Sweden, 171
Workplace: attitudes toward parental leave in Sweden, 98–101, 103, 109; attitudes toward parental leave in the U.S., 211–12; problems caused by parental leave in Sweden, 131–32, 143, 145–47, 150
Work-related barriers to taking parental leave, in Sweden, 98–106, 109–12, 223–24
World Almanac, 200, 288

Yogev, Sara, 97, 288
Yogman, Michael, 4, 9, 10, 97, 288
York, Carolyn, 204, 288
Young, John, 285

Zacur, Susan, 190, 194, 285
Zigler, Edward, 11, 192, 206, 273, 274